Scottish Opera

The first ten years

Foreword by Lord Harewood

Scottish Opera

The first ten years

CONRAD WILSON

Collins London and Glasgow

William Collins Sons & Co Ltd
London . Glasgow . Sydney . Auckland
Toronto . Johannesburg

On the title page: The Three Ladies
(Patricia Hay, Josephte Clément and
Claire Livingstone) in a scene from
Scottish Opera's production of
The Magic Flute during the Edinburgh
Commonwealth Games in 1970

First published 1972
© Conrad Wilson 1972
ISBN 0 00 410584 2
Set in Monotype Spectrum
Made and Printed in Great Britain by
William Collins Sons & Co Ltd Glasgow

CONTENTS

Note and Acknowledgements

WHEN ALEXANDER GIBSON returned to Scotland in 1959, and when Scottish Opera was founded in 1962, I was working in London and abroad and was unable to share—except at a distance—the excitement of this early period in the Company's history. Like many people at the time, I wondered if all this could really be happening in Scotland, if a real professional company had at last been created.

In the pages that follow, I hope I have managed to communicate the pleasure of discovering the quality of this brave young Company, of admiring its ideals, and of journeying with it, if only as a critic, from season to season, from city to city, from one remarkable success to another, experiencing performances of *Così fan tutte*, *The Trojans*, *The Ring*, and much else that has left an indelible impression. Scottish Opera, during its first decade, is one of the things that have made life worth living; and this book, tempered with criticism though it sometimes is, voices my gratitude to a Company which has given me so much to remember and so much to look forward to.

Gratitude must also go to all who helped me in writing it: to Alexander Gibson, Peter Hemmings, Robin Orr, Richard Telfer, Ainslie Millar, who spent time answering my questions; to Thomson Smillie and Catherine Deas in the Company's publicity office, who gave me unlimited access to crates of newspaper clippings and files of photographs, verified quantities of facts, and compiled the Cast Lists included in these pages; to Magnus Magnusson, one of Scottish Opera's first supporters, whose survey of the Company's early years in the *New Saltire* magazine was a mine of valuable information ; and, especially, to William McLeod, my editor at Collins, who presided with skill and patience over the birth of this book. Himself a real operamane, he made innumerable useful suggestions during late-night sessions at his home, where we studied pictures and discussed subject matter while listening to his remarkable collection of old opera recordings.

CONRAD WILSON, Edinburgh 1972

The author and publishers wish to express their indebtedness to Scottish Opera who supplied nearly all the illustrations and to the photographers who took the pictures, as follows:

Colour: All the colour photographs were taken by Bob Anderson.
Monochrome: Bob Anderson (9; 152; 153; 154; 156); Bryan & Shear Ltd. ((iii); 6, l.; 18, t.; 46; 47, both; 52; 53, b.l. and r.; 54, all; 59, all; 60; 61, both; 74; 75; 76, all; 79, all; 82, both; 83; 84; 85, both; 97, l.; 113; 117, b.; 124; 125; 129; 130; 131; 132; 133; 142, both; 143; 146, all; 148; 149; 150; 151); David Farrell (14); Ronald Gunn (17; 18, b.r.; 48, r.; 51; 53, t.l. and r.; 86, all; 93, all; 97, r.; 99; 100, both; 101; 107, both; 108, t. and b.r.; 114; 116; 117, t.; 118, both; 121; 126, both; 135; 137, both); Bob Johnson (108, b.l.); Robert L. Nicholson ((viii); 42; 43, both); G. Rule (18, b.l.); The Scotsman Publications Ltd (22; 24); Paul Shillabeer (6, r.); David Newell Smith, courtesy The Observer (145); Donald Southern (38); Städitsche Bühnen Augsburg (115); Vista (29; 31; 33, both; 34; 37, both; 48, l and c.); Reg Wilson (65, all; 67; 68, both; 69; 70; 89, r.; 90, all; 102; 103, all; 104)

Foreword by Lord Harewood

OF COURSE, whatever you may say or think, Scottish Opera remains one of the outstanding confidence tricks of modern musical history—and by 'confidence trick', I mean, I need hardly say, a trick brought off because of the sublime conviction of its performer. Nothing in Scottish operatic history truly justified the founding-fathers of Scottish Opera in their venture; operatic chronicles list amateur activities if the origin is local, and emphasise the touring or imported label attached to anything professional seen and heard north of the Border. Even the relative and postwar cases of successive Edinburgh Festivals only pointed the difference between the prices which could be charged for foreign-grown as opposed to British operatic products, a source of potential dismay to the organisers of Scottish Opera, not of comfort.

Except maybe on one solitary score: statistics, normally unreliable but in this case I always felt likely to be pragmatically right—just listen to them talk in the intervals—suggested all along that audiences for Festival opera in August-September were predominantly Scottish, certainly to a higher percentage than at concerts in the Usher Hall. But if Edinburgh audiences may have been subject to the law of operatic exposure which converted so many servicemen in wartime Naples to the most visceral of all reputedly intellectual pursuits—if you once get them into the Opera House for a half-decent performance of a good opera, they'll return; the problem is to get them there in the first place—such a syndrome did not apply in Glasgow, at the time of writing Scottish Opera's home. Here and elsewhere in Scotland, I can only imagine that the instinct for quality and the nose for a bargain drew an innately musical people to what Scottish Opera had over the years to offer. But to have kept going at all amounts really to the confidence trick I referred to earlier.

Certainly, it is a fairly remarkable achievement to go from a Box Office return of 66% for three performances each of *Madama Butterfly* and *Pelléas et Mélisande* at medium prices in 1962 to 100% for the complete *Ring* cycle at nearly six times the price per seat in 1971.

I have been lucky enough to be connected with Scottish Opera since the start, a by-product so to speak of my years working for the Edinburgh Festival and not the least of the incidental pleasure and benefits I had from those years, and I welcome Mr Conrad Wilson's faithful and illuminating study of an organisation which has not only advanced from the state of a venture to that of an institution in ten short years but is now in a position to give advice to other aspirant operatic bodies in the British Isles. With a full *Ring* under its belt, to say nothing of earlier triumphs, no group is better qualified.

HAREWOOD November 1971

1. The Background

THERE WAS OPERA in Scotland before Scottish Opera. By 1807, *The Beggar's Opera* had made its way across the Tweed. Rossini's *La Gazza ladra* reached Edinburgh not many years after its Italian premiere in 1817 (sooner, indeed, than British operamanes can often expect to see a new foreign opera today). In 1848, Jenny Lind made her famous appearances in Donizetti's *La Fille du Régiment* and Bellini's *La Sonnambula* in Edinburgh, Glasgow and Perth. Therese Tietjens, the burly German soprano, sang the title role in Donizetti's *Lucrezia Borgia* in Glasgow in 1872; five years later her career ended when she collapsed on stage in London while singing the same part. Meyerbeer's *Les Huguenots*, *Robert le Diable*, and *Dinorah*, Bellini's *I Puritani*, and more provincial fare such as Macfarren's *Robin Hood* and Cowen's *Pauline* were all seen in Scotland around then.

It was not, however, until the Carl Rosa Opera Company began to make regular visits to Scotland that the kind of repertoire which today would be considered viable reached the stage in Edinburgh and Glasgow (which is not to say that works like *Lucrezia Borgia* have dropped entirely from favour, but simply that they now flourish better under festival conditions than as bread-and-butter pieces). Between 1890 and 1910, the Carl Rosa performed Mozart's *Figaro* and *Don Giovanni*, Beethoven's *Fidelio*, Berlioz's *The Damnation of Faust*, Bizet's *Carmen*, Gounod's *Faust*, Wagner's *Tannhäuser*, *Lohengrin*, and *Die Meistersinger*, Verdi's *La Forza del destino*, *Otello*, and *Falstaff* – a choice of works remarkably similar to what Scottish Opera was to provide more than half a century later.

Then to all this was added, in 1910, the founding of the Denhof Opera Company by Ernst Denhof, an Austrian musician resident in Edinburgh, who wanted to pioneer performances of Wagner's *Ring* in English outside London. By 1913 the company had appeared in Manchester, Liverpool, Birmingham, Leeds and Hull, as well as in Scotland, and had staged not only *The Ring* but also Wagner's *The Flying Dutchman*, *Tristan*, and *Meistersinger*, Mozart's *The Magic Flute*, Gluck's *Orpheus*, Debussy's *Pelléas et Mélisande*, and Strauss's *Elektra* and *Der Rosenkavalier*. Obviously, by today's standards, the productions must have been very basic – as, no doubt, were the orchestras Denhof raised in each city. Yet this must have been a fascinating chapter in operatic history, albeit a short one: in 1913 the company went bankrupt and was taken over by the Beecham Opera Company, who added further to Scotland's operatic experience with

Alexander Gibson at rehearsal.

such events as a mammoth three-week season at the King's Theatre, Edinburgh, when *The Magic Flute*, Mussorgsky's *Boris Godunov*, Wagner's *Tristan*, Verdi's *Il Trovatore*, *Aida*, and *Otello*, Puccini's *Madama Butterfly*, *Tosca*, and *The Girl of the Golden West*, a double-bill of *Cav* and *Pag*, Gounod's *Faust*, Saint-Saëns's *Samson and Delilah*, and Charpentier's *Louise* were performed one after another.

After further seasons, including an Edinburgh one that featured Verdi's *Falstaff*, Mussorgsky's *Khovanschhina*, Puccini's *Manon Lescaut*, and Rimsky-Korsakov's *Golden Cockerel*, the Beecham Company likewise fizzled out, though not before making appeals for money to the corporation of each city – Glasgow, which was asked somewhat optimistically for £6000, offered (with what at that time must have seemed remarkable generosity) only £1600. By 1922, however, the British National Opera Company had risen from the ashes of the Beecham one, and came almost immediately to Scotland with a dozen operas, including Wagner's *Parsifal* and Offenbach's *Goldsmith of Toledo*. During the 1930s, Sir Thomas Beecham returned at the head of a Covent Garden company whose repertoire included *La Bohème*, a work Sir Thomas always conducted incomparably. This production, which Glasgow saw in 1932, had an additional historic value, for the settings that were seen then are the ones still used by the Royal Opera today.

Meanwhile, until its demise in 1957, the Carl Rosa continued to visit Scotland, bringing a wide range of pieces, including Offenbach's *The Tales of Hoffmann*, with the tales in their proper order, and George Lloyd's *John Socman*, the company's ill-fated "modern opera with tunes," whose main trouble was that the tunes were such poor value in comparison with the supposed nontunes of a work such as *Wozzeck*, which had not yet had its British premiere. Though most of the performances were crude in comparison with what we should now expect – the idea that an opera needed a producer was regarded by the Carl Rosa as absurd – the company nevertheless sometimes pulled off something memorable, when all forces conspired to work tellingly together, as in a magical *Bohème* conducted by Maurits Sillem in the early 1950s.

During that period, too, the Covent Garden company was not quite so firmly entrenched in London as it is now, and was to be seen in Scotland from time to time. In Edinburgh the broad stage of the Empire Theatre was preferred to that of the King's; and though some of the productions, including the inevitable *Carmen* and *Bohème*, were unadventurous, risks were occasionally taken. For instance, the Bliss/Priestley opera, *The Olympians*, was brought to Edinburgh soon after its London premiere in 1949 and left a strong enough impression to make one wonder why no one has recently thought to revive it. But perhaps the most memorable Covent Garden performances to have been given in Scotland were the *Tristan* and *Aida* conducted by Barbirolli in 1951 – one of the rare occasions, cherished by all who experienced it, when Sir John allowed himself to be lured back into the orchestra pit and reminded us tantalisingly of what a great opera conductor he could have become.

Sadler's Wells, who agreed to take over the Carl Rosa's touring obligations, came to Glasgow in 1957 with vivid performances of Tchaikovsky's *Eugene Onegin* and Puccini's *Gianni Schicchi* under Alexander Gibson, who was already, as the youngest musical director in that company's history, well on his way to becoming one of Britain's leading opera conductors. Subsequent visits to Glasgow, Edinburgh, Aberdeen, and (until the theatre was transformed into a cinema) Dundee, served to stress the increasing problems of touring opera – production standards were rising and were placing greater strain on the resources of Britain's inadequate theatres. Yet, like the Carl Rosa, Sadler's Wells provided through the years many operatic experiences one would have been sorry to miss; and though its Scottish seasons have now been gradually replaced by those of Scottish Opera, the two companies worked for a while in productive alternation, the one complementing the other, and the two between them providing a rich and satisfying repertoire which ranged, in the case of the Wells, from Mozart to Britten's *Gloriana* and Richard Rodney Bennett's *The Mines of Sulphur*.

Then, from 1947, there has been the Edinburgh Festival, which from the outset has striven to present – in a poorly-equipped theatre – the best of operatic events from all over the world. In the early years, Rudolf Bing (who soon left to become administrator of the New York Metropolitan) and his successor Ian Hunter created a special link with Glyndebourne, whose Sussex activities would have taken far longer to re-establish themselves after the Second World War if Edinburgh had not stepped in and provided the necessary financial and artistic encouragement. In return, Glyndebourne gave Edinburgh some of the choicest Mozart performances of the period (*Figaro, Don Giovanni, Così fan tutte, Idomeneo*, with singers of the calibre of Suzanne Danco and Sena Jurinac), a superb *Ballo in maschera*, with the flame-haired Ljuba Welitsch memorably climbing the hill to meet her lover beside the gibbet, a *Forza del destino* compellingly conducted by Fritz Busch, and the famous Beecham *Ariadne auf Naxos*, staged in the now rare original version with Molière's *Le Bourgeois gentilhomme* as prologue.

But before long Edinburgh found it could not afford Glyndebourne every year, and in 1952 came the Hamburg State Opera, the first of an increasing number of foreign companies with "hidden" subsidies from the countries to which they belonged, thus lightening the strain on the Edinburgh purse-strings. The Hamburg Opera, on that first visit, brought no fewer than six productions, including Günther Rennert's moving post-war *Fidelio*, with Inge Borkh in the title role, a *Magic Flute* conducted by Georg Solti, a *Freischütz* which many people found perplexingly abstract (though it was one of the harbingers of a whole new era in German opera production), and the belated but important British premiere of Hindemith's *Mathis der Maler*, a work which, disgracefully, no British company has even now added to its repertoire.

Thereafter, although the King's Theatre became increasingly notorious all over Europe for its deficiencies, many other companies came to the Edinburgh Festival, and some of them were even prepared to pay a second visit. The Hamburg Opera returned in 1956 with a repertoire including Stravinsky's *Oedipus Rex* and *Mavra*, and Cornelius's *Barber of Baghdad*, and again in 1968 with *The Flying Dutchman, Elektra*, and *Ariadne*. The Stuttgart Opera came twice, the first time with Weber's *Euryanthe*. The Stockholm Opera in 1959 brought the space opera, Blomdahl's *Aniara*, along with *Die Walküre*, *Wozzeck*, and the famous "authentic" production of *Un Ballo in maschera*. The Belgrade Opera arrived in 1962 with Prokofiev's *The Gambler* and *The Love of Three Oranges*; the Prague Opera in 1964 made the first of two visits with a splendid Czech repertoire based mainly on Smetana and Janáček; and the Florence Opera in 1969 presented some samples from the Maggio Musicale, including Donizetti's *Maria Stuarda*, with Leyla Gencer and Shirley Verrett as the rival queens. But by that time, of course, Scottish Opera was well and truly founded and was itself beginning to appear regularly in the Festival.

Earlier, in the absence of a resident professional Scottish company, these visiting productions were – and in the case of the Edinburgh Festival still are – a valuable source of operatic experience. But what of homegrown opera, the amateur companies who served to form the true pre-history of Scottish Opera until that company was founded in 1962? Though these are no longer the force they once were, they scored some important successes in their time. No British operamane can be unaware that it was in Glasgow in 1935 that the local Grand Opera Society gave the British premiere of Berlioz's *The Trojans* under the conductorship of Erik Chisholm. A special train was run from London for the occasion – even at that time Berlioz had devotees in Britain as nowhere else in the world – and the following year Chisholm went on to give the British premiere of the same composer's *Beatrice and Benedick* (in 1933 he had also earned gratitude for staging Mozart's *Idomeneo* for the first time in Britain). Nor did the enterprise of the Glasgow Grand stop there. Over the years the company also staged such works as Goldmark's *The Queen of Sheba*, Ponchielli's *I Promessi sposi*, Lalo's *Le Roi d'Ys*, Boito's *Mefistofele*, Gluck's *Armida*, Rossini's *William Tell*, Meyerbeer's *Les Huguenots*, and Verdi's *Luisa Miller* and *Les Vêpres siciliennes*.

The Edinburgh Opera Company, and its predecessor the Edinburgh Grand Opera Society, did not boast a repertoire quite so rich as Glasgow's, but nevertheless succeeded in staging Borodin's *Prince Igor*, Massenet's *Hérodiade*, Goldmark's *Queen of Sheba*, and, in more recent years, Donizetti's *Lucia di Lammermoor*, Verdi's *Nabucco*, and, as late as 1958, a Meyerbeer *Huguenots*.

No one, in the heyday of these amateur companies, could have guessed that out of them a fully professional, national company would ultimately spring. Yet, wise after the event, we can now discern a few clues. It was the Glasgow Grand, after all, which first made use of a professional orchestra, the SNO, in the pit of the King's Theatre, and this idea in later years was to become a basis of Scottish Opera's success. It was Richard Telfer, musical director of the Edinburgh Opera Company from 1950, who was one of the key figures in the creation of Scottish Opera in 1962 (and whose idea it was to stage *Pelléas et Mélisande* that year). And it was also Mr Telfer who, in 1957, had invited Alexander Gibson to be guest conductor of the Edinburgh Opera Company's *Nabucco* and had talked the Scottish bass, David Ward (whose career was already firmly launched in London) into singing a leading role. In that production, makeshift though it was, the flames which were to burst into life five years later had already begun to smoulder.

2. The Beginning

HOW THE FIRE came to be fuelled and the flames to be fanned has been described by various people in various, sometimes conflicting, ways. But all the accounts of the formation of Scottish Opera have been consistent in one cardinal detail: that when Alexander Gibson returned to Scotland in 1959 to become musical director of the Scottish National Orchestra, he was already determined to start a national opera company at the earliest opportunity. This visionary aim, as he later confessed, was one of the crucial factors in his decision to quit the rich musical pastures of London in favour of the patchier ones of Glasgow.

His task, at the time, seemed a Herculean one, but his qualifications for fulfilling it were outstanding. Opera had been in his blood from the age of twelve, when he was taken by his parents from his home town of Motherwell to see his first professional production (a Carl Rosa performance of *Madama Butterfly*, with Joan Hammond and Parry Jones) at the Glasgow Theatre Royal. As a music student in London he had conducted *Così fan tutte* and made history by recruiting his own orchestra instead of using the two-piano accompaniment traditionally favoured by the authorities at the Royal College of Music. This revolutionary act put him into temporary disgrace, but it doubtless strengthened his desire to embark on an operatic career. At any rate, after winning a Tagore Medal as best student of his year, with subsequent tuition from Igor Markevitch in Salzburg and Paul van Kempen in Siena, he joined Sadler's Wells as a repetiteur and at the age of twenty-five conducted *The Bartered Bride*. His work in professional opera had begun.

Next, by way of change, came a spell as Ian Whyte's assistant with the BBC Scottish Orchestra (a marvellous educational post, which Colin Davis in due course was likewise to hold), but the lure of opera remained powerful. By 1954 he was back at Sadler's Wells, first as staff conductor, and then, when he was thirty-one, as musical director. During his Wells years he conducted no fewer than twenty-six operas, ranging from Mozart to Bartók's *Bluebeard's Castle*, Menotti's *The Consul*, and the world premiere of John Gardner's *The Moon and Sixpence*.

No doubt his career at the Wells would have continued much longer had not the Scottish National Orchestra, after its supply of Czech and Austrian

(Left) Peter Hemmings, general administrator since 1963. "Had a lesser man been chosen, someone less courageous, less imaginative, less resourceful, less fully devoted to his cause, then Scottish Opera might never have grown to international prominence the way it has."

(Right) Richard Telfer, the first person in Scotland to support Alexander Gibson in forming Scottish Opera, shared Gibson's vision of a great Scottish professional company. He suggested Pelléas et Mélisande in 1962, and was Scottish Opera's first company manager. Today he is a valued member of the Board of Directors.

conductors had run dry, offered him the chance to become its first British-born conductor since the days of Barbirolli in the 1930s. It was a post which plainly involved an element of risk. To leave the London limelight at the very moment when he was becoming established could have had an adverse effect on his career. Yet this very aspect of the Scottish appointment was one of the features that specially attracted him. For some time he had felt uneasy that a young musician such as himself should be giving all his performances in the glare of metropolitan critical opinion and international audiences. What he wanted was a more private atmosphere in which to work out his musical ideas, and this, he felt, was something he might achieve in Glasgow.

There were, of course, other incentives. In 1959 musical life in Scotland was not the vital force it is now. Mr Gibson, with his London experience behind him, wanted to do all he could to develop music in his homeland. Above all, the conductorship of the SNO appealed to him because it seemed something really constructive. Here was an orchestra which had hitherto been directed by musicians who treated it merely as a stepping-stone to other things and who in several cases made no attempt to plant roots in Glasgow – George Szell in the 1930s knew no more of the city than the street from his hotel to the concert hall. To Mr Gibson this seemed a sadly negative attitude to a country's national orchestra, and his first resolution was to bring, as far as he was able, a real sense of purpose to music in Scotland.

In his first season he endeared himself to his audiences by conducting a complete cycle of Sibelius's symphonies, works towards which the Scottish public felt deeply sympathetic but which had been cold-shouldered by Mr Gibson's two Austrian predecessors; and to this achievement he presently added a Musica Viva series which included such important British premieres as Schoenberg's violin concerto and Stockhausen's *Gruppen*.

Exactly when the idea of a national opera company first struck him he is not quite certain. But he vividly recalls that several of the Scots who were fellow-members of Sadler's Wells in the 1950s – David Ward, Harold Blackburn, William McAlpine, to mention three – shared his pipedream and often discussed ways and means of bringing it about. He also remembers the encouragement given him by John Donaldson, the London company's Glasgow-born staff producer who, on hearing that the young conductor was heading back north to take command of the SNO, immediately urged him to start an opera company.

But between the idea and its outcome a good many hurdles had still to be cleared. Mr Gibson knew that the SNO would be a magnificent basis for opera – he had already had its services in 1954 when he conducted the Glasgow Grand Opera Society in Gounod's *Faust* and Wolf-Ferrari's *The Jewels of the Madonna*. But this time his ambitions were much greater, and he wanted to make clear that what he envisaged was not another Scottish amateur opera company with the SNO to provide a professional limbering. It was to be a professional company through and through, and nothing less would be acceptable to him.

The first person in Scotland to support his idea was Richard Telfer, the Edinburgh music teacher, organist, conductor and opera enthusiast who had invited him to conduct *Nabucco* with the Edinburgh Opera Company in 1957. Mr Telfer's operatic background may have been with amateur companies, but he shared Alexander Gibson's vision of a great Scottish professional company, and he was henceforward to play an almost Svengali-like role – commenting, suggesting, advising – in Mr Gibson's career and in the early development of Scottish Opera.

The two men had first met in 1954 when Mr Telfer sought Mr Gibson's help over a production of *La Traviata* which the Edinburgh Opera Company was then preparing. The story goes that Mr Gibson invited him to London so that they could go through the score together, and that Mr Telfer arrived promptly with a carefully-packed champagne and chicken picnic lunch to save the time of having to eat in a restaurant. Thereafter their friendship blossomed quickly. Later Mr Telfer was to become godfather of one of the Gibson children; he was also to be the conductor's sternest, most private critic. It is said that between Acts One and Two of *Die Walküre* in 1966 Mr Telfer went round to the conductor's dressing-room. "How does it sound out in front?" asked Mr Gibson. Mr Telfer cleared his throat. The conductor repeated the question. Mr Telfer replied that he did not think the conductor was yet completely inside the music. No one else, in the middle of an important premiere, would have got away with it. But Mr Telfer did, and the much more authoritative Wagner performances which Mr Gibson conducted in subsequent years bore out his words.

Meanwhile, back in 1959, Mr Gibson's ambition to form a Scottish company had won the enthusiasm of Norman Tucker, the then administrator of Sadler's Wells. Mr Tucker promised that the Wells would give all the help it could in the formation of the new company, and this assurance – which was soon to be generously fulfilled – was an enormous encouragement to Mr Gibson at the time. But greater Scottish support was needed, and the next man to join the team was Ainslie Millar, a well-known Glasgow chartered surveyor, amateur singer, and supporter of the arts. Mr Millar had recently become the Scottish director of the Sadler's Wells Trust, an appointment which quickly put him in touch with Mr Gibson. Like Richard Telfer he was soon filled with enthusiasm for the creation of a Scottish company, and during his visits to London he pledged his support and discussed for hours on end how their hopes might be achieved.

So now, as Magnus Magnusson wrote in his *New Saltire* account of the birth of Scottish Opera, they were three. The next step was Mr Gibson's move to Scotland in the summer of 1959; and although, for the first few months, he was completely immersed in orchestral work, the plans for the opera company continued to simmer. Secret meetings were held in various places – secret, because many a valiant Scottish scheme has been brought to its knees by excessive public argument, and Mr Gibson and his two colleagues did not want the same to happen to their opera project. But from W. R. Fell, the SNO's administrator at the time, they received the assurance that there would be a gap each spring when the orchestra might be able to play for opera. From Stewart Cruickshank, director of Howard & Wyndham, they won warm support and excellent terms for the hiring of the King's Theatre in Glasgow. A midnight meeting at the home of Alastair Dunnett, editor of *The Scotsman*, proved equally encouraging and led some time later to what was to be the most crucial event in the launching of the company: the promise of a subsidy from *The Scotsman*'s sister organisation, Scottish Television.

Optimism was now running high enough for an opening repertoire to be decided upon, for casts to be chosen and dates suggested. It was agreed, prudently, that the first season should be confined to a single week in Glasgow. In this way public response could be assessed while costs would be kept to a minimum. The first idea was to stage *Il Trovatore*, but in the end this was felt to be too expensive and awkward an undertaking, especially if – as was hoped – the season was to include more than one opera. Other possibilities were Donizetti's *Don Pasquale*, Wolf-Ferrari's *School for Fathers*, and a triple bill of Mozart's *Impresario*, Stravinsky's *Soldier's Tale*, and Bartók's *Bluebeard's Castle*.

Most of these were works which Mr Gibson had conducted successfully during his London days, and the choice had another advantage too: each opera provided roles suitable for a number of the Scottish singers who had established themselves in London and who were eager to help Mr Gibson in his new venture. Thus David Ward was pencilled for the part of Bluebeard, Ian Wallace and Duncan Robertson for *Don Pasquale*, Harold Blackburn (plus David Ward again) for *School for Fathers*. And from Miami, where he was filming *Mutiny on the*

The board of directors in conference in 1971. At the left are Frederick Rimmer, professor of music at Glasgow University (he was senior lecturer when Scottish Opera was founded in 1962); Peter Ebert; and Ainslie Millar. At the top (left to right) are Peter Hemmings, general administrator; Robin Orr, chairman (and by that time professor of music at Cambridge); and Lord Grant, vice-chairman. On the right are Colonel P. M. Thomas, chairman of the finance committee; Renton Thomson, accountant; Aubrey Halford-MacLeod; and Ian Rodger, company secretary. An eleventh director, Richard Telfer, is out of sight between Lord Grant and Colonel Thomas. Along with Professor Orr, Mr Millar and Mr Rodger, Mr Telfer is one of the four founder directors of the company.

Bounty, the Scottish actor Gordon Jackson reported that he would be delighted to be the narrator in the Stravinsky.

By now the week beginning 5 June 1961 had been fixed as the opening date; but since all Scottish operamanes already know that the company was not born until 1962, it will be plain that there must have been some reason why the projected 1961 season sank disastrously without trace. Perhaps the first hint of gathering clouds was when a detailed budget was drawn up for the repertoire and it was found that *School for Fathers* would be too expensive to be included (Mozart's *Impresario* had been dropped earlier for the same reason). But on the basis of *Don Pasquale* and a double bill of the Stravinsky and Bartók it was hoped to keep the total cost down to £3460, about half of which would be paid from box-office revenue. This left about £1700 still to be raised, and in December 1960 a formal application was made to the Scottish Committee of the Arts Council for a grant to cover the estimated loss.

At the same time, steps had been taken to put the company on a proper legal footing, and the three-man team of Gibson, Telfer and Millar had become a quartet through the addition of Ian Rodger, a Glasgow solicitor with a special interest in the arts. Mr Rodger drew up a provisional constitution, based on that of Sadler's Wells and the SNO, for a non-profit-distributing company, limited by the guarantee of its members, and to be called the Scottish Opera

Society Limited. This, then, was to be the legal status of the company: a cultural Trust registered, if possible, as a charity.

All these details were set down in the application to the Arts Council, and since the outcome of that application was one of the most regrettably myopic incidents in Scottish musical history, it may seem pertinent if I quote the document in full.

A SCOTTISH NATIONAL OPERA ORGANISATION

OBJECT: To further the cause of Opera in Scotland by providing short seasons of first class Opera in the four main centres and to supplement the work of the Sadler's Wells Touring Organisation, which can only provide a limited repertoire in Scotland. To this end it is proposed to launch the scheme by a week of Opera in the King's Theatre, Glasgow, during the week of 5th June, 1961.

The Scottish National Orchestra has been reserved for the period and pencilled bookings have been made with principal artists. The Director of Sadler's Wells, Mr Norman Tucker, CBE, and the Opera Manager of the Royal Opera House have agreed the availability of artists. Scenery, costumes, properties and musical scores are to be loaned by Sadler's Wells.

PRODUCTIONS 1961: Three performances each of two bills will be presented as follows:
  (a) DON PASQUALE (Donizetti), which has not been presented professionally in Scotland since the Carl Rosa's performance of 1931.
  (b) A double bill of THE SOLDIER'S TALE (Stravinsky) and Bartók's BLUEBEARD'S CASTLE, two great international masterpieces with an appeal for the more discerning opera-goer.

These productions will be in every sense professional, and the very highest standards will be the aim. Artists will be drawn from among the country's leading singers, and of the eleven principals, four will be of Scottish birth. David Ward, who will sing Bluebeard, is now principal bass of the Royal Opera House, and during this past summer sang at Bayreuth, Glyndebourne, and the Edinburgh Festival. Ian Wallace of Glyndebourne and the Edinburgh Festival sings Don Pasquale. Gordon Jackson, our leading Scots film artist, will play in the *Soldier's Tale*, a role he undertook recently at Sadler's Wells. Duncan Robertson of Motherwell, who sings in *Pasquale*, is a much sought-after singer today.

ARTISTIC DIRECTION: The complete artistic and musical direction of the Scottish National Opera Organisation will be in the hands of Alexander Gibson, Musical Director and Principal Conductor of the Scottish National Orchestra, a position he is contracted to hold until 1964, thus ensuring reasonable continuity for the direction of the project. Mr Gibson's experience as Musical Director of Sadler's Wells will ensure a very practical outlook on the problems of Opera in Scotland.

COMMITTEE OF MANAGEMENT: Steps have been taken to register the name 'Scottish National Opera Ltd.' as a non-profit-making limited liability company, and prominent figures in the musical and theatrical life of Scotland have been invited to join the board.

Along with the application, the company sent the Arts Council a budget of estimated expenditure, based on the knowledge that many of the people involved were prepared on this occasion to accept reduced fees. This budget ran as follows:

Artists		Production Personnel	
David Ward	£100	Colin Graham ⎱	£100
Victoria Elliott	100	Anthony Besch ⎰ Producers	100
Marion Studholme	80	Wendy Toye	60
Ian Wallace	80	John Gledhill, *Stage Director*	40
Denis Dowling	80	Charles Bristow, *Stage Director*	30
Duncan Robertson	80	James Lockhart, *Assistant Conductor*	
Small part artist	50	*and Chorus Master*	60
Gordon Jackson	80		
Soldier	50		£390
Devil	50		
Princess	50	Orchestra	£800
	£800	Scenery and Transport (as per	
		estimate from Wells)	700
		Wardrobe charge (includes	
		personnel)	100
		Rehearsal Rooms	60
		Royalties	250
		Advertising	250
		Insurance (includes N.I. for staff	
		and all other cover)	50
		Chorus (20 at Equity fee of	
		£1 1s. per show)	63
			£2273

Total cost of Opera Week:	Artists	£800
	Production	390
	Other costs	2273
		£3463
Less estimated share of theatre take		£1750
Estimated deficit on week		£1713

Brave, exciting and far-reaching though the document was – not since the founding of the Edinburgh International Festival had its like been seen in Scotland – the Scottish Committee of the Arts Council turned it down on the grounds that it had arrived too late to be included in the Council's annual financial budget. No doubt the Committee's director at the time, Dr George Firth, was not to guess how rapidly Scottish Opera would expand once it got going, nor how enormous its international prestige was soon to become. He would certainly have been astonished to know that by 1971, a mere ten years later, his successor, Ronald Mavor, would be happily disgorging an annual subsidy of more than £200,000 to the Company. But excuses apart, the fact remains that, as Ainslie Millar has put it, "the Arts Council simply didn't get the message." Thwarted and depressed, but fortunately undaunted, the Company set about planning a season for the spring of 1962; and by that time a *deus ex machina* had arrived in the guise of Scottish Television.

3. First Season
—Why *Pelléas*?

FOR ALEXANDER GIBSON, disappointment was softened by a three-week tour of North America in February 1961, from which he returned with an invitation for the Scottish National Orchestra to perform there – provided that funds could be raised in Scotland to pay for the transport. So now he had two major projects on his hands, and this time his attempts to raise the money resulted almost instantly in a thrilling offer. Over lunch in a restaurant near the Glasgow office of *The Scotsman*, he learnt that Scottish Television was prepared to donate £1000 towards the SNO's American tour. The orchestra's Board of Directors, alas, got cold feet and declined the offer. As a result it went instead to Scottish Opera. It was just what the Company was waiting for. "Without it," as Richard Telfer has remarked, "we would never have got off the ground."

Meanwhile, in the background, some further consolidation had been going on. Recognising that the Scottish Committee of the Arts Council might become a serious stumbling block to the development of the opera company, Mr Gibson and his three fellow-pioneers had decided that the appointment of a powerful Advisory Council might prove beneficial. Mr Gibson recalls that "we invited all the people we could think of who might be helpful." Among them (and this was an early example of Scottish Opera's instinctive flair for choosing the right person) was Robin Orr, Professor of Music at Glasgow University, who was soon to become the splendidly forthright and dedicated chairman of the Company. Others, in alphabetical order, were Ernest Boden, a director of the SNO and member of the Scottish Committee of the Arts Council; William Fell, general manager of the SNO; Dr Mary Grierson, lecturer in music at Edinburgh University and a member of the Sadler's Wells Advisory Council; Dr Henry Havergal, Principal of the Royal Scottish Academy of Music in Glasgow; Hugh Marshall, vice-chairman of the SNO and Scottish Representative on the National Committee of the Arts Council; Sidney Newman, Professor of Music at Edinburgh University; Frederick Rimmer, senior lecturer in music at Glasgow University; Noel Stevenson, managing director of STV; and Graham Wark, Glasgow solicitor and opera-lover.

All these agreed to join in. Next it was decided to appoint an honorary president, and with this in mind Mr Gibson wrote to Lord Harewood saying:

"From the moment I left Sadler's Wells I have felt that if I have a mission in life it should be to further the cause of opera in my present sphere of activities." Eloquent words, to which Lord Harewood responded by immediately sending his acceptance.

Also around this time, John Boyle, a Glasgow solicitor and friend of Alexander Gibson, joined in the Company's deliberations, first as publicity officer, later as chorus secretary, and always as one of Scottish Opera's most dedicated enthusiasts.

The next task was to plan and cost a 1962 season and then once again to seek the support of the Scottish Committee of the Arts Council. With a little more time to play with, and with a fresh spirit of optimism generated by STV's promise of support, the pioneers were already beginning to think more ambitiously. Instead of a repertoire founded largely on Sadler's Wells, as the abortive 1961 season had been, something bolder was beginning to form in their minds. *Tristan and Isolde* was seriously considered at this time. So was an operatic rarity, *Tiefland*, by Eugen d'Albert, the Franco-German-Scottish composer who had been born in a hotel only a few yards from the King's Theatre, Glasgow. With its title translated as *The Lowlands*, this piece of nineteenth-century blood-and-thunder might have had – might yet have – a success in Scotland.

But in the end it was Richard Telfer, who had lived and worked for a period in France and had a special affection for the French repertoire, who thought of the work with which Scottish Opera sprang to fame and caught the imagination of opera-lovers all over Britain. Magnus Magnusson, in his *New Saltire* account of the company's early days, has related how, at the end of a Saturday evening concert at the now defunct St Andrew's Hall in Glasgow, Mr Telfer was waiting for Alexander Gibson with the words: "I think I have an idea for you." The idea took root at once. It was for a Debussy centenary production of *Pelléas et Mélisande*, an opera which had not been seen in Scotland for about forty years and which was not then in the repertoire of Covent Garden. The fact that the world's earliest and most famous Mélisande, Mary Garden, was at the time living in retirement in her home ground of Aberdeenshire at the age of eighty-four, gave an added fillip to the idea.

But because, even in an era that recognised Debussy's genius, a work as delicate and subtle as *Pelléas* remained a connoisseur's masterpiece, it was felt that it should be performed in alternation with a more basically popular work. Romantically, Mr Magnusson has suggested that Mr Gibson's thoughts then went back to the first opera he had ever seen. At any rate the choice was *Madama Butterfly*.

An immediate problem to be faced was that of rehearsals, and what they might cost. To mount a season based to some extent on Sadler's Wells was one thing; to prepare two productions from scratch, one of them of a strange and difficult masterpiece, was another. Would the King's Theatre in Glasgow be available for a sufficient period of rehearsal? Would the company be able to afford it, even if it were? Fortunately there was at the time a fresh avenue worth exploring. Recently a theatre project had been launched in Glasgow in which

"Is this how you want it to sound?" Alexander Gibson, conductor and musical director, in discussion with Robin Orr, chairman and composer of Full Circle, *Scottish Opera's first Scottish opera.*

the old Empress Theatre had been renamed the Falcon Theatre and chosen as the site of a valiant if short-lived enterprise which involved its serving as a centre for touring drama companies and local amateurs. The Falcon Theatre, it was ascertained, would be available – and at a price far below that of the King's.

By now Mr Gibson had ensured that the SNO would be free at the beginning of June 1962; but rather than book singers at this point, and get into bad odour two years running if bookings had to be cancelled, it was felt that the Scottish Committee of the Arts Council would have to be consulted as soon as possible. This was already a matter for some trepidation, because costs had risen steeply since the time of the 1961 plans. Although once again it was hoped that the performers would accept reduced fees, the week's season was expected to run up a bill of as much as £4500. Of this, it was hoped, about £2000 would come back from the box-office, and there was also the vital grant of £1000 from STV. Nevertheless, this left £1500 unaccounted for. Would Dr Firth, who had been unhelpful when asked for £1700 the previous year, come up trumps when asked for £1500?

At first, things seemed unpromising. When Mr Gibson, along with William Fell of the SNO, called on him, they found he was thinking at most of an £800 guarantee against loss. In the end this was increased to £1000 – after all, in the circumstances, it would have been shameful if the Arts Council had offered less than STV – but this left £500 still to be found. An added worry was the fact that the Falcon Theatre was now said to be in financial difficulties and was not expected to survive until June 1962. Sadly, the company began to fear they would have to drop the idea of mounting *Pelléas* and instead present something cheaper – say, a ready-made double-bill of Bartók's *Bluebeard's Castle* and Ravel's

L'Heure espagnole, which could be imported reasonably cheaply from London.

This, however, was felt to be a weak-kneed solution, which might result in the Arts Council reducing or withdrawing its guarantee (which had been offered specifically for the sake of *Pelléas*). Instead it was decided to invite a number of private individuals and organisations to make guarantees against loss, and in this way a further £725 was promised – enough to make the 1962 season at last seem viable. The press were notified and on 29 January 1962 the glad tidings were splashed across the front page of *The Scotsman*. "NEW OPERA GROUP FOR SCOTLAND" was the heading, and the report ran as follows:

"A new professional Scottish opera company has been formed. Its first programme of two operas will be presented in Glasgow's King's Theatre on June 4 for one week.

"The company is supported by an impressive advisory council, involving some of the most eminent figures on the Scottish musical scene. The whole project is built on the growing strength and reputation of the Scottish National Orchestra, whose conductor, Alexander Gibson, will be musical director of the company.

"The first programme is in the nature of a pilot scheme. If it receives an encouraging response in Glasgow, the scheme will immediately be extended to provide Edinburgh and other Scottish centres with short opera seasons to supplement the work of Sadler's Wells Opera, which can only bring a limited repertoire on its Scottish tours.

"A new organisation, Scottish Opera Ltd, a small company limited by guarantee, will act as the nucleus of the scheme, arranging the season's programme under the guidance of the advisory council. Leading roles will be sung by singers of national or international standing, and local choruses will be enlisted as required.

"The sponsors of the project believe that it is a logical part of the development of musical culture in Scotland, which has shown so marked an advance in post-war years and which is receiving splendid support from the education authorities."

The report went on to list the members of the advisory council, to name the operas being performed, and to express the hope: "If all goes well the scheme will become a significant feature of the musical and cultural life of Scotland in general and Glasgow in particular."

Not only did *The Scotsman* that day give the project twenty-four inches of space on its front page, but it contained on an inside page a lengthy article by Magnus Magnusson entitled "This is Scotland's chance." In this, in characteristically enthusiastic prose, Mr Magnusson declared that he could "see this as one of those immensely bold and imaginative breakthroughs that can revitalise an area of a nation's cultural life, the final act of faith that caps long months, even years, of dreaming and planning – an act that could be as decisive and fertilising as the foundation of the Scottish National Orchestra itself."

In comparison, the *Glasgow Herald*'s tribute to the scheme was surprisingly meagre – a perfunctory single-column announcement, seven inches long – but within a few months that newspaper, too, was to recognise just what the new company might mean to Scotland. On 6 April 1962, in a leader headed "The Scottish Opera," the *Herald* at last welcomed the Company and remarked that it was "a measure of the integrity of Scottish Opera's aims that we should be given the chance of hearing Debussy's masterpiece." However, with good Glasgow caution, the writer added apropos of the Debussy that "Rarity value in artistic matters should in theory always ensure interest, but in practice rarely does." And as if already fearing the worst, he commented darkly that "People responsible for promoting the arts in Scotland claim that public taste is disconcertingly fickle," and summed up his argument by saying: "Whether the eventual aim of four or five weeks of opera is ever achieved will depend on the support given in June."

Meanwhile, now that the green light had been given, the company was going ahead with casting its two productions. Denis Arundell, one of Britain's senior opera producers, agreed to stage both pieces and to accept a reduced fee for his services for the sake of working on a work as rare and inviting as *Pelléas*. Alexander Gibson would conduct most of the performances, and James Lockhart, another young Scot (he was a former assistant organist at St Giles' Cathedral in Edinburgh), was engaged to handle the remainder. Subsequently Mr Lockhart likewise developed his operatic powers: in 1969 he became musical director of the Welsh National Opera.

From the start, Mr Gibson's aim had been to make Scottish Opera the Covent Garden rather than the Sadler's Wells of Scotland; and it was doubtless with this in mind that he insisted on *Pelléas* and *Butterfly* each being performed in its original language by an international cast. For the title-roles in the Debussy a French soprano, Micheline Grancher, and a French-Canadian tenor, Emile Belcourt, were chosen. King Arkel was to be sung by another French-Canadian, Joseph Rouleau, who was already establishing himself at Covent Garden and was to sing many times again for Scottish Opera. The important role of Golaud at first posed problems, but after a lengthy search a further Frenchman, Louis Maurin, was selected. In 1962, as in 1972, the shortage of good French singers was severe, and the role of Geneviève went to an Italian, Laura Sarti, who at one time set up a record for appearing in more Scottish Opera productions than any other singer.

Originality of casting was soon to be hailed as one of Scottish Opera's strong suits, and in *Butterfly* as in *Pelléas* it was already noticeable. The need for a really credible Cio-Cio-San was obvious, since the success of Puccini's opera stands or falls on that requisite. First choice for the part was the British soprano, Marie Collier; but as she was already fully booked (the Company's decision to delay its casting arrangements until it was sure of help from the Scottish Committee of the Arts Council was now causing difficulties), Mr Gibson decided to act on a suggestion of Lord Harewood's that the young New York soprano, Elaine Malbin, might be worth considering. In Britain she had already sung in a television version of *I Pagliacci* and had appeared in the Glyndebourne *Ariadne auf Naxos* at the 1954 Edinburgh Festival. She accepted the invitation (the story

Wardrobe department at Stobcross Hall, with Arthur More, head of wardrobe in 1966, at work on the costumes for Falstaff. *Though dark and dingy, Stobcross played an important part in the development of Scottish Opera and many people retain a sentimental affection for the time spent there. Glasgow Corporation bought it for the company in 1964 for use as a production centre. The first floor, once a Boys Brigade drill hall, was turned into a rehearsal room. Above was the wardrobe, and in the basement the carpentry and prop-making department—all a hive of industry until the company moved in 1968 to the Scottish Opera Centre at Elmbank Crescent. Thereafter Stobcross Hall was demolished to make way for Glasgow's new roadway system.*

goes that she paid her own air fare from America) and was teamed with Charles Craig as Pinkerton, John Cameron as Sharpless, and William McCue as the Bonze. Mr Craig, a Beecham discovery who had earlier sung with the Carl Rosa, was then on the brink of creating an international reputation. He had recently scored a hit as Pinkerton at Covent Garden, had won the International Opera Medal for 1961–62, and during the next decade was to play major tenor roles for Scottish Opera and in some of the leading German houses. Mr Cameron was an established Australian baritone – Scotland was to see him again later as Punch in the English Opera Group's production of Harrison Birtwistle's *Punch and Judy* – and Mr McCue was one of several young Scottish singers who were henceforward to get their chances from Scottish Opera. Little did this promising young bass, who had once been an electrician in a colliery at Shotts, know that within a few years he would be singing such parts as Rocco in *Fidelio* and Fasolt and Hunding in *The Ring*. Other local singers, John Shiels and Norma Goldie, were given the roles of Goro and Kate Pinkerton.

In Wales, the success of the Welsh National Opera rested in the first place on its magnificent chorus; and it was on great choral operas, such as Verdi's *Nabucco* and Rossini's *Mose*, that that company sprang to fame. Scottish Opera, however, did not have choral roots of this kind; and although in later years,

(*Above*) The carpentry department at work at Stobcross Hall on Adam Pollock's settings for Albert Herring *in* 1966. *These were to become Scottish Opera's most widely-travelled settings, and in subsequent years they withstood frequent performances of Britten's opera in various parts of Europe.*

(*Below, left*) *John Stoddart, who designed Scottish Opera's famous* Così fan tutte *in* 1967, *talks to Jane Bond, the costume supervisor at the time, amid the ravishing dresses and tunics worn in Anthony Besch's production of Mozart's opera.*

(*Below, right*) *Sewing at Stobcross. Bruce Millar, son of Ainslie Millar, was one of many early volunteer helpers. Others included Veronica Gibson, Morag Millar, and Jane Hemmings, wives of important company personalities, who together worked on the final sewing sessions for Falstaff in 1966 and earned themselves the nickname of the Three Norns.*

in productions such as *The Trojans, Peter Grimes,* and *Fidelio,* the Scottish chorus was to become just as famous – if not more so – as the Welsh one, it did not occupy the key place in the early productions that the Welsh chorus did. Nevertheless, right from the start, a chorus was needed, and early in 1962 Dr Henry Havergal began to recruit singers from among his past and present students at the Royal Scottish Academy of Music, with Iain Campbell as chorusmaster. In subsequent seasons, when Mr Campbell was succeeded by Leon Lovett, recruiting was broadened to take in a wider range of Scottish vocal talent and a small professional nucleus was formed, all ultimately under the dynamic guidance of Arthur Oldham. In the second half of the 1960s, with his activities as chorusmaster split between Scottish Opera, the newly-formed and outstanding Edinburgh Festival Chorus, and the London Symphony Orchestra Chorus, Mr Oldham was to establish himself with extraordinarily rapid success as Britain's Wilhelm Pitz.

Meanwhile, back in April 1962, the musical scene in Glasgow was abuzz with preparations for the first spring season. The Scottish Opera Society Ltd was officially constituted and registered under the Companies Act, and an executive was appointed consisting of Alexander Gibson (Artistic and Musical Director), Ainslie Millar (Administrative Director), Richard Telfer (Company Manager), Ian Rodger (Company Secretary), Professor Robin Orr (Chairman), and Professor Sidney Newman (Vice-Chairman). The object of the company was simply stated: it was to create "opportunities for the people of Scotland to see and hear opera." News stories and think-pieces began to appear with increasing frequency in the Glasgow and Edinburgh newspapers, and even farther afield. The day before the box-office opened, a large photograph in the Glasgow *Evening Citizen* showed two students camping outside the King's Theatre in order to be first in the queue for seats. One of them was Thomson Smillie, who five years later became the Company's full-time publicity officer; the other was Anne Pringle, later to become Mrs Smillie. "Allanton bass realises lifelong ambition," proclaimed the *Wishaw Press* in a story about William McCue. "From baby-sitter to opera lead," said the Glasgow *Evening Times* of Elaine Malbin. "International opera cast gather in Glasgow," stated *The Scotsman,* and this and other papers displayed photographs of Miss Malbin looking scrumptious.

The *Daily Record,* in reports headed "Why the leading lady threw a tantrum" and "Star in tears," attempted to discover a clash of temperaments between Micheline Grancher and Miss Malbin. *The Scotsman,* in a more sober and relevant appraisal of the forthcoming season by Christopher Grier, begged audiences to do their homework on *Pelléas* before going to the theatre. The *Glasgow Herald,* in its most substantial article so far on the company, invited Robin Orr to provide an inside view of the approaching season.

In Scotland, opera had suddenly become news – maybe not so completely so as in Germany or Italy, but in a way which by British standards had refreshingly few class barriers about it. The message, which by now had got through even to the Arts Council, was plain: something was happening in Scotland which had the ability to enhance and transform the lives of many people.

4. Floreat Opera Scotica

ACTIVITIES WERE NOW accelerating towards the opening night, which had been postponed until 5 June 1962 – one day later than originally announced. During May, Alexander Gibson had steered the SNO for the first time into the rapt, delicate music of *Pelléas*. Denis Arundell had flown to Paris for rehearsals with the French singers; then the French singers had flown to Glasgow to find themselves rehearsing in, among other places, the Astoria Ballroom in Sauchiehall Street. *Madama Butterfly*, too, was well under way. At the first orchestral rehearsal with the principal singers at the St Andrew's Hall, the SNO had spontaneously applauded Elaine Malbin and Charles Craig at the end of the love duet. "That sort of thing," a spokesman for the company informed *The Scotsman*, "is almost entirely unknown in highly professional rehearsals of this sort."

Elsewhere in the city, in an abandoned workshop in Garscube Road, the sets for the two operas were being rapidly assembled by the designer, Mark King (they proved, alas, less durable than some of the company's later designs, which is why that 1962 *Pelléas* was never revived). Elsewhere again, the costumes were being stitched together by Mrs June Baker, a member of the phonetics department of Edinburgh University, who happened also to be a useful seamstress.

In later years, when all the departments of Scottish Opera were fully professional and housed in the big Scottish Opera Centre behind the King's Theatre, the arrangements for 1962 came to seem in retrospect decidedly makeshift. Yet the spirit of idealism which existed at that time, the feeling that miracles were being worked on a shoestring, was something very real and precious. For some people, those were the golden years of Scottish Opera; and when the Company grew better, richer, stronger, and ever more ambitious, that free unfettered feeling of pioneering, of striking water from the rock, like Moses in the wilderness, was thought by a few of the founder-members to have been lost.

But not yet. Magnus Magnusson has related how the final lighting rehearsals for *Madama Butterfly*, with which the season opened on 5 June, were still taking place while the audience was filing into the King's Theatre, and how at the very last moment volunteers were still dashing round town collecting low tables and vases with which to dress the stage. Yet in fairness to Scottish Opera at that point in its history, it must be said that such last-minute panics are not necessarily tokens of inexperience where opera companies are concerned; and all who have heard of what prefaced the rising of the curtain on Covent Garden's production of *Tristan and Isolde* in June 1971 will know that even the most established opera houses are not immune from them.

The box-office, too, had been kept busy in those last days. "Big success forecast for opera venture," predicted *The Scotsman* at the beginning of June. Advance bookings had suddenly jumped in two days from £1000 to £2000 and there were large queues for tickets – though earlier a Company official had reported that one of the biggest tasks had been to convince the public that the productions were going to be something more than "amateur shows with a professional in the leading role." But the public were soon able to see for themselves just how high Scottish Opera had set its sights. "Scottish Opera's fine debut" and "A Scottish landmark in opera" were the headings in *The Scotsman* and the *Glasgow Herald* on 6 June; and even people who at first had stated snootily that they did not and would not attend "provincial opera productions" were sooner or later won over when they realised that provincial productions were just what Scottish Opera's were not.

"June 5, 1962, may well prove to have been a very important date in the mottled history of Scotland's artistic affairs," stated Christopher Grier, the then music critic of *The Scotsman*, in his review of *Madama Butterfly*. "Nobody at this juncture can foresee what the future has in store for Scottish Opera," he continued, "but it made its debut last night in the King's Theatre, Glasgow, before a crowded audience with unmistakably impressive results. The enthusiasm of the applause at the end was not a gesture of politeness but the genuine expression of gratitude and admiration for professional services rendered. Admittedly, *Madama Butterfly* is a popular favourite, but because of that very fact audiences were not likely to let themselves be fobbed off with a limp performance. Nor were they."

Neither Mr Grier nor his anonymous colleague on the *Glasgow Herald*, however, regarded the performance as an occasion for blanket praise. Both of them treated Scottish Opera as a professional company, to be judged by professional standards, with its flaws duly noted alongside its virtues. Exciting and rewarding the performance certainly was; but, as Mr Grier pointed out, there was still work to be done. "An opera company is, of course, no Minerva to be brought into being fully armed and fit to beat La Scala at its own game overnight, over weeks or over months," he reminded his readers. And among the shortcomings of the performance, he noted that the chorus, though well trained, was "slightly undernourished vocally"; that Elaine Malbin's Butterfly was "in some ways better acted than sung"; that Charles Craig, though the "best Italian-type tenor in the country," was "still a comparatively stilted actor"; that the smaller roles were decently but not ideally cast; and that Denis Arundell's production, while very adequate, lacked positive distinction.

On the other hand, he found plenty to praise in Alexander Gibson's conducting: "Without disrespect to his colleagues, it was really his evening." And

"*Elaine Malbin*," said The Scotsman, "*was no kittenish, pattering Cio-Cio-San, full of winning ways, but more of an intrepid, though graceful, little person of strong character.*" *A special asset of all Scottish Opera's performances of* Madama Butterfly *has been the casting of a real child, instead of a dummy, as Butterfly's son. In 1962 the part was played by four-and-a-half year old Lindsay Marshall.*

in spite of reservations about Miss Malbin's voice ("rather thin on top and without a wide range of expressive colour"), Mr Grier found her characterisation compelling. "This was no kittenish, pattering Cio-Cio-San, full of winning ways," he said, "but more of an intrepid, though graceful, little person of strong character who could withstand the cruel shocks that were her lot with a finely drawn, desolate dignity. Furthermore, she was almost unique in looking the part."

Mr Grier also drew attention to what was to become a special feature of Scottish Opera's performances of *Madama Butterfly*, both then and in the later 1965 production and its revival in 1968: this was the decision, permitted under Scottish law, to have a real child to play the part of Trouble – a small, non-speaking role, potentially poignant, but in practice rarely so, for reasons set down by Mr Grier. "It was a clear gain," he said, "to have a 4½-year-old boy instead of a dummy or a stunted teenager as Butterfly's child."

The *Glasgow Herald* shared Mr Grier's reservations about Miss Malbin's voice and pointed out that although "of unquestionably international stature, she was nevertheless slow to establish the vocal assurance and dramatic conviction which the part of Butterfly demands." Not until "One fine day," said the *Herald* critic, was she "able to impart to her upper notes the effortless delivery and unforced tone which characterised the lower half of her range. Thereafter she became increasingly implicated in the drama, and in the climactic third act every gesture and every utterance was deeply felt and profoundly moving." Again there was praise for Mr Gibson's conducting. "It was a joy," the review ended, "to hear the ample sonorities of a full orchestra (the Scottish National) in place of the thin, undernourished sounds which too frequently issue from orchestra pits in provincial theatres."

Musical organisations in Scotland often complain about being neglected by the London press, but right from the start Scottish Opera made its presence felt, attracted metropolitan critics to Glasgow, and won their enthusiasm. The music critic of *The Times*, at that time still supposedly anonymous, included in his review of *Madama Butterfly* the happy assertion: "It is the most natural thing in the world that Scotland should have its own opera." And in his assessment of the performance, he showed that he was judging the Company's achievement by standards neither higher nor lower than those of his Scottish colleagues. Of Miss Malbin's Butterfly he wrote that she was "of ideal build and fine-grained tone, until she forced her voice into a wobble – but she matured before our eyes and ears, in the last act, into a commanding figure." Like Mr Grier, he reserved his highest praise for the conductor. "The hero of the evening," he proclaimed, "was Mr Alexander Gibson, who conducted a reading of remarkable operatic quality, in which singers and orchestra were so spurred that their efforts balanced automatically (even without a proper orchestra pit) and in which Puccini's effects shed grease-paint and became human, cogent and astonishingly new." Summing up, *The Times* critic wrote that "London has lost a good opera conductor in Mr Gibson; but the audience seemed tonight to appreciate that Glasgow had gained one."

From the start, Alexander Gibson's aim was to make Scottish Opera the Covent Garden rather than the Sadler's Wells of Scotland; and it was doubtless for that reason that he insisted on Pelléas et Mélisande *being performed in its original language by an international cast. Mélisande (centre) was sung by the French soprano, Micheline Grancher; King Arkel (left) by the French-Canadian bass, Joseph Rouleau; and Golaud (right) by the French baritone, Louis Maurin.*

Noël Goodwin, making the first of many visits to Glasgow to review Scottish Opera for the *Daily Express* and the magazine *Music and Musicians*, agreed with the other critics about the performance but was only half in favour of the repertoire for that first season: *Pelléas* was fine, but "whether *Butterfly* was a wise choice is a matter for the Scottish Opera Society and its conscience." Already Mr Goodwin was so much an admirer of the idea of Scottish Opera that he felt the company should set its sights higher than pieces he plainly regarded as tiresome warhorses; in subsequent seasons he was to express similar sentiments about the company's decision to perform Gounod's *Faust* and Puccini's *La Bohème* – but more of that later.

Certainly, though *Butterfly* won Scottish Opera ample praise, *Pelléas* the following night won it both praise and prestige. "Even in Debussy's centenary year," said *The Times*, "*Pelléas et Mélisande* is not an obvious choice for a new opera company. The Auld Alliance must be thanked for Glasgow's boldness in presenting it as one of the two operas which are this week inaugurating the venture of Scottish Opera, and for the sympathetic character of the performance it received."

The ability to rise to an occasion has always been one of Alexander Gibson's virtues as a conductor, and his first *Pelléas* was no exception. As *The Times* pointed out, the problems faced in performing *Pelléas* – a work whose greatness lies in the subtlety and understatement of text and music alike – can be daunting ones. "A movement or grimace too many, a personality too assertive, the merest suggestion of contrivance or banality in a piece of scenery – and away goes the illusion that these people, so insubstantial and unpredictable, have an existence and a significance, away goes the tragedy in the conflict between Golaud, the realist, and the innocents who surround him, away goes the magic of Debussy's score, its power to take root in the mind and dwell there for the rest of life."

In Scottish Opera's case, the risk of failure was obviously high. To quote *The Times* again: "A production, such as this one by Mr Denis Arundell, with decors by Mr Mark King, on a small stage and to a limited budget, with an orchestra and conductor quite new to the work, was more likely than not to suffer some of these shortcomings; astonishingly it leaps clear of them as if they were not there, and grasps the magic easily on the wing."

For the singers, *The Times* had nothing but enthusiasm and saw nothing unnatural about comparing Scottish Opera's cast with that for the Glyndebourne production which had opened that same year. "At Glyndebourne this season, Mélisande is the least convincing member of the cast, but in Glasgow Miss Micheline Grancher looks and sings the part almost ideally; she is all pre-Raphaelite innocence and eagerness to please, and invests the widest-eyed platitudes with credibility, even to 'Je suis heureuse, mais je suis triste.'" Emile Belcourt's Pelléas, "a gangling but romantic-looking hero," also won approval, though ringing roundness of tone was felt to be missing from his singing. Louis Maurin's Golaud was described as "a banked bonfire . . . all dignity and restraint, whose movements of violence happen as if without his volition." As for Laura Sarti and Joseph Rouleau, they "made no secret of the sublime things in their smaller roles."

This was high praise, but *The Times* had not finished yet. "There is an absence of pretentiousness about the whole production that allows the truth of the work to declare itself," the review of *Pelléas* concluded, "and this too was the distinction of the musical interpretation which Mr Alexander Gibson conducted. The orchestral score was sensitively and euphoniously played for him by the Scottish National Orchestra who have covered themselves with credit these last two evenings. *Floreat Opera Scotica!*"

The rest of the press confirmed *The Times*'s appraisal of the evening. In *The Observer*, Edmund Tracey remarked that when he first heard that a short season of Scottish Opera was to be given, he grew faint with apprehension: "Tovey's *The Bride of Dionysus*, perhaps, was on the list, and then, mightn't there be *Jeanie Deans*, by Hamish MacCunn – the Scottish Tchaikovsky as he used to be called?" But Mr Tracey's phantoms were rapidly put to flight when he discovered that the scheme was born not of nationalist fervour but of deep musical need. And musically, he said, the standard of the *Pelléas* performance was "very high, encouraging one to foresee a most promising future for the new venture." Mr Gibson, he added, evoked the "night and light and the half-light" of Debussy's score with exceptional sensitivity, and the confident playing of the SNO suggested "long and careful rehearsal."

However, Mr Tracey was less happy with the visual side of the evening. Mr Arundell's production, he thought, tended to be "vague and shapeless," though he was prepared to place some of the blame for this on Mark King's "inapt and dowdy settings." This point was made also by the *Daily Telegraph*, whose critic, Donald Mitchell, declared that the "major weakness of the production was the indifferent decor of Mark King, which must, one assumes, have actively hampered the work of the producer, Denis Arundell." But the musical standards, he said, promised well for the future. Alexander Gibson was an "always painstaking and often persuasive exponent of the score," even if "a suppler shaping of the rhythmic ebb and flow of the composer's invention" would have been welcome.

Anthony Hedges in *The Guardian*, on the other hand, thought that Denis Arundell's production "underlined the restraint in Debussy's score," and he described Alexander Gibson's conducting as "splendidly flexible and sympathetic." The critic of the *Glasgow Herald* thought the production restrained to the point of being elusive, but Noël Goodwin in the *Daily Express* felt that it had successfully caught the uncanny twilight mood of the opera – though he complained that the lighting had lagged behind its cues. Christopher Grier in *The Scotsman* likewise referred to the lighting deficiencies (a subject which was to recur in later seasons, when it became plain just how inadequately the switchboards of the Scottish theatres were equipped to cope with high-quality professional opera), but in a long and detailed review he found the general "stylised simplicity" of the performance very much to his taste.

By the end of that first week of Scottish Opera, in an auditorium seating 1700, nearly 3000 people had been attracted to *Pelléas* and nearly 5000 to *Butterfly*. The public had given the company a vote of confidence. The critics had paid tribute to its artistry. Dame Maggie Teyte, a great and beloved Debussy exponent of an earlier generation, had come to Glasgow at the age of seventy-four to attend the gala opening of *Pelléas* – she herself sang Mélisande with the old British National Opera Company in Glasgow in 1923. And for Alexander Gibson the opening night of the Debussy was made additionally memorable because – as he learnt at a civic reception after the performance – his wife (who had had to leave the performance in haste) had just given birth to their second son. Resisting the temptation to call him Pelléas, and for obvious reasons rejecting Golaud, they settled in the end for the name of Philip.

And so, as Christopher Grier summed up in *The Scotsman*, the good ship Scottish Opera was duly launched. In the months ahead it was to find itself in stormy seas; but meanwhile the captain and his crew were able to pride themselves on the smoothness with which they had set out from port and the seaworthiness of their sturdy little vessel.

5. Expansion

No COMPANY COULD have hoped for a happier start than Scottish Opera. On the last day of the short season, everybody involved must have felt a glow of pleasure that things had gone so well. But tomorrow, as Don Alfonso shrewdly remarks in *Così fan tutte*, comes the sorrow. Soon the bills for the two productions were flowing in and amounted in the end to almost £7000 – some £2500 in excess of the initial estimate. True, the situation was not quite so bad as it looked. The box-office returns, too, were higher than predicted – £2500 instead of £2000. Profits from the souvenir brochure brought in a further £580 (those were the days when people could still make a profit from souvenir brochures); Glasgow Corporation was persuaded to contribute £250; guarantors were called upon to fulfil their promises to the hilt.

But after all possible money had been raised, the Company still found itself £1400 in the red. "Funds needed to boost opera" was the glum heading in *The Scotsman* only a few days after the season ended. The accompanying news story, however, revealed that the funds in question were not for the season past but for the succeeding season. Already Scottish Opera was learning the lesson that if an opera company is to survive in Britain, it must look constantly ahead and somehow contrive to live with its losses. Not that Scottish Opera's losses were – or even now are – substantial in comparison with those of other British companies. Even while the writing of this book has been in progress, the Welsh National Opera has had to be saved from what seemed imminent extinction, and Sadler's Wells has run up a mounting overdraft. But by dint of good administration, stirring speeches, and a certain amount of civilised blackmail, backed up by a quickly-established reputation for musical excellence, Scottish Opera has always succeeded in raising most of the funds it has needed.

Fortunately, as early as that first summer, the Company recognised that if it was going to develop strongly and speedily it would need a forceful professional administrator to soldier side by side with its forceful professional conductor. To say, simply, that the job went to Peter Hemmings would be to underplay the arrival of the second of the two remarkable protagonists in our narrative. Had a lesser man been chosen, someone less courageous, less imaginative, less resourceful, less fully devoted to his cause, then Scottish Opera might never have grown to international prominence the way it has. Today it would still perhaps be stuck with a small subsidy, and a season of a few weeks every year. But from the start Mr Hemmings was determined to get the company on to a full-time footing. Later in these pages I shall quote some of the battle-cries with which he led Scottish Opera to one victory after another in his attempts to keep his singers and staff active for ever longer periods. Suffice it for the moment to say that the arrival in Scotland, at the age of twenty-eight, of this zealous and already experienced young operamane was one of the key moments in the Company's history.

Mr Hemmings did not as a matter of fact attend the first season of Scottish Opera. He was on his honeymoon at the time. But he recalls very clearly the day in mid-September when Alexander Gibson, whom he did not yet know very well, came and asked him if he would like the post. Mr Hemmings was then the Repertory and Planning Manager of Sadler's Wells, where he had been working for three years after reading Classics at Cambridge and serving as president of the University Opera Group (there is a photograph of him, savoured by members of his staff, showing him singing in *The Rake's Progress*). He had also been gaining valuable experience as General Manager of the New Opera Company, a London-based venture with a reputation for enterprising productions of important operas outside the standard British repertoire.

In the first place his Scottish appointment was to be a part-time one, involving an annual five weeks in Glasgow, for which Sadler's Wells agreed to release him, plus a certain amount of administrative work in London during the rest of the year. Not until 1965 did his appointment become full-time. By then it was plain that Scottish Opera was here to stay, and that its activities were exciting and challenging enough to justify Mr Hemmings moving his home to Glasgow.

Meanwhile, in the autumn of 1962, the Company was already preparing to expand. By November *The Scotsman* had announced the glad tidings that although Scottish Opera was "not very secure financially," the 1963 season would last twice as long and would include Edinburgh as well as Glasgow. By January it was stated that there would be three new productions instead of two. In 1963, as on many occasions later, Scottish Opera was to respond to its financial troubles by simply announcing an even more ambitious programme than the previous one and trusting that the money would be raised somehow. It always was.

Had the Company for a moment relaxed, had it failed to maintain the confident, assertive approach which enabled Mr Hemmings and Mr Gibson to push through their ideas, ably backed by Robin Orr and the Board of Directors, there would surely have been no *Albert Herring* in 1966, no *Trojans* in 1969, no *Ring* in 1971, no foreign tours or trips to England, no autumn and winter seasons added to the traditional spring one, no Scottish Opera Centre in which to work. If only Edinburgh Corporation had possessed a similar self-confidence over its long-postponed opera house and had simply started building it in the 1960s, the money for that project, too, would surely have been found and the theatre would now be open.

Peter Rice's setting for Il Seraglio *was, according to* The Scotsman, *"a sort of revolving portico-cum-patio." In the foreground, Adrian de Peyer and Marion Studholme as Pedrillo and Blonda. The London press hailed the production as a "Seraglio of smiles" and a "Salzburg on the Clyde."*

Not that all Scottish Opera's ambitions have materialised precisely as planned. Choice of repertoire has inevitably depended many times on the availability or non-availability of important singers. The 1963 programme, like that of the previous year, went through a variety of changes before being finally settled. At first a new production of *The Flying Dutchman* was considered, in honour of the 150th anniversary of Wagner's birth, but this idea was abandoned when it was learnt that David Ward could not be released by Covent Garden at the required time to sing the leading part. The fact that Verdi was born in the same year as Wagner, however, inspired another idea, or rather two ideas. The first was to do *La Traviata*, but this was dropped in favour of a bolder, more imaginative choice, which once again showed the sort of idealism for which Scottish Opera was already becoming famed. Instead of playing safe with standard box-office Verdi, the Company decided on *Otello*, a work which was to some extent a connoisseur's piece yet which had the special allure of being one of the four great masterpieces of the composer's full maturity. The fact that it had not been seen in Scotland for about forty years made the choice all the more exciting.

Wolf-Ferrari's *School for Fathers* was another early contender in 1963, but for the second year running had to be abandoned because of casting problems (a pity, though, that there was no subsequent attempt to stage this charming comedy, which has been absent from the British repertoire for far too long). *Così fan tutte* was also on the list around this time but it, too, was dropped – which was perhaps just as well, for if *Così* had been mounted in 1963 the great production of 1967, with Elizabeth Harwood and Janet Baker as the two sisters, would surely never have occurred. Instead *Il Seraglio* was picked.

However, the "prestige" production of the year was not intended to be the Mozart, nor even *Otello*, but the British premiere of Prokofiev's *Angel of Fire*, a little-known masterpiece which had made sporadic appearances in Europe and thereby gained the kind of reputation among Prokofiev devotees which *King Stag* has succeeded in gaining among Henze's. The work, with its incisive music and its mysterious, vision-tormented heroine, was said to exert a powerful spell on all who heard it. In Britain it already had a number of eager champions, among them Lord Harewood. Here, then, was a marvellous chance to let people experience at first hand an opera whose qualities they knew only by hearsay, yet which had been hailed as one of the most unusual, striking, and masterly works of the present century.

Because of the special nature of the opera, the Company hoped it might rate a special subsidy – perhaps from the Calouste Gulbenkian Foundation, which was known to support visionary ventures such as this. Accordingly, application was made and the Foundation responded with the offer of a grant more generous than any the company had so far received. But the money, £4500, was to be given on one condition: the Scottish Committee of the Arts Council would be required to play its part by donating a similar sum.

This condition was miraculously fulfilled (the Company in fact asked the Arts Council for £10,000 but no doubt felt itself lucky to receive £4500 – an amount, nevertheless, substantially smaller than the £22,000 which the Welsh National Opera was by then receiving from the Welsh Committee). But the production, alas, never took place. At this point in the Company's history, the difficulty of putting on Prokofiev's opera proved too formidable and the honour of giving the British premiere went two years later to Peter Hemmings's other team, the New Opera Company, whose production received a series of performances at the Sadler's Wells theatre in London.

In 1970, however, Scotland did get its chance to see *The Angel of Fire* when a sensational German production – complete with a gratuitous orgy of naked nuns but not at all complete so far as the actual music was concerned – was brought to the Edinburgh Festival by the Frankfurt Municipal Opera. But sensationalism was no substitute for the opera's deeper qualities, to which the truncated Frankfurt production, even with Anja Silja in the leading part, did scant justice; and so, although Scottish Opera failed to capture *The Angel of Fire* in 1963, the field is still open for a further attempt in some future year.

In 1963, however, the immediate problem was to find an alternative to the Prokofiev which would be important and exciting enough to stop the Gulbenkian Foundation from withdrawing its support. So one January morning, Alexander Gibson, Robin Orr and Ainslie Millar flew to London in the hope of

Constanze in the course of her taxing double-aria in Act Two of Il Seraglio. *Rae Woodland played this role in Scottish Opera's 1963 production; the Scottish actor Moultrie Kelsall, played the speaking role of the Pasha Selim.*

persuading the Foundation that the British premiere of Luigi Dallapiccola's *Volo di notte* (Night Flight) would be an equally worthwhile proposition. Certainly there was a good case to be made for the piece. Dallapiccola was a senior Italian composer who had never had the attention he deserved in Britain; and *Volo di notte*, based on Saint-Exupery's novel about an airline pilot heading for a fatal crash, promised to catch – if only in a small way – the imagination of a public that had never been particularly dedicated to the cause of modern opera.

Happily, the Foundation agreed to the change of plan; but as the Dallapiccola was only a one-act opera, a second piece was required to fill out the evening. Fortunately for the Company's finances, Peter Hemmings was able to supply a ready-made coupling in the form of the New Opera Company's production of Ravel's comedy, *L'Heure espagnole*, and it was decided to bring this to Scotland to form a nicely contrasted twentieth-century double-bill.

The 1963 repertoire was now complete. But a good deal more money had still to be raised if the season was to go ahead as planned. Though the 1962 deficit had by then been wiped out with the aid of a bank overdraft of £651 guaranteed by Ainslie Millar, the estimated cost of the forthcoming season threatened to be in the region of £22,360 – more than three times the amount of 1962. Of this sum, the Company expected to recoup about £8000 from the box-office. In addition, there was the combined contribution of £9000 from the Gulbenkian Foundation and the Arts Council, but this left more than £5000 still to be found.

Would the programme after all have to be curtailed? Luckily, other sources of revenue again proved available. Scottish Television, the Company's saviour the previous year, offered a further £1000. Glasgow Corporation again agreed to give £250, and some new and sizable grants came from elsewhere. The Musicians' Union, recognising the long-term value of an organisation such as Scottish Opera to musicians in Scotland, contributed £500; and now that the company's activities were extending eastwards, Edinburgh Corporation set Glasgow an example by chipping in very handsomely with £1000. No doubt the fact that the Lord Provost at the time, Sir Duncan Weatherstone, was an opera fanatic served to help this generous grant being pushed through (Sir

Duncan, it is worth recording in passing, all but succeeded in getting the Edinburgh opera house started but went out of office too soon to see his hopes materialise; his successor, Sir Herbert Brechin, was more interested in pushing through a scheme to bring the Commonwealth Games to Edinburgh than in giving the city its much-needed theatre).

One other major contribution to the 1963 season has yet to be mentioned; and because it was a particularly touching one, it deserves a paragraph to itself. This was the sum of £1191 donated by the long-established Edinburgh Opera Trust. If the amount seems an odd one, there was a reason for that: the £1191 represented the Trust's total funds.

With only £1500 still to be raised, Scottish Opera could now feel confident enough to press ahead. This time, in place of Denis Arundell and the ephemeral Mark King, the Company opted for a team of young producers and designers whose names were soon to become closely linked with the development of Scottish Opera and, indeed, with the progress of opera in general. The producers were Anthony Besch and Peter Ebert, the designers Ralph Koltai and Peter Rice. As examples of good shopping, the choice would have been hard to beat – though at the time Scottish Opera could hardly have forecast that in 1967 Mr Besch's *Così fan tutte* would be hailed as one of the finest Mozart productions of the century, nor that Ralph Koltai was even then in the process of revolutionising British operatic decor by stripping it of tiresome and inessential bric-à-brac and giving audiences superbly expressive abstract designs on which to feast their eyes. Peter Ebert, of course, had already established himself at Glyndebourne as Carl's heir, and in Glasgow had won local recognition for some work he had done with the Glasgow Grand; but as a producer of important big-scale pieces, of *The Ring* and *The Trojans*, he had yet to make his name, and it was Scottish Opera above all which helped him to do so. In tribute to his abilities, the Company before long appointed him Director of Productions; and with his foreign contacts – in America, in Holland, and in Germany, where he became Intendant of the Augsburg Opera in 1968 – he has helped Scottish Opera throughout most of its first ten years to maintain its adventurous international outlook.

Anthony Besch and Peter Rice, as it happened, had already worked together on *L'Heure espagnole* for the New Opera Company, and it was this that gave Scottish Opera the idea of using them for other productions in 1963. Mr Besch, this time with Ralph Koltai as designer, was allotted *Otello*. Mr Rice, this time with Peter Ebert as producer, was given the chance to bring to *Seraglio* the wit and flair he had already displayed in his delightful toytown settings for the Ravel. By a further permutation of the available talents, *Volo di notte* went to Mr Ebert and Mr Koltai.

Alexander Gibson, who had conducted the first nights of both productions in 1962, decided in 1963 to limit himself to the two major events, *Otello* and *Volo di notte*. *Seraglio* he passed on to Leon Lovett, his recently-appointed assistant with the SNO; and the Ravel was conducted by Brian Priestman, a familiar figure at Sadler's Wells. As for the casting, the Verdi was to feature Charles

Two scenes from The Turn of the Screw. To illustrate the prologue (above) the producer, Anthony Besch, conceived an ingenious tableau, enacted by Catherine Wilson and Gregory Dempsey as Governess and Guardian, with John Robertson (left) as narrator. Below: the closing scene with Timothy Oldham as Miles and Catherine Wilson as the Governess.

Much of the atmosphere of The Turn of the
Screw *derived from John Stoddart's filmy, floral,
softly dappled settings, subtly lit by Charles
Bristow. The scene (left) shows Miles (Timothy
Oldham) in the garden and Flora (Nan Christie)
at the window while the ghosts (Gregory Dempsey
and Milla Andrew) lurk in the background.*

Above: *Catherine Wilson, who sang the Govern-
ness in* The Turn of the Screw, *was also a delightful Nancy in* Albert Herring. *Here she is
seen in Mrs Herring's shop.*

A remarkable feature of the Scottish Opera production of Albert Herring was the way the large cast was held together, almost intact, season after season. Above: in Lady Billows' parlour, are six of the most familiar faces: Patricia Clark as Miss Wordsworth, Francis Egerton as Mr Upfold, William McCue as Superintendent Budd, Judith Pierce as Lady Billows, Johanna Peters as Florence Pike, and Ronald Morrison as Mr Gedge. Below: Miss Wordsworth and Mr Gedge in close-up.

(Left) Osmin (Inia Te Wiata) and Pedrillo (Adrian de Peyer) in Il Seraglio. *The modern stepladder was presumably a deliberate anachronism.*

(Right) Blonda in altercation with Osmin. Marion Studholme and Inia Te Wiata in Il Seraglio.

Craig, Peter Glossop, and a young and then little-known Lebanese soprano, Luisa Bosabalian, as Otello, Iago, and Desdemona. *Seraglio* was to have Rae Woodland, Marion Studholme, John Wakefield and Adrian de Peyer as the two pairs of lovers, with the amiable Maori bass, Inia Te Wiata, as Osmin, and the dour-faced Scottish actor, Moultrie Kelsall, in the speaking part of the Pasha Selim.

Marie Collier, whom the Company had failed to get in 1962 for *Madama Butterfly*, was this time safely secured to sing Concepcion in the Ravel (the Glasgow *Evening Citizen*, fired with enthusiasm for her good looks and for her role in an opera which Ernest Newman had nicknamed "The Immoral Hour," later printed a giant photograph of her with her toes in the air, lounging on a raft on Loch Lomond). Peter Glossop, Emile Belcourt, Howell Glynne and Edward Byles made up the rest of the cast, and in *Volo di notte* the main part was sung by Don Garrard, with William McCue, Marie Collier and Laura Sarti in support.

In the weeks before the season opened, the Scottish Opera Chorus – which had a more important part to play this year than in 1962 – was strengthened and enlarged by Leon Lovett, who had taken over the job of chorusmaster. The scenery, which had been constructed in London, was brought north by train. The newspapers were again filled with information and gossip about the Company's activities. "As sweet as she sounded . . . so singer Peter fell for Joyce" was the *Evening Citizen*'s way of introducing the Glossops to its readers. "Second glowing season of Scottish Opera" was the heading for Magnus Magnusson's now predictably excitable preview in *The Scotsman*. "Verdi, Boito, and *Otello*" was the refreshingly sober title of an extensive essay by "a special correspondent" on the *Glasgow Herald*'s leader page.

But much space was deservedly given around this time to the efforts Scottish Opera was making to attract a new and youthful public. Among many titbits of news was the fact that pupils in some thirty Glasgow schools were receiving special lessons in *Seraglio* before being treated to a special matinee performance at the King's Theatre. The Glasgow Education Committee enterprisingly gave a grant of £750 towards grooming a new generation of opera-lovers, and some of the leading singers devoted time between rehearsals to visiting schools and performing excerpts from the operas.

In subsequent years, school matinees were to become a regular and valuable feature of Scottish Opera's work, and in 1969 the Company pioneered a scheme – the brainchild of Ainslie Millar – in which some of the younger singers toured Scotland with a mixed programme of talk and music under the title of Opera for Schools. At first the presentation seemed a little too square and stilted to make many converts; but by 1971, with Michael Maurel as an engaging host,

Finale of Il Seraglio. Pasha Selim (Moultrie Kelsall) forgives Belmonte (John Wakefield). In the background, to the right of the staircase, stand Pedrillo (Adrian de Peyer), Blonda (Marion Studholme), and Constanze (Rae Woodland).

and with the programme devoted in its entirety to Antony Hopkins's amusing Peter Ustinov-like *Doctor Musikus*, Opera for Schools had got promisingly into its stride.

Certainly, in 1963, there was sufficient of an audience problem to make the wooing of a new generation seem vital. "It would be no service to pretend that audiences for the recent Scottish season were as large as they should have been," remarked David Drew severely in a retrospective article in the *New Statesman*; and a glance at the box-office returns indeed suggested that Scottish Opera had perhaps at this time overestimated the operatic sophistication of its public. *Otello*, it is true, attracted full houses in both Glasgow and Edinburgh; but *Seraglio* failed to rise above 54 per cent, and for the double-bill the theatres were only a quarter full. One interesting fact to emerge from the box-office figures, however, was that in Edinburgh – reputedly a less operatic city than Glasgow – the average attendance for the week was 59 per cent, whereas in Glasgow it was 6 per cent lower.

But whatever the disappointment over the failure of the Mozart to attract large houses (in the case of the double-bill, only a total idealist could have expected Dallapiccola to be a draw), it was clear from the start that *Otello* was going to be a sure-fire success. "TONIGHT, OTELLO," proclaimed the poster outside the King's Theatre, Glasgow, on 27 May; and as one London critic remarked, still dazed at the idea of a city like Glasgow creating its own production of late Verdi, those blunt, confident capitals made an extraordinary sight as he arrived for the opening of the company's second season.

Then, when Alexander Gibson stepped into the pit and unleashed the storm, and the curtain rose on Ralph Koltai's striking hexagonal ramp, the directness of the poster was quickly confirmed by the performance, which went straight for the essentials of the score. "This was not *Otello* the supreme lyric tragedy, the appalling study of human nobility gutted by its own destructive urges, the music-drama that Shakespeare would have written if he had had the luck to be a composer, nor could it be expected to be," stated David Cairns in the *Financial Times*. "What it was was simply a superb Italian opera, the greatest of them all, performed *con fuoco* in an atmosphere of high dedication."

If a slight reservation could be detected in Mr Cairns's first sentence, this was because he felt that Mr Gibson's conducting was as yet "rather quick, light, lacking in grandeur and expansiveness," and that some of the singers were still too new to their roles to probe the depths of Verdi's masterpiece. Charles Craig's "firm, mellifluous and well-shaped" singing won praise; not so his acting abilities as the Moor, which "carried soldierly dignity to the point of absent-mindedness." Of Mr Craig's exit after the vengeance duet, watched all the way by the gloating Iago, Mr Cairns wrote that it was "as measured as a colonel leaving his club."

Even Peter Glossop's Iago, suggested Mr Cairns, was a "brilliant first sketch rather than a complete and fully realised portrait." Nevertheless, it was "already an almost unrecognisable advance on his wooden Rigoletto [at Covent Garden] of a season or two ago," and among the words Mr Cairns chose to describe it were "physical," "excitable," "gross," "not often lapsing into conventional villainy," "thought out," and "sung with intelligence and variety as well as force." To have a performance called intelligent is thought by many singers to be the ultimate insult, but plainly Mr Cairns liked Mr Glossop's portrayal enormously and described "Era la notte" as "flesh-creeping in its enjoyment of the bloated vision of the babbling Cassio."

Concerning Miss Bosabalian's qualities, Mr Cairns seemed inclined to reserve judgment, but he thought she was at least "comfortably above average," and that "without starting at all badly, [she] got better as the evening progressed." Like Mr Craig, however, Miss Bosabalian proved to be no great shakes at acting; and to accept this chubby little soprano as Desdemona, credulity had to be stretched fairly far (it had to be stretched farther still when she turned up in 1967 in the role of Mimi). Yet the overall vivacity of the performance, the strength of Mr Koltai's settings, the sweep of Mr Besch's production did much to carry those members of the cast who, visually speaking, could be regarded as passengers.

Among a number of vivid dramatic touches to which Mr Cairns and other critics referred was Iago's tense, quivering pose as he gazed at the handkerchief dropped by Desdemona. Similarly, the sight of him kicking the prostrate body of Otello, so that it rolled down the ramp and sprawled several yards below, left an indelible impression. By operatic standards, too, there was an uncommonly good duel in Act One. These, however, were details. In the end, whatever the little flaws and virtues of this *Otello*, it was an evening that had its priorities right. To quote Mr Cairns once more, "Throughout the performance there is a feeling that the music is in command, chastening and inspiring all concerned, including the Scottish Opera Chorus and the Scottish National Orchestra and their conductor, Mr Gibson, to whom much of the credit for this bold and remarkably successful enterprise must belong."

If I have quoted freely from Mr Cairns's review, it is because it stated so lucidly most of the points which were raised, either in praise or in blame, and to a greater or a lesser degree, by other critics at the time. These views ranged from Colin Mason's unexpectedly harsh appraisal in *The Guardian* (unexpected because, in the years before his sadly early death, Mr Mason was becoming an increasingly benign and happy critic) to what were tantamount to rave notices in the *Sunday Telegraph*, the *Glasgow Herald*, and *The Scotsman*. *The Times* and the *Daily Telegraph* came somewhere in between. Most of the critics lavished the bulk of their praise on the conductor, producer and designer, and on Mr Glossop's Iago; and in surveying the season with considerable enthusiasm for *Music and Musicians*, Noël Goodwin made the important point that "in a venture of this sort the second year is crucial, depending for success on something more than novelty value and good intentions." Scottish Opera, it was plain, had passed Mr Goodwin's test.

The good features of this *Otello* apparently induced in some critics a state bordering on euphoria; for when *Il Seraglio* opened the following evening, it inspired Peter Stadlen, of all unlikely people, to prattle in the *Daily Telegraph* about "a Salzburg on the Clyde," and "a *Seraglio* of smiles." *The Times*, not to be

Volo di notte, *Dallapiccola's setting of Saint-Exupery's novel about the early days of flying, was the first of many operas by living composers to be staged by Scottish Opera. Marie Collier and Don Garrard played Mrs Fabien and Riviere, two of the leading parts.*

Keeping tabs on the night flight which provided the dramatic framework of Dallapiccola's Volo di notte. *Ralph Koltai's geometric designs, with their use of ladders and metal rods, gave a foretaste of some of his later work for the company.*

outdone, urged those Glaswegians who stayed away from the opening performance to "hasten to repair their folly" because "it would be hard to find a more enjoyable presentation anywhere of this good-humoured work."

The success of the evening, continued *The Times*, lay in the complete fusion of music and stage action. "There was no conscious striving for effect of any kind: everyone behaved with a lifelike plausibility, and sang of their pain and pleasure as if it were the natural and inevitable thing to do." Peter Ebert was commended for creating people rather than puppets. Peter Rice was thanked for devising a utility set which at the same time preserved the necessary fairy-tale fantasy. "A mere pull of a rope changed walled exteriors into inviting interiors in his cunning, revolving Pasha's palace, yet without ever destroying our illusions." Leon Lovett won gratitude for "invariably finding the natural pace of every aria and ensemble, and for persuading the Scottish National Orchestra to play with the suave urbanity that is more than half the secret of Mozart's style." Singers and chorus were accorded similar praise.

So far, more than good. The *Glasgow Herald*, too, seemed pleased, but other members of the home team of critics proved less enthusiastic. John Currie, *The Scotsman*'s Glasgow correspondent, began his review promisingly enough with the statement that the company's "un-parochial standard" was being maintained on all sides. But his praise for the performance was punctured here and there by some sharp little barbs. Constanze's big Act Two aria, for instance, was "ruined by the needless fussing of Pasha Selim"; and Peter Rice's ingenious

As a companion piece for Volo di notte, *Scottish Opera imported the New Opera Company's production of Ravel's* L'Heure espagnole. *The witty décor, with its cutout clocks, was by Peter Rice and the cast included Marie Collier as Concepcion.*

set, "a sort of Turkish revolving portico-cum-patio," was "initially a delight, but latterly a pest and a nuisance."

A week later, when the production reached Edinburgh, Christopher Grier backed up his Glasgow colleague. Referring to the "tremendous acclaim" with which the production had been greeted by the London press, he declared: "Bully for Scottish Opera, but at the risk of appearing like a death's head at a feast, I cannot be quite so enthusiastic." Just why Mr Grier saw himself as a harbinger of doom, his review did not in fact make clear. True, he did not exactly rave about the performance; but he found nothing to say in its disfavour and the nearest he came to complaint was perhaps his description of Leon Lovett's conducting as "absolutely straightforward."

Anthony Hedges in *The Guardian* was somewhat more outspoken. "Neither Peter Ebert's production nor Leon Lovett's conducting seemed sufficiently in command of things," he said; and in the *Sunday Telegraph*, John Warrack likewise deemed Mr Lovett to be disappointing. "Here," he recalled, "was little of the lyricism and rhythmic brightness that first drew attention to him at Cambridge." Nevertheless, the balance of opinion suggested that Scottish Opera's first shot at Mozart was a pretty good one. Whether it came anywhere near the standard of the remarkable 1967 *Così fan tutte*, however, nobody by that time felt disposed to remember.

With the arrival, on the third night of the season, of the double-bill of Dallapiccola and Ravel, it was obvious that the Company had pulled off an artistic hat-trick. Some years later, in *Opera* magazine, Harold Rosenthal was to refer warmly to Scottish Opera's repertoire policy – so much more enterprising, he claimed, than that of one or two other British organisations. And indeed, to have staged by 1972 four operas by Britten, one by Henze, and two by Scottish composers, plus Stravinsky's *Rake's Progress* and *Soldier's Tale*, speaks volumes for the Company's courage in the face of what threatened at first to be public apathy.

Yet the fact that nearly 2000 people saw the Dallapiccola in 1963 was surely an achievement of sorts – enough to justify the performances and the sizable grant that was needed to put them on. Here Scottish Opera firmly laid the foundations for the rest of its modern repertoire with a work (composed in 1939) whose British premiere had been long overdue. Two performances were given in Glasgow, another two in Edinburgh; and in each city, the piece (aided, no doubt, by the Ravel) made a strong enough impression to attract a larger house for its second performance than for its first. Had it been put on a third time, attendance might have been better still – for by then the newspaper reviews and word of mouth would have had time to make their effect.

As the Company's first choice of a modern opera – not counting the ill-fated Prokofiev project – it was a thoughtful and sensible one, being neither too conventional nor too advanced for the kind of public Scottish Opera was trying to encourage. In *Music and Musicians*, Noël Goodwin placed it somewhere between Puccini and Berg in style. In *The Scotsman*, Christopher Grier warned his readers not to expect big, fruity tunes; "nor," he added, "need anyone fear that they are being kept at arm's length by the score." And in the *New Statesman*, commending the Company for choosing Dallapiccola, David Drew remarked that in the field of modern opera, "the only roads to easy success are disreputable, and the Company was well advised to avoid them." To include a modern opera in a season of this kind, Mr Drew continued, "only makes sense if it demonstrates the continuing vitality and creative relevance of the operatic form. Any other criterion, whether it leads to the choice of a worthy failure for the cachet it may bring or an unworthy success for the cash it may bring, is an insult to the audience."

Nevertheless, Mr Drew (who, being one of Britain's leading Dallapiccola authorities, had a special interest in the project) confessed to some "preliminary alarm" at how the piece might be handled by the freshly fledged Company. "In vocal score," he said, "Dallapiccola's adaptation of Saint-Exupery's famous novel might seem a typical early effort of a talented composer who is not yet sure of his intentions, musically or theatrically." Would Scottish Opera have the know-how to see beyond what might be construed at first sight as elements of uncertainty in the music? The answer, in Mr Drew's opinion, was yes. "Understandingly produced by Peter Ebert, cunningly set by Ralph Koltai . . . and for the most part well sung, the piece came to life in the theatre, and was more moving than I had believed possible. Among the leading roles Marie Collier – also the heroine, in every sense, of *L'Heure espagnole* – was particularly good, and in the smaller part of the Radio-telegraphist Raymond Nilsson was outstanding."

Summing up, Mr Drew decided that any complaints about *Volo di notte* being untheatrical could be safely discounted. "The question depends on what is meant by theatre – what is meant in this case is an Italianate fusion of Expression-ism and Symbolism, via *Pelléas* and the Berg operas. The work has its own, slowish, tempo; and this, by the way, was perfectly set off by *L'Heure espagnole*. It was an almost ideal programme of its kind."

Commenting on the size of the audience, Mr Drew added that "even the BBC stayed away, thus neglecting not only an important British premiere but also a company in need of every support." Perhaps the BBC could not forgive Scottish Opera its links with STV. At any rate, although by now a number of productions have been broadcast over the years, the Company has never received from the Corporation the consistent support it has deserved – in 1969 only the Carthaginian part of *The Trojans* was recorded, and in 1971 the December *Ring* cycle was ignored altogether, in spite of the fact that this was the first complete alternative *Ring* to Covent Garden's to be presented in Britain since the days of the British National Opera Company.

In general, the rest of the press shared David Drew's views on the production of the Dallapiccola, but not everyone agreed with him about the excellence of the opera itself. Thus Peter Stadlen in the *Daily Telegraph* thought it dramatically ineffective and far less moving than the score of Dallapiccola's more famous one-act opera, *The Prisoner*; and although Alexander Gibson conducted "an extremely well-prepared and authoritative performance," Mr Stadlen said he "simply could not take an interest in the protagonist Rivière, an airline director who imagines that it is his obsession with aviation (and with progress in general) that is responsible for the death of one of his pilots."

The loss, perhaps, was Mr Stadlen's, though Anthony Hedges in *The Guardian* likewise found himself out of sympathy with the piece. "Almost unbroken lyricism and heavy orchestration," he suggested, "makes the music less flexible to the demands of dramatic pace than one could wish, and it seemed at times that faster tempi could generate more tension." Peter Ebert's production, he thought, was "rather hampered" by the difficult libretto, though "within those limitations it was effective, as was Ralph Koltai's stark, geometric set." *The Times* felt that the opera "just failed to make its mark as music drama," and John Warrack in the *Sunday Telegraph* considered that the music, "pleasantly atmos-pheric" and "fluently scored," gave scant idea of the tensions raging in Rivière's breast. *The Scotsman* also thought there was "perhaps a flaw at the heart of the matter, the character of Rivière himself"; and the *Glasgow Herald*, while stating the production to be "a further feather in the cap of Scottish Opera," felt that "contrary to expectation," the Dallapiccola yielded to the Ravel in terms of dramatic effectiveness.

Still, if one accepts the theory advanced by Dr Alan Walker in his book, *An Anatomy of Music Criticism* – that the views of a critic who reacts positively to a piece of music are more valuable than, and not simply the opposite of, the views of a critic who reacts negatively – then David Drew's assessment of *Volo di notte* was the most important the work received in 1963. In any event, both Scottish Opera and the Gulbenkian Foundation could pride themselves that they enabled an underrated masterpiece to gain a hearing.

6. Consolidation

THE HISTORY OF Scottish Opera can be divided so far into two phases. The first culminated in 1965 with *Boris Godunov*, the second in 1971 with the complete *Ring*. Of the Company's first four seasons, that of 1964 was perhaps the least "progressive." Since the choice of works the previous year was felt to have shot fractionally ahead of local taste, with a noticeable effect on bookings, a policy of consolidation was now deemed advisable. And so, in a written introduction to the 1964 programme-book, the chairman, Robin Orr, delivered what seemed tantamount to an apologia admitting that the music was "deliberately more conservative," but adding in explanation that "if Scottish Opera is to fulfil its ambition to become a national company for Scotland it must build up a reperoire of standard works which will provide a foundation for the future." Earlier, Peter Hemmings had made the same point another way when he announced at a press conference that the decision to give "classics only" was taken in order to prove that there was "massive support" for the basic idea of opera in Scotland, on a professional scale and at an international level.

The standard works for 1964 were to be Gounod's *Faust* and Mozart's *Don Giovanni*, with a revival of the previous year's *Otello*. The thought of a *Faust* from Scottish Opera struck some critics as odd, not to say unsatisfactory, and the sharpest comments on the subject came from Noël Goodwin in *Music and Musicians*. In a column entitled "Step-aside strategy," he opined that for Scottish Opera to present Gounod along with Verdi and Mozart seemed comparable with a nascent theatre company putting its faith in Shakespeare, Shaw and *East Lynne*. Asking whether *Faust* could really be considered a reliable guide to public support ("except among elderly nostalgics for whom nothing is ever as good as it used to be"), Mr Goodwin said he doubted if the younger opera-goer, whatever his or her individual tastes, was in any frame of mind to take Gounod seriously any more.

"If this opera gets by at all today," he pointed out, "it is as a vehicle for star singers and nothing else, and that is not Scottish Opera's purpose. Their concern ought to be mainly with developing a young audience for opera, who will increasingly sustain it in future years. If that audience derives its image of opera as an entertainment from *Faust*, the task of attracting it to Stravinsky or Britten or whatever will become correspondingly more difficult, whether it happens

Aged Faust (André Turp) in the prologue to Gounod's opera.

to like *Faust* or not. It is not a question of duty but of strategy, at the box-office as much as elsewhere. For the sake of its future I hope Scottish Opera will reconsider its policy – and quickly, before too much ground has been lost."

Musical organisations never like being publicly informed by critics that their policies are wrong, and *Music and Musicians* soon received a reply from Scottish Opera jointly signed by Peter Hemmings and Alexander Gibson. On the whole it was tactfully worded. Mr Goodwin's gentle strictures, it said, were so obviously the result of a desire to see Scottish Opera developing along the right lines that "we should like to assure him that his fears are groundless." The letter then referred to the lack of public enthusiasm for modern opera, but added that the Company all the same intended to include modern works in future seasons. As for the 1964 repertoire, *Otello* was, by Verdi standards, a "rarely seen opera" and "the obvious choice for the Shakespeare centenary year"; *Giovanni* had not been seen in recent years in Scotland and had been out of the Sadler's Wells repertoire for several years; *Faust* was "even more of a rarity today," and the decision to perform it in French was "a logical outcome of Scottish Opera's successful initial production of *Pelléas et Mélisande*." But not only that: *Faust* in its time had been "the most frequently performed opera ever written and it is surely right that a new generation of opera-goers should have the opportunity of endorsing their parents' opinion."

As far as they could, Mr Hemmings and Mr Gibson made a good case for their choice, but Mr Goodwin remained unconvinced. In a reply to the reply he said: "Scottish Opera argues that only standard operas will enable the Company 'to judge how broad-based is the Company's potential support.' On the contrary, if it indicates anything at all, it will be the narrowest basis of support, for it restricts potential interest to one small sector of the operatic repertoire. The choice of *Faust* in this context is all the more astonishing since its past success belongs to a vanished era. It has demonstrably failed to hold the repertoire for the 'new generation' except in a few of the most backward-looking opera houses. Moreover, has any new generation ever *endorsed* its parents' opinion in anything – particularly in matters of taste?"

Mr Hemmings and Mr Gibson refrained from carrying the correspondence further. They had made their point; as had Mr Goodwin. Certainly, whether conservative or not, the 1964 season did not look like being any cheaper than the 1963. Indeed, preliminary calculations suggested that the total bill might be as high as £31,000 – £8000 more than the previous year. But by now the Company (and also fortunately its benefactors) was coming to accept the fact that costs were bound to keep leaping upwards each year; and after all, in spite of some poor attendances in 1963, Scottish Opera had emerged from that season with a deficit of less than £1000 – which, as *Opera* magazine pertinently pointed out, "represents under 5 per cent of the season's expenditure, compared with the 10 per cent which is shown at Sadler's Wells."

Consolidation, not only in repertoire but also in money, was a theme of 1964. From the Gulbenkian Foundation came a splendid vote of confidence: a grant of £15,000 to be spread over three years. From the Scottish Committee

(Above) Robert Savoie as Valentin sings his famous air in Faust.

(Below) Joseph Rouleau as Méphistophélès is temporarily quelled during the Kermesse scene when the other singers advance on him using their sword-hilts as crucifixes. In this picture, Peter Rice's Gothic setting is seen to good advantage.

of the Arts Council came a similar prize for good conduct: a grant of £9000 – twice the sum given the previous year. The Musicians' Union this time contributed £2000. Glasgow Corporation, perhaps recalling that Edinburgh had made it look mean in 1963, stepped up its grant from £250 to £2000, thereby overshooting Edinburgh which this time supplied £1250. And just as the Edinburgh Opera Trust in 1963 had donated its entire funds, so the Glasgow Arts Theatre Trust in 1964 handed over £1400 which had been set aside for the by then defunct Falcon Theatre project. Between them, these grants amounted to almost £21,000 – two-thirds of the estimated cost of the season. The other third, it was hoped, would come from the box-office.

When booking for the Glasgow part of the season opened in April, it was plain that support for the Company was going to be greater than in 1963, and perhaps even broader-based than Mr Hemmings and Mr Gibson had dared to expect. During the first week, ticket sales reached a record £2000 in Glasgow. By the beginning of May, with the first performance still a fortnight ahead, this figure had risen to £3000. "Opera bookings heavy," exclaimed the *Glasgow Herald*. "Boom bookings for Scottish Opera," stated the *Daily Mail* in an article which revealed that there had been demand for tickets from south of the Tweed and from as far north as Elgin. "People are realising," said Robin Orr in an interview, "that we are presenting full-scale international standard productions, equal to those of the great centres of opera."

Certainly, in 1964, the performances consistently bore out his remarks. *Faust* opened the season in Glasgow on May 14, and whether you regarded it, like Noël Goodwin, as a reprehensibly retrogressive step or as a timely revival of a once-favourite opera, it was clear that here was a masterly piece of musical and dramatic rethinking. Once again, Anthony Besch had been invited to work as producer, and Peter Rice as designer; and they, with Alexander Gibson as conductor, succeeded between them in injecting strong new life into the piece. So far as the cast was concerned, there had been – as with *Pelléas* in 1962 – some considerable raking among the available French singers, but in the end a good team was recruited, which included a French-Canadian Faust, André Turp, a French Marguérite, Andréa Guiot, and a Belgian Valentin, Julien Haas. For the role of Méphistophélès, another and more familiar French-Canadian, Joseph Rouleau, was borrowed from Covent Garden. Laura Sarti, in Scotland for the third year running, was Siebel, and the roles of Marthe and Wagner went to two Scottish singers, Johanna Peters (whose subsequent appearances with the Company were to become even more frequent than Miss Sarti's) and John Shiels.

David Cairns, back for the *Financial Times*, thought that Mr Turp was "not the most histrionically compelling Faust one can imagine, even allowing for the unusual feebleness of the role." But – except for the opening night, when an inflamed tonsil was causing him to sing flat – he brought what Mr Cairns admitted was "an attractive mixture of ardour and sweetness" to his music. Again Mr Cairns thought that Miss Guiot might have made a little more of the character of Marguérite, but she "sang stylishly, with a clear, firm, crystalline tone" – not qualities one necessarily expects from a product of the Paris Opéra-Comique.

Like most of his colleagues, Mr Cairns considered that the most interesting performance was Mr Rouleau's Méphistophélès – "a hard, rangy, slightly buccaneering figure, with a touch of Don Giovanni impersonating Leporello." Mr Rouleau, as Mr Cairns was pleased to note, "did not try to come the formidable Satan over us more than once or twice. There was a gleam in the eye, a bounderish swagger, an almost waggish sense of humour and a frank vulgarity which made the sudden insane laughter in the Serenade almost spine-chilling if such a sensation were not quite beyond the range of Faust's chaste pleasures."

Mr Rouleau apart, the evening's principal assets lay with the team of Messrs Gibson, Besch and Rice. To the music, Mr Gibson brought a pulse and colour, a sense of timing that displayed Gounod's score to unexpected advantage. Mr Besch, though inevitably hampered by the opera's cardboard characters in a way he would not be three years later when he entered the much deeper world of Così fan tutte, nevertheless made something of the big, famous moments of the piece – the kermesse, the soldiers' chorus, the church and prison scenes. These were superbly presented, the soldiers' chorus in particular being a striking splash of colour, with scarlet tunics and white banners imposingly arrayed against a turquoise sky.

For this, of course, Mr Rice shared the honours; and indeed his decision to present the bulk of the opera in and around a single omni-purpose set (a sort of Gothic lift-shaft, which served effectively as a fountain in the kermesse scene, a tree-house in the garden scene, and had a Dali-like crucifix lowered diagonally into it in the church scene) helped to give Faust a sharpness and unity it normally lacks. Even Noël Goodwin, who had few kind words to spare for this episode in the history of Scottish Opera, felt disposed to pay tribute to the "praiseworthy idea" of staging the opera "in the austere style of a medieval morality instead of a romantic spectacle."

Decor, this time by Ralph Koltai, was again a special feature of the new production of Don Giovanni. For this, Mr Koltai characteristically chose to reduce the scenery to its essentials: two large sliding panels, powerful and menacing, one pure white with a hint of brickwork, the other all shiny black daubs and mirror effects, which together served to suggest the contrast between darkness and light which is a particular feature of Mozart's drama. These, with the addition of a number of smaller, copper-coloured panels and shapes, which were raised and lowered from time to time, tended perhaps to make the opera seem as if it was taking place in the middle of a modern exhibition at the Tate Gallery, yet the result was immensely exhilarating and inspired the producer, Peter Ebert, to create a fresh and lively production.

The only snag was that Mr Koltai's settings, which slid back, forward and sideways, gliding and interweaving in a way that made them almost characters in the drama, proved almost too overpowering for the rather motley cast that was assembled in 1964. Giovanni is ever an awkward opera to cast, and many a fine production has been seriously damaged by just one singer looking or sounding

Ralph Koltai's designs—large, abstract, black-and-white sliding panels—were a special feature of Scottish Opera's Don Giovanni, *enabling the production to move with unusual smoothness. This scene shows the arrival of the masked guests at Giovanni's party: Peter van der Bilt (left) is Giovanni, Stafford Dean (hands outstretched) Leporello.*

wrong; and in fairness to Scottish Opera, it must be said that a serious attempt had plainly been made to find a fresh and plausible team. In a leader article months before, the *Glasgow Herald* had asked: "Where will they get all the soloists from?" The question was a good one, and Scottish Opera answered it by importing a Dutch baritone, Peter van der Bilt, for the title role, and a Dutch-American soprano, Marilyn Tyler, for Donna Elvira. The part of Donna Anna was shared between two British-based singers, Elizabeth Fretwell and Jennifer Vyvyan; Zerlina, Leporello and the Commendatore went to three London Scots, Elizabeth Robson, Harold Blackburn and David Ward; and Masetto and Don Ottavio were sung by two English singers, Michael Maurel and Alexander Young. Some of these, among them Mr Van der Bilt and Mr Maurel, were later to become pillars of the Company, returning season after season to sing a variety of important roles.

On the whole, in spite of some good individual portrayals, the team did not really hang together satisfactorily. Most of the critics, while admiring the general conception of the piece and the thoughtfulness of the casting, nevertheless found themselves having to play the part of modern Beckmessers, chalking up faults. Thus *The Times* complained that Miss Fretwell had "slightly too heavy a vibrato to allow her to achieve a truly Mozartian line," that Miss Tyler's singing was "rather gusty and uneven," that Mr Blackburn was "inclined to be woolly in tone." The *Financial Times* thought that Miss Fretwell commanded the high notes of her part all right, but "not the sense of fanaticism and cold,

(Left) Michael Maurel (Masetto) with his later Zerlina (Margaret Price).

(Right) Finale of Don Giovanni. In this picture of the supper scene, Stafford Dean is Leporello and Peter van der Bilt is Giovanni. Ralph Koltai's designs, which caused some critics to suggest that this was a Giovanni performed in the Tate Gallery, played their part strikingly in this section of the opera.

desperate fury that inspire them." Mr Blackburn was a "colourless but efficient" Leporello, Mr Young a "stylish but rather vacant" Don Ottavio.

Almost everybody, however, recognised Mr Van der Bilt as a real discovery. A member of the Netherlands Opera, he was then in the process of joining the Deutsche Oper am Rhein in Dusseldorf, and Scottish Opera was attracted to him by that nose for quality which was to be revealed again in later seasons when such singers as Helga Dernesch and George Shirley made their first British appearances with the company. *The Times* described him as a "splendid, upstanding young man, noble alike in voice and mien," and the *Financial Times* spoke of his "imposing height" and "strong, warm, clearly focused voice," but felt he needed to screw up the intensity of his performance a little more. Mr Van der Bilt's was very much a velvety, baritonal Giovanni, with some exquisite top notes, and in that respect he made a pleasant change from the performances by bass singers that seemed in favour around that time with the record companies.

With a stronger-minded, more experienced conductor than Leon Lovett, the cast might have been bound together into a more effective ensemble. As it was, he gave a rather too agreeable and lightweight account of the score, choosing tempi which many critics felt to be ill-judged. This point was neatly made by David Cairns in the *Financial Times*, who declared that Mr Lovett had "too swift a way with the *andantes*," which moved "too easily" and lacked intensity. On the other hand, said Mr Cairns, "where the music suggests frenzied speed, wild exuberance, he tends to hang back: the Champagne Aria, taken at a very measured tempo, sounded almost decorous.'' The Company, it seemed, shared the opinion of the critics about the virtues and flaws of the evening. When the production was revived the following season, Mr Van der Bilt still headed the cast, but many of the other singers and the conductor had been replaced. As it happened, the 1965 version did not work ideally well either, and when the piece was next revived, in 1970, there was a further substantial change of cast.

Otello, in 1964, did not call for such major surgery, and all three of the previous season's principals were retained – though this time Charles Craig shared the title role with Ronald Dowd, who was henceforward to perform a number of Scottish Opera's leading tenor roles. Vocally, he lacked Mr Craig's ease of delivery; but in recompense he was able to bring to the part a fierce intensity which Mr Craig lacked. "It was," remarked David Cairns, "a performance. There was a haunted quality, a dramatic eagerness, a sense of violent physical tension exploding into violent physical abandonment, and also a commanding presence and dignity." At the end of Act Three, Mr Dowd also succeeded in suggesting – as surely few other singers can have done so effectively – that Otello's personality problems included not only jealousy but also epilepsy. Of the rest of the cast, Peter Glossop was a still more self-confident Iago and Luisa Bosabalian had warmed considerably to the part of Desdemona –

(Left) In the 1964 revival of Otello, *Luisa Bosabalian warmed considerably to the part of Desdemona—"an extremely appealing portrayal," remarked* The Times, *"with presages of greatness in the last act."*

(Centre) Peter Glossop's self-confident Iago in Otello, *here seen with Emile Belcourt as Cassio.*

(Right) Peter Glossop as Iago, with Pier Miranda Ferraro as Otello in the background.

"an extremely appealing portrayal," said *The Times*, "with presages of greatness in the last act."

Box-office calculations at the end of the season revealed that Edinburgh had once again done better than Glasgow, with an average attendance of 80 per cent as against Glasgow's 67 per cent (Glasgow, it is true, had eight performances in 1964, whereas Edinburgh had only six; but then, the population of Glasgow is twice that of Edinburgh). *Faust*, it was found, had attracted attendances of up to 90 per cent. Did this suggest that Scottish taste was lazy, Victorian, and provincial? Or that people had heard that, as a production, Scottish Opera's *Faust* was something special? No one could say for sure, though the fact that *Don Giovanni* drew houses of up to 97 per cent at least showed that Scotland had its priorities right.

The length of season, which had been increased in 1964, was increased still more in 1965 when for the first time the Company decided to add Aberdeen to its itinerary. There, His Majesty's Theatre was already known to be in some ways the most attractive of the three main Scottish houses. It boasts what are arguably the best acoustics; its shallow, horse-shoe shaped balconies give it a real opera-house look; its circle bar (which is literally circular) is better serviced and has a pleasanter ambience than its rivals in Glasgow and Edinburgh. The only snags are that the stage facilities are inferior – the theatre lacks a proper counterweight system – and that Aberdeen has too small and too unadventurous a population to enable Scottish Opera to perform to the size of audience it needs.

In the weeks before the Aberdeen portion of the season opened, there were gloomy predictions in the press that response was going to be wretched, and Robin Orr felt compelled to utter threats and rallying cries to chivvy people up. It was not as if the repertoire was grossly over-specialised: with *Boris Godunov* as the main attraction, and *Madama Butterfly* and *Don Giovanni* forming the rest of the bill, it should have had considerable drawing power. The trouble was (or so it was said) that in Aberdeen Scottish Opera was still an unknown quantity, and people wanted to wait and hear how good it was before paying what they reckoned to be excessively high prices (the top was £1) for seats. In the end, however, they succumbed to temptation and bookings averaged 76 per cent, with a record 91 per cent for *Boris*. Compared with Glasgow's 83 per cent that year, and Edinburgh's remarkable 98 per cent, the overall Aberdeen returns were not outstanding but at least they seemed to justify adding the granite city to the Company's schedule.

The inclusion of Aberdeen, of course, raised the cost of the season still higher. This time it was estimated at £44,000 – some £12,000 more than 1964 – of which £26,000 was to be met by grants and £18,000 was expected from the box-office. This pattern, with a substantial rise on one side balanced by a substantial rise on the other, was to become a natural feature of the Company's development, until by 1972 sums in excess of £200,000 were being asked for and received from the Scottish Arts Council (which had been functioning under that, more independent, title since 1966, when Dr Firth retired from the Scottish Committee and was succeeded by Ronald Mavor, playwright, erstwhile drama critic of *The Scotsman*, son of James Bridie, and a dedicated man of the theatre, who in 1965 had stated in print that Scottish Opera was the best thing that had happened to Scotland for at least fifteen years).

The 1965 season, though it included no modern opera, revealed nevertheless some slackening of the conservative policy of the previous year. *Boris Godunov*, after all, was a more enlightened choice than *Faust*; and the choice was made to seem more enlightened still when it was announced that the Company would not be performing the familiar Technicolor version of the opera, prepared by Rimsky-Korsakov from Mussorgsky's original (and widely favoured by Europe's opera houses, including Covent Garden), but a version which as far as possible reverted to Mussorgsky's own ideas on the piece. Once again Scottish Opera had made one of those visionary decisions which were to win it fame and admiration, and no one admired it more warmly than Andrew Porter, the chief music critic of the *Financial Times*, in his first appraisal of a Scottish Opera production for his newspaper.

"This," he said, "was a *Boris* unlike any other I have seen; a quieter, darker, more lyrical one. And the reason, I suppose, is that most of our *Boris* performances stem eventually from Diaghilev and Paris, and the whole notion of the glittering, exotic Russian art which burst on the astonished West. *Boris* conjures up images of magnificent spectacle: a brilliant Coronation Scene in the Kremlin Square with bells pealing and costumes gleaming, and the heavy mantles of Chaliapin falling on whoever is singing the title role. And even now that we have learnt to prefer Mussorgsky's original score, which has a starker, more pungent, less sophisticated sound than the Rimsky-Korsakov revision current for so many years, the idea of a *Boris* centred around its tremendous hero still persists.

"It is not an untrue idea, but it is less than the whole truth. Michael Geliot, Ralph Koltai and Alexander Gibson, producer, designer and conductor of the Scottish *Boris*, have sought to amplify it. Equally, they have in this presentation reformulated the common statement that 'the real hero of *Boris* is the Russian people.' As I pointed out when reviewing the last Covent Garden revival of the opera, the Russian people in *Boris* are a fickle, brutal, stupid, untrustworthy, and pretty contemptible mob. Certainly we can feel compassion for their sufferings, and understand what has driven them, in the final scene, to torment poor Khrushchev so viciously. But to glamorise them runs contrary to that 'truth' which was ever Mussorgsky's professed aim.

"This Scottish *Boris* is unglamorous; and in its very seriousness of intention it may have gone too far. It is one thing to argue that the crowd of the opening scenes is a listless, apathetic group, another – and in the theatre a very hazardous thing – to ask an inexperienced chorus to portray this. The Prologue, to put it bluntly, fell flat – and dark thoughts about the quality of the large, amateur Scottish Opera Chorus were dispelled only in the final Kromy Forest

Coronation scene, with chorus of Boyars, in Boris Godunov. Ralph Koltai's austere, uncluttered settings, dominated by the motif of a Russian eagle, added powerfully to the atmosphere of the opera.

scene, where their singing and movement were vigorous, ringing and confident.''

In spite of these hazards, however, the Company's decision was obviously the right one. The producer, Michael Geliot, who was working for the first time with Scottish Opera, may have had his troubles in marshalling his amateur chorus on the small Scottish stages, but he achieved some striking effects nevertheless – in the opening scene the soldiers bore down on the mob in a brutal re-creation of the Odessa Steps sequence of *Battleship Potemkin*. Ralph Koltai's austere, powerful, typically uncluttered settings, dominated by the motif of a Russian eagle, must have been a considerable help in staging the piece and giving people room to move.

Yet although the emphasis was rightly on the chorus, that is not to say the production neglected the role of Boris himself; and indeed it was David Ward's deliberately subdued, introspective, anguished portrayal of the Czar that enabled an almost ideal balance to be achieved between the great public scenes

David Ward, the Dumbarton-born bass, was Scottish Opera's inspired choice for the title-role in Boris Godunov. Emile Belcourt, who two years earlier had appeared in L'Heure espagnole, was a suitably slimy Shuisky.

(Above, left) The aged Pimen, as portrayed by William McCue, in the 1968 production of Boris Godunov.

(Above, right) Duncan Robertson as the Simpleton has his penny stolen by the children in Boris Godunov.

David Ward's introspective, anguished portrayal of the Czar helped an almost ideal balance to be achieved between the great public scenes of Boris Godunov *and the intimate private ones. Below, (left) he is seen with Anne Pashley as his son, Feodor, and with Emile Belcourt as Shuisky. (Right) Godunov's reign moves towards its tormented close.*

(*Above*) Madama Butterfly *in 1965 was graced by the coloured American soprano, Felicia Weathers, in the title-role. Here she makes her entrance in Act One.*

(*Below, left*) *In 1965, as in 1962, Scottish Opera's production of* Madama Butterfly *had the advantage of a real child to play the part of Cio-Cio-San's son.*

(*Below, right*) Madama Butterfly *moves towards its tragic close. An expressive study of Felicia Weathers as the lonely Cio-Cio-San.*

and the intimate private ones. Had Mr Ward merely given a big, traditional, histrionic performance, the special quality and poetry of the Scottish production would have been lost. Here was a *Boris* in which the private tragedy of the Czar was strongly framed, as it should have been, by the rest of the opera, and which did not burst that framework apart.

The rest of the cast, without being outstandingly memorable, included good performances of Varlaam by Donald McIntyre, Grigory by William McAlpine, and Feodor by Anne Pashley. Alexander Gibson conducted thoughtfully, delicately, catching both the sharpness and poignancy of Mussorgsky's scoring. In the annals of Scottish Opera, this was a very special event indeed.

The *Madama Butterfly* that year was not a revival of the one that was seen in 1962 but a whole new production, again by Peter Ebert, but with fresh settings by David Wilby; a new Cio-Cio-San, Felicia Weathers; and a new conductor, Norman Del Mar, who tended to overpress the music but won praise all the same for the warm, vital playing he drew from the SNO. Miss Weathers, a young coloured American soprano who had been making her career in Germany but had not so far sung in Britain, turned out to be another Scottish Opera discovery. To quote Andrew Porter again, she had "unselfconscious charm of appearance, movement, personality and utterance. One's heart goes out to her at once. Yet it was not a performance that depended merely on charm: she is an accomplished singer and a sensitive, intelligent interpreter. . . . The timbre is perhaps not very distinctive except in a beautifully rounded lower register, but the whole performance was uncommonly distinguished. It lived along each line."

Charles Craig was again the Pinkerton, but there was a new Goro, Francis Egerton, who was soon to establish himself as one of the company's finest character actors, and who was already a superb Missail in *Boris*.

Don Giovanni, the third production of 1965, was an improvement on the first attempt of the previous year, but once again it was Ralph Koltai's settings that dominated the evening. Of the three new ladies, Janice Chapman, Ava June, and Margaret Price, it was Miss Price's Zerlina that seemed the most natural portrayal, as well as the most delicately sung – no one who saw her in 1965 could have failed to spot that here was a superb Mozart singer in the making. Michael Maurel, a promising Masetto in 1964, developed his portrayal of him as a fully-fledged revolutionary, no mere buffoon. Peter van der Bilt's Giovanni, too, had developed, and though the new Leporello, Ian Wallace, and the new Don Ottavio, Donald Pilley, both leaned towards caricature rather than character, their portrayals were adequate enough. This time the conductor was Alexander Gibson, firmer-handed and more vivacious than his predecessor, but without yet having at his disposal the sort of material to work on that would transform this *Giovanni* into the electric evening it ought to have been. But if the drama did not tell strongly enough, at least the comedy did. Like *Boris*, this *Giovanni* was sung in English translation (Dent's), and the responsiveness of the audience must have made it clear to the Company that the decision to break away once in a while from original-language versions was well worth making.

7. The *Ring* Begins

IN CHOOSING *Boris Godunov* for its 1965 season, in preferring Mussorgsky's *Boris* to Rimsky-Korsakov's familiar disarrangement of it, and in presenting the work so tellingly, Scottish Opera set itself a new standard of achievement that caught the imagination of its audience more keenly even than the *Otello* of 1963 or the *Pelléas* of 1962. This meant, however, that as much, if not more, was expected of the Company in 1966; and the plans, to say the least, were courageous.

For a start, it was decided to take the plunge into Wagner, a composer who obviously deserved a prominent place in the Company's repertoire, and who – partly as a result of an audience opinion poll, which came down firmly in favour of his music – was given that place maybe sooner than expected. *The Flying Dutchman* at first seemed a likely candidate, just as, in 1963, it had been a possible alternative to *Otello*. And certainly a good case could have been made for staging it, for it is a work commonly regarded as a useful starter for a company inexperienced in Wagner's ways, and for an audience it has the appeal of brevity, simplicity and straightforwardness. But as in 1963 so in 1966 the idea was dropped.

Tristan and Isolde, which had not been seen in Scotland since the Stuttgart Opera brought it to the Edinburgh Festival in 1958, and *The Mastersingers*, with its opportunities for the Scottish Opera Chorus (some of whom, long before Scottish Opera was thought of, had served as extras in the Hamburg production at the 1952 Edinburgh Festival), were also considered at this time. But in the end, by an imaginative stroke which was to have far-reaching effects, *Die Walküre* was chosen. Whether, at the time, the Company intended to go that far and no farther into *The Ring*, whether consciously or subconsciously they were already thinking in terms of a complete cycle, has never been completely clear. But I can remember a conversation with Peter Hemmings early that year when he told me of the designs that had been drawn by Michael Knight, and of how they could be adapted for all four music dramas.

Gradually, in spite of occasional statements from one or another of the Company's organisers to the effect that there could be no guarantee of a complete *Ring*, the contrary idea began to take root: that there would indeed be a complete *Ring* and that anything less would be an act of pusillanimity un-

Among the new productions launched in 1971, The Barber of Seville served as a delightful summer "show", produced by Ian Watt-Smith at the Royal Lyceum Theatre, Edinburgh, and later taken on tour. Bernard Culshaw's practical structure of a stage-within-a-stage added to the character of the presentation by making it seem something of a Brechtian Barber. Among its highlights was the presence of the Texan bass, Elfego Esparza, as Dr Bartolo, seen above listening to Don Basilio's slander song, performed by William McCue. Below: Michael Maurel as Figaro sings the "Largo al factotum".

Two more scenes from The Barber of Seville. Above: *an ensemble from Act Two, with Elfego Esparza caught between Michael Maurel (Figaro) and David Hillman (Almaviva in his disguise as Don Alonso); in the background, Patricia Hay as Rosina. Below: finale to Act One, with David Hillman, Anne Howells, Michael Maurel, Elfego Esparza, Judith Pierce, William McCue.*

typical of Scottish Opera. As it happened, *Die Walküre*, on reaching the stage, did not prove an unqualified success – for reasons I shall come to presently – nor was it at first anything like the box-office draw for which the Company had hoped. Yet it left many people hungry for something which Scotland had not experienced for nearly half a century: the chance to see the complete tetralogy on their own doorstep, without the expense of having to go to London or Bayreuth or Stuttgart for it. And by the time the next instalment, *Das Rheingold*, was launched the following year, the audience had indeed begun to increase to such an extent that it was possible to foresee in Scotland the kind of *Ring* mania which Georg Solti had created in London and Wieland Wagner at Bayreuth.

Die Walküre, however, was not the only major new production of 1966. With an almost insolent cockiness, this young Company – still only four years old – decided to follow its *Otello* of 1963 and 1964 with a *Falstaff* in which (several years before the Welsh National Opera got round to doing the same) the title role in this most subtle and mellow of Verdi's operas was to be played by Geraint Evans. But even that was not all: a further, and as it turned out extremely important, addition to the Company's activities enabled the charming little Perth Theatre to be included for the first time in the spring season along with Glasgow, Edinburgh and Aberdeen. The auditorium (like a King's Theatre in miniature) being too small for any of the established productions, an opera suitable for Perth had to be chosen; and so it came about that Britten's *Albert Herring* entered the repertoire of Scottish Opera, a production which, though no one could have guessed it at the time, was to become one of the Company's major successes, was to have more performances than any other work during the first ten years, and was the first Scottish Opera production to be seen abroad – at the Florence Maggio Musicale in 1968, and later in Germany and Iceland.

Meanwhile it was at Perth, on 11 April, that the 1966 season was launched, thus setting a pattern that was to be maintained almost continuously up to the present (only once was it altered when, in 1970, the spring season opened in Aberdeen instead). At first it was decided not to bank too heavily on Perth's support. The visit was to be regarded as an experiment, which in the opinion of various people, including the then manager of Perth Theatre, was doomed to failure. Consequently, only two performances of *Albert Herring* were scheduled; and Perth Corporation's prudence was such that it was prepared to donate only £350 to the venture – though bearing in mind the size of the city, and the fact that Perth had been contributing money to Scottish Opera for years without ever really expecting a visit from the Company, the sum was by British standards not a bad one. At the same time the Scottish Arts Council, as it now was called, was eager to inject new blood into Perth Theatre in order to prevent its transformation into a chain store – as seemed for a period all too possible. The Council consequently encouraged Scottish Opera to go there, and agreed to increase its annual subsidy to cover the loss that would be the inevitable result of staging a professional production in so small a theatre.

As expected, neither performance was a sellout. Yet by the standards of

modern opera, whereby rows of empty seats are regarded as the natural outcome of staging, say, Shostakovich's *Katerina Ismailova* at Covent Garden, *Albert
Herring* did outstandingly well in a town which hitherto had had scant experience of opera of any kind, let alone a modern work. At the first performance,
65 per cent of the 500 seats were sold. At the second performance the figure rose
to 88 per cent, and it became plain, even to the most casual or pessimistic of
observers, that 1966 in Perth was the start of something important, and that, in
selecting *Albert Herring*, Scottish Opera had drawn the bung from a barrel that
was soon to pour forth other, similar riches. Indeed, the opportunity to present
a work on that small stage in that intimate theatre set the Company more
firmly than before on the road to treating opera not just as song and spectacle
but also as drama. That quality, for which one can look in vain in some of the
world's most famous "traditional" opera houses, was henceforward to become
one of Scottish Opera's special characteristics and a tenet of the Company's
artistic thinking. Audiences began to expect it as a matter of course, and when,
as occasionally happened, it was not forthcoming (as in the 1970 *La Traviata*,
which was an unashamed "star" attraction, and an unexpected throwback to
the opera-as-song school of thought) complaints were soon to be heard.

At first *Albert Herring* seemed an odd choice for the launching of Scottish
Opera's chamber repertoire, for it had come to be deemed one of Britten's
weaker pieces, with an unconvincing principal role, some fairly dated jokes,
and music which sometimes degenerated to the level of intimate revue. Most
of these judgments, however, had been based on experience of the long-standing English Opera Group production, a much-travelled, well-seasoned affair
(it was seen at the 1965 Edinburgh Festival, by which time it was already no
chicken) which had grown broader with the years until it included such exaggerated portrayals as Sheila Rex's Mrs Herring – a part she performed in the
manner of the witch from *Hansel and Gretel* – and such vulgarities as some
gratuitous knicker-dropping by one of the schoolgirls during the garden party.
Nor had the question of making Albert's character seem plausible ever been
properly thought about, partly, no doubt, because the role had come to be
considered an impossible one: it had always been principally associated in
people's minds with Peter Pears, whose portrayal – as the Decca recording bears
witness – was too sanctimonious, too well-bred to offer a convincing picture
of an East Anglian greengrocer's boy breaking out and sowing his first wild oats
(Albert, for readers still vague about the plot, has had a sheltered, mother-
dominated upbringing, and his hitherto good behaviour makes him the only
person in town eligible to become the local May King; but if he is played too
primly at the outset, it is hard to accept that he will later be capable, when the
opportunity arises, of snapping the apron strings and embarking on an all-
night spree).

Scottish Opera succeeded in vindicating the piece, making the personality
of Albert at last seem credible, striking a natural balance between comedy and
seriousness, and preventing as far as possible the Aldeburgh townsfolk from
teetering too far into caricature. The most imaginative stroke was the decision

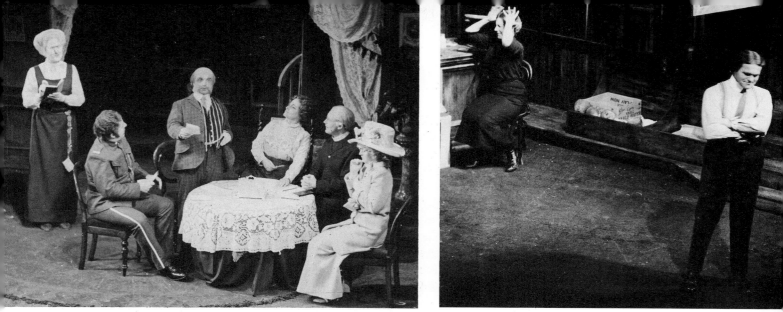

(Above, left) In Act One of Albert Herring the committee attempt to nominate a Queen of the May while Florence Pike (far left) provides reasons for the rejection of each candidate. In the 1966 performances, Johanna Peters sang the part of Florence; the other characters (left to right) are William McCue as the police superintendent, Francis Egerton as the mayor, Rae Woodland as Lady Billows, Ronald Morrison as the vicar, and Patricia Clark as Miss Wordsworth.

(Above, right) The most imaginative stroke in Scottish Opera's production of Albert Herring was the casting of the Australian tenor Gregory Dempsey in the title role. The role of Albert's Mum was no less credibly played by Anna Reynolds.

(Below, left) To the strains of Tristan and Isolde, Sid laces Albert's lemonade with rum—and thereby helps to achieve the May King's emancipation. In this scene from Act Two of Albert Herring, Michael Maurel and Catherine Wilson are seen as Sid and Nancy. Their delightful naturalness, seen also below, right, was one of the assets of Scottish Opera's Albert Herring.

to cast the Australian tenor, Gregory Dempsey, as Albert. He had not until then sung the part, nor had he so far appeared with Scottish Opera; but he had already won praise in Britain for his portrayal of the villainous Boconnion in Richard Rodney Bennett's *The Mines of Sulphur* at Sadler's Wells. On the strength of that he was an obvious candidate for the role of, say, Peter Grimes, but would he not perhaps be too tough, too abrasive and extrovert for the over-mothered Albert? Maybe so; but only for an audience hopelessly tied to a Pearsian conception of the part. In fact, as John Warrack was later to declare in the *Sunday Telegraph*, Mr Dempsey turned out to be an Albert "in whose emancipation one really believed." And for Andrew Porter, in the *Financial Times*, Mr Dempsey brought to his performances the kind of intensity and conviction that might have been expected of a Jon Vickers. In other words, here was a "heroic" Albert, with something of a Florestan about him. As for Anthony Besch's production, it was, said Mr Porter, the most brilliant and sensitive imaginable. It turned, he added, on a knife-edge between comedy and tragedy. "The pressures on Albert are almost those on the heroine of *Katya*; they might have destroyed him: it is almost by luck that he is 'saved'."

Before long, Mr Dempsey was being widely proclaimed to be the first singer ever to make sense of the role of Albert. The intensity he brought to his big monologues made many people suddenly realise that locked inside *Albert Herring* there is a serious opera screaming to get out, and that potentially Albert is as profound a hero as Peter Grimes or Billy Budd. Like them he is an outsider victimised by society; unlike them he wins in the end. Mr Dempsey's intensity of feeling was reflected in the conducting of Roderick Brydon, a young Scot who the previous year had been put in charge of three of the performances of *Madama Butterfly* and who had now become, after a period of training with Sadler's Wells, Scottish Opera's first staff conductor. A dedicated Brittenite,

(*Opposite*) Lady Billows (*Judith Pierce*), with a sullen Albert (*Gregory Dempsey*) on one side and a benign vicar (*Ronald Morrison*) on the other, delivers her address during the tea party in Act Two of Albert Herring.

(*Right*) Adam Pollock's designs for Albert Herring, and the poetry of Charles Bristow's lighting, were much in keeping with the spirit of the opera. Here, in a memorable scene, Albert (*Gregory Dempsey*) skulks in a corner of the darkened shop while Sid and Nancy (*Michael Maurel and Catherine Wilson*) embrace beneath the lamp-post outside the window.

(*Below*) Climax of Act Three of Albert Herring: as treated by Scottish Opera, the "dead" Albert's return at the height of the threnody sung in tribute to him was moving as well as amusing. In this scene, the cast (left to right) are Johanna Peters, Judith Pierce, Anna Reynolds, Catherine Wilson, Francis Egerton, Ronald Morrison, William McCue, Gregory Dempsey, Patricia Clark, and Michael Maurel.

Mr Brydon was convinced even before performing it that *Albert Herring* was a fascinating and underrated score, which had long been misunderstood; and by the time rehearsals were in progress, he confessed that he was beginning to wonder if *Albert Herring* could really be called a comedy at all, so full of undertones was its music. That is not to say that his resultant performances lacked wit or humour; but he shared with Anthony Besch (who the following year was to bring a similar perceptiveness to *Così fan tutte*) the belief that the opera's fun should grow naturally from serious roots, and not seem merely superimposed.

Only once or twice did Mr Besch's hand falter a little in that respect. The fluttery, though deftly performed, portrayal of Miss Wordsworth, the schoolteacher, which he drew from Patricia Clark was arguably more exaggeratedly characterised than the rest of the production, and missed the role's element of pathos; and there were a few, happily very few, unnecessary sight-gags, such as when, in Act Three, the police superintendent reached his lines about "a criminal case of rape," and William McCue, who played the part, was made to underline the words by accidentally spearing a turnip with the point of his umbrella.

Concerning vegetables, too, there was also at one point a minor misinterpretation of the libretto, resulting from the fact that no one involved in the production was an expert in East Anglian customs; for when Albert, in Act One, was asked to supply "twopennorth of pot-herbs to make a stew in a hurry," he should have known, as a native of Aldeburgh, that that meant a mixture of carrots and onions (I am indebted to Colin Graham for this information). Mr Besch, however, fell into the trap, and made Albert dutifully pour out mixed herbs. Still, at least it made sense to a Scottish audience who, in their ignorance, would have been baffled if Albert had illogically started serving carrots.

The broader issues of the opera were admirably dealt with. Mr Besch had obviously kept in mind the fact that *Albert Herring* was based by Britten on a Maupassant story whose outcome was far less happy: there the hero, having won his emancipation, soon dies of *delirium tremens*. Again and again, as the opera unfolded, one got the impression that it might just conceivably end tragically, that Albert might meet his death during his night on the tiles. So when the big threnody arrived at the climax of Act Three, one could savour it on two levels – as the superb parody it unquestionably is, and (by dint of Mr Brydon's eloquent conducting) also as a genuine threnody, heartfelt and affecting. Consequently Albert's reappearance at the height of this passage was moving as well as amusing, and the closing pages of the opera – which on other occasions have seemed weak – were given a fresh glow, a strong sense of release, so that the children's jingle at the close actually succeeded in bringing tears to the eyes.

A remarkable feature of this *Albert Herring* (though at the time no one was to guess it) was that of the thirteen members of the original cast, almost all were to reappear, season after season, in the production's various revivals. Seldom, in the annals of British opera, has so large a cast been held together for so long. As a result, a very special sort of teamwork developed, which succeeded in avoiding the mannerisms which tend to grow like barnacles on long-standing productions and which concentrated instead on spontaneity and perfection of timing. If there were in-jokes among the singers – and what production of a comic opera has been entirely without them? – they were invisible to the audience. To begin with, at Perth, the only potential weakness of casting appeared to be Rae Woodland's Lady Billows: finely sung (as one would expect of a distinguished Mozartian), but a trifle low-keyed for so imperious a part. The following season she was replaced by Judith Pierce, who shaped her lines less purely but looked and sounded formidable enough to hold her place in the production from then until now.

One of the weaknesses of Britten's score, it is sometimes said, is the stiffness of the love music he wrote for Sid, the butcher's boy, and his girl-friend Nancy; but again one of the assets of the Scottish production was the delightful naturalness with which these roles were played by Michael Maurel and Catherine Wilson, who succeeded in making not only the characters but also the music fully convincing. For once it was possible to believe in their relationship, and to believe also that Nancy might just conceivably be willing to swap Sid for Albert at the end of the opera (Nancy's affection for Albert, and Albert's secret longing to be in Sid's shoes, was one of the skilfully-drawn details of Mr Besch's production).

Of the other characters, Ronald Morrison's portrayal of Mr Gedge, the vicar, and Francis Egerton's mayor were beautifully judged, and managed to stay on the right side of caricature; and Johanna Peters turned Lady Billows's housekeeper, Miss Florence Pike, into a gaunt, joyless ancestor of Mrs Mary Whitehouse's National Viewers and Listeners Association. But next to Albert himself, perhaps the most revealing portrayal was that by Anna Reynolds of Albert's domineering mum – a role which can be, and usually is, treated very broadly, but which on this occasion was curiously touching as well as simply querulous and bossy. Though she distorted her voice in order to convey the nagging characteristics of Mrs Herring, the effect was not (as it can be in some productions of Così fan tutte when the disguised Despina places too much emphasis on singing nasally) merely irritating; and she rose expressively to her big moment near the start of Act Three, when Mrs Herring is asked to supply a photograph of the vanished Albert "for identification" and lapses nostalgically into family reminiscence while a tinkling little waltz-tune underlines her memories.

The scenery, which was to have to stand up to a considerable battering in later seasons as it was transported from country to country, was by Adam Pollock, a young designer whom Scottish Opera had not previously used. Its period atmosphere, its Aldeburgh townscapes etched against the sky, and the poetry of Charles Bristow's lighting (the sight of Sid and Nancy embracing beneath the lamp-post outside the window, while Albert skulked in a corner of the darkened shop, lingers specially in mind), were all in keeping with the spirit of the opera. But because it involved the lowering of the house curtain between each scene, it failed to solve one of the recurring problems of Albert Herring:

how to prevent the audience from lapsing into chatter during the instrumental interludes, tellingly though these were performed by what was described in the programme as the Scottish Opera Chamber Ensemble but which turned out to be mainly members of the Scottish National Orchestra, led by Sam Bor. By the time Mr Besch came to produce *The Turn of the Screw* in Scotland four years later, he had learnt this lesson and devised a way of holding the audience's attention throughout the interludes in that work.

Each of the first ten years tended to be a key year in Scottish Opera's development, and none at the time seemed more so than 1966. Not only was the repertoire larger and more ambitious ("four operas in four languages" was one of the ways in which the Company, with almost Glyndebourne-like cosmopolitanism, proclaimed its offerings that season), but there were also more performances – apart from the Perth opening, Edinburgh and Glasgow were each given an extra week of opera, and there were other important signs of roots being strengthened. For the first time the Company had a proper office, up a stair near the Glasgow King's, and a full-time administrative staff had begun to be recruited by Peter Hemmings, who had moved north at the beginning of the year and was now resident in Glasgow. By today's standards the premises were decidedly cramped; but with their photograph displays, their general buzz of ideas and enthusiasm, the small staff gave the rooms a real feeling of an opera company in the making, and no one could then have known how soon (a mere three years later) a palatial Victorian office-block was to come their way, or that the rate of expansion would be such that this block – proudly named the Scottish Opera Centre – would soon seem not a square foot too large.

It was in 1966, too, that the Scottish Opera Club was launched on the lines of the Friends of Covent Garden, thus helping to provide a nucleus of permanent supporters who, for a small annual fee, were offered various perks: advance booking for performances, monthly recitals or lectures, a quarterly house magazine, regular news letters, and the chance to take part in opera-going tours to Germany, Austria and Italy. In addition, by arrangement with the Arts Council, the Company took over the running of the northern section of Opera for All, whose aim was maybe a lowly one – to tour utility opera productions, with piano accompaniment, to towns and villages without the facilities for full-scale opera – but one which henceforward provided Scottish Opera with a useful training ground for young singers who could serve as understudies and in time be absorbed into the main Company.

All these innovations contributed to the sense of excitement and confidence that sprang up in 1966, and in the background there was the hope that by 1970 both Edinburgh and Glasgow would possess proper opera houses for the Company to perform in. It was, of course, a vain hope; but it seemed strong enough at the time, and several London critics made special mention of it in their reviews that season. Thus, in the *Sunday Telegraph*, John Warrack felt free to write: "Two opera houses promised and audiences agog – it all has the ring

"Here was one of the great Falstaffs of our time, Sir Geraint Evans, not in any way dominating the rest of the singers—as would have happened in a production that made economies in order to have a star in the lead—but taking his place as part of a superb ensemble." With sharp character sketches from Francis Egerton, as Bardolph (above, centre and right, below, left), Ian Wallace as Pistol (above, left), and Dennis Brandt as Dr Caius (below, left)—and with John Shaw as a firm-toned and unusually bitter Ford (below, right)—this was a Falstaff which any permanent opera house would have been proud to stage.

of an enterprise in its heroic days." And, reviewing the new *Walküre* in the *Financial Times*, Andrew Porter declared: "This was a Scottish *Ring* well-founded, and by 1970, when the Glasgow Opera House opens, it may well be drawing pilgrims from London." By 1970, however, Edinburgh's plans remained on the drawing board and Glasgow's had been scrapped altogether.

Yet the thrill of that period in Scottish Opera's development, when everyone involved was still in his first flush of enthusiasm, sticks indelibly in the mind; and it was Andrew Porter who, above all, placed his finger on the pulse of the times when he wrote: "A seven-week season puts Scottish Opera, now in its fifth year, on as 'regular' a basis as, say, the more famous Chicago or San Francisco companies; and for the London-based opera-goer in this country, there is an extraordinary exhilaration in being able to slip away for two nights and (by taking in a matinee) see three productions by another company with a character of its own. Almost – not quite – one might be in Germany!"

The operas a visiting operagoer could have seen that year were the new *Herring*, *Walküre* and *Falstaff*, and a revival of the 1964 production of *Faust*, with a complete change of principals. *Falstaff*, in Glasgow, opened the main spring season. On the first night, Peter Ebert's production and Peter Rice's settings seemed a little too rich and elaborate for the King's Theatre stage, but otherwise the scale of the performance seemed about right. *Falstaff*, after all, though it had had its premiere at the Scala, Milan, was originally intended by Verdi for a small theatre. Today, it is true, we have grown accustomed to "big" performances of it, and in Britain the Zeffirelli production at Covent Garden has for many years been our yardstick. Yet much of the score has the intimacy of chamber music, just as many of the libretto's comic and amorous situations are best savoured at close range, and it was a pleasure to be reminded of all this by a performance such as Scottish Opera's, which was geared, as Glyndebourne's had been in the 1950s, for Scottish-sized theatres. A still closer rapport between singers and audience might have been established, however, if the opera had been performed in English instead of Italian.

With *Walküre* and *Faust* also sung in the original language, the pros and cons of translation proved a major talking point of the season. Clearly, if Scottish Opera wanted to attract – as was hoped – a new young audience, then good English translations would be important. Would it be difficult to get international stars to learn their roles in English? Tradition said yes – yet the Dutch baritone, Peter van der Bilt, had learnt a translation of *Don Giovanni* specially for Scottish Opera, and David Ward had sung Boris in English, although, for the international market, he might well have preferred to learn the part in Russian. But in general, at that stage in its history, Scottish Opera did not possess the bargaining power to tell singers that if they wanted an engagement they might have to learn their roles in the vernacular (Mr Ward presumably sang Boris in English because he wanted to, and Mr Van der Bilt was not so well known in 1964 as he is now); and, as John Warrack pointed out in an article in *Opera* magazine (July 1966), in order to achieve the reputation and authority to dictate terms, Scottish Opera would have to "justify its existence with the very finest

Luisa Bosabalian's "radiant peach" of an Alice (right) in discussion with Laura Sarti's vivid Meg Page (left) and Elizabeth Robson's Nanetta.

musical presentation by the best international artists it can get." By 1966, of course, the Company was already well on the way to doing so; and by 1971 it was able to talk Helga Dernesch, Karajan's new Brünnhilde at Salzburg, into learning the role of the Marschallin in English for a new production of *Der Rosenkavalier*. But meanwhile the problem remained, and seemed highlighted by the fact that one of the few big laughs raised by Verdi's opera was when Falstaff shouted "Protesto" – partly because that was one of the few words the audience understood.

Still, *Falstaff* in Italian – which in any case at least part of the audience favoured – did guarantee a first-rate cast of international calibre. It was, most unusually, a *Falstaff* without a single weak link, with the smaller roles as carefully cast as the major ones. Here was one of the great Falstaffs of our time, Geraint Evans, not in any way dominating the rest of the singers – as would have happened in a production that made economies in order to have a star in the lead – but taking his place as part of a superb ensemble. The rich artistry of his portrayal, the conviction with which he depicted Falstaff as an energetic man sadly saddled with a massive drinker's paunch, was a pleasure to watch and hear; and with John Shaw's firm-toned and unusually bitter Ford (already known from Covent Garden), Luisa Bosabalian's radiant peach of an Alice (perhaps the best performance she has ever given Scottish Opera), Laura Sarti's vivid Meg Page, and Elizabeth Bainbridge's relaxed and humorous Mistress Quickly, with Elizabeth Robson and Ryland Davies as an enchantingly lyrical Nanetta and Fenton, and with sharp character sketches from Francis Egerton, Ian Wallace and Dennis Brandt, this was a *Falstaff* which any permanent opera house would have been proud to stage.

Alexander Gibson's experience of the score dated back to his Sadler's Wells days, and his understanding of it was revealed in a thousand little details of line and pace and texture. Some conductors make *Falstaff* all brass and glitter. Mr

(*Above*) "*I can't call myself Peaceful; I wish I were called Cheerful; but Woeful has to be my name.*" *In this scene from Act One of* Die Walküre, *Hunding (Donald McIntyre) and Sieglinde (Elizabeth Fretwell) listen to Siegmund (Charles Craig) describing his adventures.*

(*Below*) *Domestic crisis: Wotan (David Ward), Brünnhilde (Anita Välkki), and Fricka (Ann Howard) in Act Two of* Die Walküre. *Fricka's "flounced white nightie" and "eighteenth-century white wig" came in for a good deal of criticism.*

(*Opposite*) *Brünnhilde (Anita Välkki) and Sieglinde (Elizabeth Fretwell) in flight from Wotan's wrath in Act Three of* Die Walküre. *Around them, the Valkyries stand on guard. Brünnhilde's bicycle-saddle wig was later dispensed with.*

Gibson's was a more tender approach, not lacking in vivacity and high spirits, but full of subtle shades. Peter Ebert's production was equally warm-hearted and detailed, though the language barrier appeared to have impelled him to underline emphatically a number of points that would have needed no such underlining if the work had been sung in English. On the whole the audience appeared to appreciate his thoughtfulness, but some of the comic touches irritated Andrew Porter of the *Financial Times*, who wrote that it was "silly for Ford to go rummaging through a laundry basket which is evidently empty except for just a few clothes at the bottom." Mr Porter also drew a fine distinction between this *Falstaff* and another of the season's productions when he pointed out that: "For Falstaff to wander round the room, inside the screen, during the hunt, is good for an easy laugh, but untrue to a situation in which his aim is to escape unnoticed. *Herring* was brilliantly successful precisely because it observed the 'truths' of comedy – which are not those of farce."

Die Walküre fared not quite so well in the poorly equipped Scottish theatres, but was nevertheless a remarkably successful first shot at Wagner. Again a distinguished cast was assembled, headed by two established Wagnerians, David Ward and Anita Välkki, as Wotan and Brünnhilde. But the casting as a whole was not just a reshuffling of the international jet set who zoom from *Ring* to *Ring* round the world. Sieglinde and Fricka, Elizabeth Fretwell and Ann Howard, were both drawn from Sadler's Wells and both were new to their roles. Hunding was Donald McIntyre, who was just beginning what was soon to become an imposing Wagnerian career (by 1970 he was singing the Flying Dutchman at

Wotan (David Ward), in pursuit of Brünnhilde, encounters the Valkyries in Act Three of Die Walküre.

Bayreuth); and for Siegmund it was decided to risk choosing a British tenor who was by then widely known in Italian roles but to whom the German repertoire was still largely unexplored territory. The choice of Charles Craig for this important part – he was later to sing Siegfried too – paid off handsomely, even although it could be said of him that if he knew little Italian (he was coached phonetically in each role) he knew still less German. The feat of learning as arduous a part as Siegmund parrot-fashion was later to impress German audiences, when he came to sing Wagner in Berlin and elsewhere, rather more than it impressed the Scots, most of whom were unaware of it anyway.

All these singers, as Andrew Porter stated in the *Financial Times*, were "very acceptable – not yet outstanding, but already a cut above what one might hear in a German provincial house." John Warrack made the same point somewhat more negatively in the *Sunday Telegraph* when he wrote that he was "not exaggerating in saying that there is many a worse *Walküre* to be seen in established German provincial houses." True enough; but considering how bad a German provincial performance of almost anything can be, Mr Warrack's praise on this occasion was perhaps unnecessarily faint. Still, he was surely right, elsewhere in his article, to issue a cautionary reminder of how Scottish artistic chauvinism had at one time enfeebled Scotland's cultural life, and how Scottish Opera was one of the natural outcomes of the erosion of that chauvinism by the Edinburgh Festival, with its introduction of new standards and new ideas, resulting in "a growing appetite for proper musical amenities." To have hailed Scottish Opera's first *Walküre* as being competitive with Bayreuth's, or even Covent Garden's at its best, might have produced undue complacency in the Company when it came to present the next instalment of its *Ring* cycle.

On the whole, then, this *Walküre* was reviewed in terms of promise rather than fulfilment. In *The Observer*, Peter Heyworth suggested that the conductor, Alexander Gibson, was "still feeling his way into a big-scale interpretation and has not yet got the hang of matching strong characterisation of lyrical ideas with the symphonic coherence he rightly takes as his starting point." But, as Andrew Porter pointed out, Mr Gibson's conducting was also "warm, lyrical, often penetrating"; and indeed the way he obtained a convincing, alive, well-sustained Wagner sound from an overworked symphony orchestra in what was by far the longest opera the Company had so far tackled was an achievement not to be gainsaid. The players, fortified with Wagner tubas, and with the over-flow of the percussion rather effectively placed aloft in one of the theatre boxes (even if this solution to the space problem demonstrated once again how badly Scotland needed proper operatic facilities), were as much the heroes and heroines of the occasion as the singers on the stage.

Most of the main complaints, in fact, were reserved for Michael Knight's settings, which on paper had seemed so promising. Peter Heyworth went so far as to declare the whole visual side "misconceived." John Warrack, less out-spoken, thought it "did not look very handsome." Andrew Porter was "a little depressed to find we were in for yet another set of dim-lit, drab abstracts, divorced from the great scapes of sky, river, crag and forest against which Wagner set his drama," and went on to deliver a timely little homily to the effect that "All *Ring* designers should be treated to a Rhine journey before they set brush to paper, and then be shown, at Bayreuth, how 'abstract' settings too can reflect enormous natural scenes." For Harold Rosenthal, editor of *Opera*, the production offered an opportunity to express a longing for things past. "Perhaps one day, soon, a producer will try a completely naturalistic approach once more," he remarked in an essay on the vicissitudes of Wagner production contributed to the first issue of the new quarterly *Scottish Opera Magazine*. "Of course," he continued, "it must not look old-fashioned yet at the same time must recapture something of what Wagner wanted in the 1870s. Perhaps one of the great Italian opera producers, like Zeffirelli or Visconti, can one day be persuaded to try his hand at this kind of approach. It certainly can be no worse than some of the recent attempts to imitate post-war Bayreuth, and it may be a great deal better."

Many who saw the Scottish *Walküre* must have felt prompted to think along the same lines as Mr Rosenthal. Though Michael Knight's aim was plainly to create an illusion of space on the cramped Scottish stages, and was therefore admirable at least in theory, his designs ironically achieved the exact opposite. The basic idea was a ring ("what else?" asked Andrew Porter), sliced into movable segments which were variously compared to an orange, to wedges of cheese, to the screw of a giant liner, and to a Chinese puzzle. As a conception it seemed very much the residue of the Wieland Wagner revolution which had taken place some years earlier in Germany – a fault it shared with Sean Kenny's designs for the new production of *The Flying Dutchman* which was launched by Covent Garden that same year (Michael Knight, perhaps significantly, had been chosen by Scottish Opera from Mr Kenny's stable of protégés). The segments, which certainly had the virtue of geometric flexibility (they could be assembled and re-assembled into various shapes, and were not in fact to be seen as a complete ring until Act Three of *Götterdämmerung*), unfortunately had the vice of seriously confining the singers' field of movement – so much so that in one performance Miss Välkki accidentally rammed her spear into a nearby rock. They also tended to make entrances and exits difficult: the singers had first to come on to the stage and then, in full sight of the audience, climb on to the rostrum, and many a dramatic point was spoilt because of this.

Nor was the lighting, at this stage in *The Ring*, all it should have been. As I wrote in *The Scotsman* at the time, productions which attempt to recreate a Bayreuth-style presentation, doing away with "naturalistic" settings in the process, must achieve their effects with lighting and props of the most subtle kind. At Bayreuth, Wieland Wagner had already by then proclaimed the lighting director to be as important as the conductor. In Scotland, Charles Bristow had at his disposal the most elaborate and expensive equipment the Company had yet used, but not even he could work magic with it in the primitive conditions of the Scottish theatres, where such things as computerised switchboards – standard fittings in the main Continental houses – were unheard-of luxuries. As a result the first act of *Walküre* looked very dreary, with Hunding's hut transformed into a muddy-coloured dugout more appropriate to *All Quiet on the Western Front*. As for the dramatic moment when the door was supposed to burst open and the lovers embrace in the moonlight as it flooded into the room, this was thrown away not just because (in accordance with modern abstract practice) there was no door, but because the lighting at this point was simply not effective enough to give a poetic impression of the scene. Happily, by the time he reached *Götterdämmerung* two years later, Mr Bristow had such matters much better under control.

Also included in the list of complaints about *Walküre* was the question of costumes. The producer, Peter Ebert, had invited Michael Knight to design these as well as the settings, and the response to them varied from "An Emma Peel look for Wagner" (Eric Mason in the *Daily Mail*) to "Costumes are ill-assorted" (*The Times*), and "The costumes are quaint" (*Sunday Telegraph*). Once again, however, it was Andrew Porter in the *Financial Times* who provided the most vivid description of them when he wrote: "The costumes are striking (and to my eyes strikingly ugly); they place 'significance' above any attempt to make the actors look pleasing, or dignified. Wotan is in gold lamé, Brünnhilde in a poisonous electric-blue wrapper, cut short above her sensible boots, with a sausage-roll of violent copper hair tricorning her head. [Miss Välkki, fortunately, imported her own wig from Finland for later performances.] Fricka wears a flounced white nightie and an eighteenth-century white wig."

In spite of all this, Peter Ebert won considerable praise for his first *Walküre*. He had mounted, wrote Mr Porter, "a clear, intelligent performance, direct, sensible and sharply-focused." All the same, like Charles Bristow's lighting, Mr Ebert's *Ring* took a while to mature: not until *Götterdämmerung* did it get confidently and excitingly into its stride.

Der Rosenkavalier *in 1971 was one of the special productions with which Scottish Opera celebrated its first ten years. The picture above shows the Italian Tenor (Derek Blackwell) singing his aria to the Marschallin (Helga Dernesch) in Act One; behind (centre) can be seen the two conspirators, Valzacchi and Annina (Nigel Douglas and Joan Davies). Right: Janet Baker as Octavian (in her Mariandel disguise) in a scene from Act One with Noel Mangin as Baron Ochs and Helga Dernesch as the Marschallin.*

Janet Baker as Octavian in full lyrical flight in a scene from Act One of Der Rosenkavalier *with Helga Dernesch as the Marschallin.*

8. The Year of *Così*

THE YEAR 1967, too, had its share of milestones. It was the year of *The Rake's Progress*, Scottish Opera's first production for the Edinburgh Festival. It was the year of *Das Rheingold*, a gilt-edged assurance that the Company was now fully committed to the idea of a complete *Ring*. But above all it was the year of *Così fan tutte*. The inspired decision to team Elizabeth Harwood and Janet Baker as the two sisters – one blonde, the other brunette – had been quietly brewing for some time. If one or other of them had been unavailable (or if Miss Baker had considered Dorabella to be out of keeping with her talents, as she was to do later when Scottish Opera invited her to sing Carmen) the production might never have reached the stage. But both agreed to appear, and with Anthony Besch as producer and Alexander Gibson as conductor, the roots were planted for what turned out to be on every level the most intelligent, satisfying and beautiful production in the Company's history.

As all Mozart devotees know, good performances of *Così fan tutte* are surprisingly rare. Brigid Brophy, in her spirited book on the operas (*Mozart the Dramatist*), diagnosed the trouble when she declared that "Official taste has always been perceptive enough to admit Mozart to the canon of perpetual remembrance; and popular taste is perfectly correct when it calls him charming, even though it giggles at the inane producer's business which so often coarsens the charm on our stages."

Or to put it another way, too many producers concern themselves with the icing on the cake rather than with the cake itself. A new Mozart production has come to mean, very often, merely the addition of new gratuitous business to a traditional approach to the work – especially if the work happens to be *Così fan tutte* – instead of an attempt to think afresh about the characters and their music. But when Scottish Opera unveiled their *Così fan tutte* at Perth Theatre on 12 April 1967, one's first thoughts were that here at last was the production we had been waiting for ever since Carl Ebert's famous Glyndebourne version at the Edinburgh Festival in 1948.

Yet in spite of glowing memories of Suzanne Danco and Sena Jurinac as the two girls, the Scottish production, if I am not mistaken, had the edge on Glyndebourne's. At one time *Così fan tutte* was deemed the most superficial of Mozart's great operas, its plot preposterous, its people mere puppets. Today

By shifting the opening scene of Così fan tutte *from the usual sunny café terrace to a Turkish bath, the producer, Anthony Besch, could well have been accused of unnecessary tampering. In fact, by this bold stroke, he made the scene more than usually realistic. At the right, extolling the fidelity of their fiancées, are Ferrando (Ryland Davies) and Guglielmo (Peter van der Bilt). Squatting behind them, Don Alfonso (Inia Te Wiata).*

we have come to consider it the most probing of all his human comedies, so much so that when we encounter Ernest Newman's comments on it in *Opera Nights*, in which he stated Mozart's genius to be not always able to "grace a poor text with fine music," and Dorabella's Act Two aria ("E Amore un ladroncello," so enchantingly sung by Janet Baker in the Scottish production) to be "so uninteresting that it is generally omitted," and Ferrando's Act One aria ("Un' aura amorosa") to be "sickly-sentimental . . . excessively long and, if the truth must be told, not merely conventional but commonplace," we simply do not know what that distinguished critic was talking about.

Were productions of *Così fan tutte* so bad in Newman's day that the truths of the opera failed to communicate themselves to him? Perhaps. For even now, when Mozart is loved and understood as never before, productions of *Così fan tutte* are often dismayingly wrong-headed. At Aix-en-Provence I have watched a famous American soprano sing "Come scoglio" as if it were a sketch by Anna Russell; and at Hamburg, Günther Rennert's production showed Dorabella (Kerstin Meyer, no less, in the performance I saw) armed with a fishing-rod which she dangled over the edge of the stage in the finale to Act One. Such misinterpretations had no place in Anthony Besch's production for Scottish Opera. Instead of tinkering around with surface details he got down to the

The first Fiordiligi/Dorabella duet took place in the girls' bedroom instead of (as in most productions) on a sunny terrace—the point being, as the libretto makes plain, that it is still six o'clock in the morning. In this scene, as elsewhere, the opera's sense of symmetry was beautifully caught by John Stoddart's black-and-white settings, by the placing of the two beds, and by the contrast between the blonde and the dark sister. Left, Elizabeth Harwood as Fiordiligi; right, Janet Baker as Dorabella.

basic issues of the piece. And as a result we were enabled to recognise *Così fan tutte* for what it is: a sublime statement about human nature and experience, about fidelity and infidelity, about what it feels like to love and be discarded – in fact an opera in which Mozart's and Da Ponte's observations are just as valid today (consider John Updike's novel, *Couples*) as they were two centuries ago.

The plot of *Così fan tutte*, and the music with which Mozart brings it to passionate life, are far more ambivalent, far deeper, than most productions make them seem. Who really loves whom? Do the men really want to marry their respective fiancées? Will they eventually do so? Will their marriages be strengthened or weakened by the events of the opera? Would they subconsciously prefer to swap partners? Could it even be that not only Guglielmo but also Ferrando loves Fiordiligi, the more "challenging" of the two sisters, and that it takes Don Alfonso's cruel practical joke to make him realise this? One of the stimulating features of Anthony Besch's production was that it did not take sides. When the curtain came down on Act Two, the field was still open and the audience was left wondering what would become of the two pairs of lovers. In an interview later with Janet Baker I learnt that she, too, as she grew into the role of Dorabella, had begun to feel increasingly disconcerted about what might ultimately befall her: she had become very conscious, she said,

(Above, left) White gives way briefly to funereal black: the lovers have departed for war and the sisters lament their fate in the mock-tragic music which Mozart here provided. Janet Baker, with a superb sense of self-parody, at this point turned Dorabella into a great classical tragic heroine.

(Above, centre) Don Alfonso (Inia Te Wiata), having bribed Despina (Jenifer Eddy) to help him in his plot, is treated to some minxish repartee.

(Above, right) With the arrival of the Albanians came the first splash of colour—strong greens and yellows and oranges for their costumes.

(Below) By the end of Act One, as Fiordiligi and Dorabella begin to show their first signs of yielding, funereal black was banished and their white dresses began to gain a few pastel accoutrements.

that perhaps both men were in love with Fiordiligi, and that her bond with her proper fiancé, Ferrando, was little stronger than her bogus bond with Guglielmo. But maybe the most satisfying aspect of Mr Besch's production was that every time you saw it you emerged with new theories about it, and noticed telling little details that had not previously struck home.

At Perth, that sunny Easter, the production did not get quite fully into its stride. The Scottish National Orchestra was not yet at home in the music, and the accompaniments needed more bloom, sparkle and fluency. But it was plain that an outstanding *Così fan tutte* was in the making, and by the time the production reached Glasgow the following month – even though the King's Theatre lacked the special intimacy of the little Perth house – it had become what David Cairns in the *Financial Times* hailed as "a lesson to all opera companies, here and in other countries."

Although not all the London critics were as quick as Mr Cairns to put their finger on the special quality of the production – it was ideal, he said, "because it comes out of the music and, so to speak, goes back into it again" – most of them found plenty to praise in it. They recognised, as Mr Cairns did, that "Besch and his designer, John Stoddart, have not in any way used the work as a vehicle for preconceived ideas, but . . . looked at it afresh, distinguishing what the libretto says from what it does not, imposing nothing but also taking nothing on trust."

That is not to say, however, that Mr Besch failed to take risks. By shifting the opening scene from a sunny café terrace to a Turkish bath, he could well have been accused of unnecessary tampering. In fact, by this bold stroke, he made the opening scene more realistic than usual. After all, a café terrace is not perhaps the place you would expect to find two men, goaded by a third, making a wager about the fidelity of their fiancées. But in a Turkish bath, sobering up after an all-night stag party, they might well have been tempted to do so. Mozart, who delighted in Turkish exotica, would surely have applauded Mr Besch's change of locale; and it proved additionally valuable in that, as Mr Besch made plain, the sight of the two young officers swathed in towels and turbans could have been just the sort of spark to fire Don Alfonso with the sardonic idea of disguising them as Albanians in order to dupe their fiancées.

Never before had one seen a *Così fan tutte* that placed so much emphasis on time and place. While the orchestra murmured the dreamy introduction to the first Fiordiligi/Dorabella duet, the girls could be seen still asleep in bed instead of, as usual, strolling in the sunshine. At first it seemed a "producer's touch," albeit a charming one; but later its point was made clear when Dorabella, having yawned, stretched, and come to life more slowly than her imperious sister (even at this stage in the opera Mr Besch was deftly building up the characters of the two girls), remarked that it was already six o'clock. Niceties of that kind abounded in the excellent, explicit English translation by the American writers, Ruth and Thomas Martin, chosen in preference to the familiar and sometimes embarrassing one by the Rev Marmaduke E. Browne, which had seen service in Britain since 1890 and is still used by Sadler's Wells.

As the story unfolded, and Don Alfonso's wager began more and more powerfully to take effect, the onset of afternoon, evening and night were all carefully suggested by Mr Stoddart's exquisite designs. But as well as suggesting time and place, these settings, with their subtle use of colour, had an important additional function. The early scenes were entirely monochrome – black, grey, and gleaming white for both the scenery and the costumes, reflecting the hitherto pure, uncomplicated relationship between the characters. With the arrival of the Albanians came the first splash of colour – strong greens and yellows and oranges for their costumes. By the end of Act One, as Fiordiligi and Dorabella were beginning to show their first signs of yielding, their white dresses gained a few pastel accoutrements. Then, with the start of Act Two, the settings suddenly gained colour, and grew steadily richer and sultrier as the sisters began to fall for their new lovers and large cut-out plants (ominously phallic-shaped) began to sprout on stage. In other circumstances the effect could have seemed tiresomely artificial; but here it served to heighten the intensity of the opera, to enhance the curve of emotion revealed as the characters cast off their inhibitions and revealed their deeper instincts – even Don Alfonso's tastes were hinted at when, in Act Two, he took to wearing a green carnation as proof perhaps of why he was so cynical about women. At the end, as the characters returned to the everyday world of the beginning, so the colours faded and monochrome resumed.

Fortunately the production's musical virtues matched its visual ones. As a token of faith in the opera, it was more complete than most performances, and it included, in Act Two, not only Dorabella's "E Amore un ladroncello" but also Ferrando's cavatina, "Tradito schernito," both frequently omitted; it also included, captivatingly, the little decorations and cadenzas that Mozart intended to be sung, even if he did not bother to write them into the score. Here, for the first time in Britain, was a *Così fan tutte* whose phrases were graced with appoggiaturas, so that the musical line curved and flowed without being weakened by ugly "blunt endings." As for the flourishes and cadenzas with which Mr Gibson filled out the score, these were added not just for the sake of "good style" but also to suit the voices of the singers who were performing them. Anything that failed to work at rehearsal was promptly discarded. As a result the decorations always sounded natural, instead of tentative and self-conscious as in the Sadler's Wells *Marriage of Figaro* of the same period (though that historic production was nevertheless a valuable one, serving as the stylistic model for Scottish Opera's *Così fan tutte* and other more recent Mozart productions.).

Mr Gibson, though criticised in some quarters for his penchant for slow speeds (Stanley Sadie, writing in *The Times*, remarked that the performance had reminded him how long an opera *Così* was), conducted the music with manifest love, catching the delicacy and sweetness of the iridescent wind parts with which Mozart filled this radiant operatic divertimento, relishing the fine-spun loveliness of the vocal line and always giving it space to breathe and blossom. Of the well-chosen cast, it was Janet Baker's Dorabella that was the most immediately

(*Above, left*) Dorabella (*Janet Baker*) begins to succumb to the eloquence of the disguised Guglielmo (*Peter van der Bilt*).

(*Above, right*) The disguised Ferrando (*Ryland Davies*), after a lengthier struggle, wins Fiordiligi (*Elizabeth Harwood*).

(*Below*) The mock wedding ceremony at the end of Così, with Ryland Davies and Peter van der Bilt (*left and right*) as the Albanians and Elizabeth Harwood and Janet Baker as Fiordiligi and Dorabella.

complete and bewitching portrayal. For a singer whom we had come to associate with darker music – with Purcell's Dido at Glyndebourne, Mahler's *Kindertotenlieder* and *Das Lied von der Erde*, Schumann's *Frauenliebe und Leben* – her touch proved astonishingly light, her flair for comedy delightfully natural. She was an adorable Dorabella, impulsive, quick to produce tears and smiles, as convincingly woe-begone when she bade farewell to Ferrando as she was roguish when, in Act Two, she placed a feather in her hair with a splendid gesture and informed her sister that she had fallen for the disguised Guglielmo.

The rest of the cast, fine though they were as individuals and as a team, did not all get quite so quickly to the heart of their roles. Elizabeth Harwood as Fiordiligi and Ryland Davies as Ferrando produced plenty of pure, smooth, beautiful tone, but seemed just a little cool and careful (though by the time Miss Harwood returned to the production, two years later, she was just as radiant as Miss Baker). Peter van der Bilt, the accomplished Don Giovanni of 1964 and 1965, proved an equally impressive, lanky, handsome, appropriately direct Guglielmo, the more basic and worldly of the two lovers, as Mozart and Da Ponte from time to time make plain (for instance, in the way each plans to spend his prize-money: Guglielmo on a good meal, Ferrando on a band of musicians). Mr Van der Bilt rose strongly to his big moment in the finale – subtly highlighted by Mr Besch – when not only did he lose his temper with the progress of the mock wedding ceremony, but also broke away from the rest of the group, until he was led back gently by the ever-watchful Don Alfonso. Jenifer Eddy, Despina, and Inia Te Wiata, Don Alfonso, completed the vocal sextet. Miss Eddy, though recovering from a black eye received when a piece of scenery collapsed during rehearsals, was crisp, spirited and sparkling, refreshingly different from all the exaggerated tasteless little portrayals that pass for Despina in so many productions of the opera. Mr Te Wiata, beamingly avuncular, lacked the edge of asperity one has come to look for in a Don Alfonso, and lacked also a real command of Mozartian style; yet, as Peter Heyworth pointed out in *The Observer*, one could not help warming to the amiable old rascal he presented.

In spite of some deterioration in the quality of lighting and staging when the production moved from Glasgow to Edinburgh and Aberdeen, the perform-ances lost none of their charm and intensity as the season progressed. But in setting Britain and perhaps the world a new standard in Mozart production, the Company had at the same time set itself some problems. Would or could its next Mozart production reach the same level of artistry? Would or should that production use the same inspired team (Gibson/Besch/Stoddart) respon-sible for the *Così*? Would Elizabeth Harwood and Janet Baker be available for revivals of *Così* in future seasons, and, even if they were available, would it be possible to recreate the magic which moved *The Scotsman*'s columnist, Wilfred Taylor, to write in *A Scotsman's Log* after one of the Perth performances of how he "came out of the theatre, after the repeated curtain calls, into the cool moonlight softly playing on a romantic little town, walking on air, as . . . everyone else did."

9. Das Rheingold

THE NEW *Rheingold*, a new *Bohème*, and revivals of *Otello* and *Albert Herring* were the other productions to be seen in the spring of 1967. The Wagner, which opened the Glasgow part of the season on May 6, brought the Company half-way round its *Ring*. Logically it was the work that should have been staged the previous year, but opera companies have a fondness for beginning a new *Ring* cycle at chapter two. Like Scottish Opera's, the current Covent Garden cycle had begun (in 1961) with *Die Walküre*; so, more recently, did Karajan's four-year plan for a *Ring* at the Salzburg Easter Festival, and the new Sadler's Wells *Ring* at the London Coliseum was also launched in that way.

Such decisions are understandable. To open with *Die Walküre* may upset the chronology of the cycle while it is in the process of creation, but the first act of that opera is the most glowingly human, the most compact, the least problematic portion of the great tetralogy, and one can appreciate why opera companies prefer to ease themselves and their audiences into a new cycle with that work. *Das Rheingold*, on the other hand, though only half as long as *Die Walküre*, imposes a special strain on its performers, for it is contained within a single act lasting about two-and-a-half hours and involving several awkward scene changes. For producer and designer it is a fussier, more detailed score, requiring a greater number of props and visual effects, and calling for the most careful grouping of characters – of dwarfs, giants, gods, and Rhinemaidens – as Wagner's great study of power politics is set on course.

Among the questions any producer of *Das Rheingold* must first ask himself are whether the more elaborate scene changes can be made without bringing down the main house-curtain (the Covent Garden *Rheingold* fails in that respect), whether the Rhinemaidens should be singers or dancers (if the latter, their voices have to be projected from off-stage), whether the gold should be made of painted wood (which makes the wrong sort of noise) or metal (which is heavier to lift and more expensive), whether enough suitable anvils can be found for the forging scene (the Decca recording used eighteen of the type and size specified by Wagner, and the Vienna Philharmonic produced eighteen percussionists to play them), whether the "magic" can be convincingly enough worked to make Alberich's transformations into a dragon and toad look effective rather than laughable, and to make the rainbow bridge emerge really spectacularly from the mist at the end of the opera.

These are some of the more mechanical problems which face any producer of *Das Rheingold*, and which for Peter Ebert and his designer Michael Knight were made especially problematic because of the technical limitations of the Scottish theatres. A visitor to the King's Theatre, Glasgow, a few days before the opening could have gained valuable insight into the efforts that were being made to give Scotland a viable *Rheingold*. Because, at the time, I was writing a special preview of the production for *The Scotsman*, I was enabled to be such a visitor; and for an afternoon I explored the theatre, soaking up the sights and sounds, watching first a group of percussionists backstage practising on the dozen anvils that had been collected for the forging scene (some were real anvils, others were bits of dismantled railway line, and though in quantity they were not so numerous as those in the Decca recording, they made a fine ringing din which was far more satisfying than the solution nowadays employed by many German companies – which is simply to tape-record the sound). Next, two of the stage staff began thwacking whips in preparation for the scene in which Mime is thrashed by the invisible Alberich. The right sound for this was proving hard to capture. "Too resonant," called Alexander Gibson from the orchestra pit when they tried striking a wooden table behind the scenes. "Why not try skin?" asked Peter Ebert cheerfully.

Upstairs in one of the foyers an American soprano, en route for Munich, was aptly singing "Batti, batti" from *Don Giovanni* while she paced up and down in solitude, awaiting an audition during the lunch break. From a workshop in the wings an old-fashioned dragon – species Hammer Film – stared hungrily at the rehearsal, tongue hanging out. Within its reach, propped against the wall, stood the gold in the shape of a ring. Nearby, in the cramped dressing-rooms,

(Opposite, left) "*When for my wife I won you, one of my eyes I gave up so as to court you.*" Das Rheingold, *in 1967, was the second instalment of Scottish Opera's* Ring *cycle. In Glasgow the roles of Wotan and Fricka were sung by Forbes Robinson and Anna Reynolds. Valhalla, in the background, was thought by some critics to have more than a hint of Wall Street.*

(Opposite, right) Loge (Joseph Ward) in political discussion with Wotan (Forbes Robinson) during the second scene of Das Rheingold. *Behind them, Donner and Froh (Ronald Morrison and Ramon Remedios), Freia and Fricka (Elizabeth Fretwell and Anna Reynolds) gaze into space.*

(Right) Later in the 1967 season the German tenor Richard Holm took over the role of Loge in Das Rheingold, *and David Ward, who had appeared in* Die Walküre *in 1966, returned to sing Wotan.*

most of the costumes hung ready: great thick rubber suits (like primeval adverts for Michelin tyres) for the giants, Fasolt and Fafner, who were also to wear four-inch lifts; a flickering, fiery robe for Loge; mesh and glitter for the Rhinemaidens; a smock with a streak of lightning on it for Donner. On stage, some of the singers, in their ordinary clothes, were checking their positions and footholds on the slopes of Michael Knight's controversial geometric rostra. Forbes Robinson, Glasgow's Wotan (he was to be replaced in Edinburgh and Aberdeen by David Ward), was balancing his ten-foot spear and seeing how much room he had to swing it without driving it into the scenery. Higher up the mountainside, Elizabeth Fretwell, who played Freia, goddess of eternal youth, was poised precariously in high heels on the edge of a chasm (but the Covent Garden production of Tippett's *King Priam* is reputed to have even steeper settings – the singers have to wear specially padded shoes in order to cling, like flies, to its slopes). Joseph Ward, Loge, was perfecting the hunched posture which many singers adopt for that role.

Yet for all the efforts to make this *Rheingold* look good, there were, as David Cairns wrote later in the *Financial Times*, things in the production and staging that could surely have been improved. "Why is it," he asked, "that producers are regularly overcome with a kind of paralysis by the demands of Wagner's stage action? Peter Ebert is no exception. In Nibelheim, for instance, it is almost as if he had gone out of his way to draw attention to Alberich taking cover a good second or two before his various transformations. Alberich's pursuit of the Rhinemaidens is also quite astonishingly feeble and implausible. And in the piling up of the gold in front of Freia a large vertical fissure is left, wide enough to put your arm through, which makes nonsense of the action."

Luisa Bosabalian as Mimi, alone and forlorn, at the gates of Paris in Act Three of La Bohème in 1967.

Nor did Mr Cairns's complaints end there. "The stage designer's answer to the problem of a rainbow bridge," he continued, "is to release an actual structure, supported on struts, hopefully across the ravine. It is hardly surprising, however, that no one actually ventures to tread on it, but stands about as if waiting for someone else to make the first move, for after a few yards the bridge simply stops and ends in air."

Nevertheless, Scottish Opera's *Rheingold* was far from being the only one to contain faults of that kind – Covent Garden's has suffered from similar blemishes – and Mr Cairns was quick to point out that the new production was a brave undertaking. Indeed, in some respects, such as avoiding lowering the curtain until the end, it managed to avoid certain familiar pitfalls; and by the time the production was revived in 1971 a number of the visual details had been improved, and the rainbow bridge no longer looked as if it had been constructed by the gods with pieces from a giant Meccano set.

As with *Die Walküre*, however, it was on the musical side that the performance worked best. Although most of the cast were still feeling their way into their parts – once again Scottish Opera was commendably determined to develop new Wagnerian voices rather than hire established figures from the international jet set – there were at least two immediately striking portrayals: the remarkably assured, expressive, glistening-voiced Fricka of Anna Reynolds (whose career as a Wagner singer was thereafter rapidly to expand) and the unusually human, touching, eloquently sung Fasolt of Victor Godfrey, a bass whom Covent Garden had had on its books for some time but whose talents had not hitherto been sufficiently recognised.

Forbes Robinson's Wotan never came quite so strongly into focus, but he sang firmly and sonorously; and if Joseph Ward missed something of the barbed, darting humour of Loge (admirably suggested by the German tenor, Richard Holm, who was imported for the later performances and gave a considerable lift to the production) his portrayal was nevertheless a very intelligent one, a strong foundation for his appearance in the revival four years later. Gwyn Griffiths's Alberich was not sufficiently baleful. Manacled in scene four, he made an oddly pathetic figure. Yet he fitted in aptly enough with a production whose virtues in general tended to be those of understatement.

In that respect, the conductor Alexander Gibson seemed to have kept in mind that *Rheingold* is the gateway to the *Ring* and not its climax, though it was not until he pieced the whole tetralogy together in December 1971 that we were to gain an idea of his thoughts on the structure of the complete work. Meanwhile he gave us a delicate, thoughtful *Rheingold*, alive to many of the undertones of the music, such as that quiet yet chilling passage where the gods are cut off from Freia's power and we see them age before our eyes.

At the opening performance in Glasgow an extra lustre was given to the evening by the presence in the audience of Friedelind Wagner, the composer's grand-daughter, who also found time during her visit to give a lecture at Glasgow City Chambers on Wagnerian stage technique. To see that noble profile, the line of the brow, nose and chin unchanged after two generations,

(Left) Musetta (Barbara Rendell) in minxish mood in La Bohème. *Behind her in the Café Momus sit Mimi and Rodolfo (Luisa Bosabalian and George Shirley).*

(Right) Two beautifully-placed trees added a touch of Utrillo to Peter Rice's designs for the Barrière d'Enfer in La Bohème. *Here Rodolfo (George Shirley) sings of his troubles with Mimi while Marcello (Robert Savoie) listens and Mimi (Luisa Bosabalian) stands unnoticed in the background.*

was startling; and in praising the musical values of the Scottish Opera performance, but pronouncing doubt about some of its visual inconsistencies (abstract settings in conflict with pantomime dragon), she stamped a Wagnerian seal on the reviews by the critics.

In a year that included so ravishing a *Così* and so fascinating an *Albert Herring* it was perhaps inevitable that the new *Bohème* would be subject to more fault-finding than might otherwise have been the case. Maybe Noël Goodwin went too far when he wrote in the *Daily Express* that "surely the cost of the Company's third new production this year would have been better justified in an opera that represents young and modern musical theatre rather than one which basically relies on a romantic memory of youth." But the fact was, in choosing one of the most familiar of all operas, the Company was automatically expected to do something special with it – as they had done in 1964 with *Faust*. On this occasion, however, what we were given was a fairly straightforward presentation, produced with vitality by Peter Ebert, effectively designed by Peter Rice, sensitively conducted by Roderick Brydon, and containing, in the Rudolfo of the coloured American tenor George Shirley, a portrayal that was

The revival of Otello *in 1967 included two major changes of cast. Joan Carlyle took over the role of Desdemona from Luisa Bosabalian, who had sung it in 1963 and 1964; and in the Edinburgh performances the title role was performed by the vehement Italian tenor, Pier Miranda Ferraro, in place of Charles Craig, who had appeared in the opera as usual in Glasgow. These three studies show Mr Ferraro's Otello gradually giving way to jealousy as the opera proceeds towards its climax.*

a worthy successor to the Madama Butterfly of Felicia Weathers. In sum, this was quite a lot for any production of *Bohème* to offer, especially as most of the smaller roles were nicely filled and the choruses in the Café Momus scene were superbly controlled and thrillingly sung. But perhaps because Luisa Bosabalian's Mimi, though often beautiful in vocal tone and line, never came dramatically to life or really looked right, the production suffered from a void at the centre; and not until Joan Carlyle took over the role for the last of the performances in Edinburgh did the full potential of this *Bohème* become recognisable.

The full potential of the Scottish *Otello*, of course, had been recognised some years earlier. The special feature of the 1967 revival was the presence of Pier Miranda Ferraro in the Edinburgh performances in place of Charles Craig. An established Italian tenor, he brought to the production a violent, richly histrionic conception of the title-role, making plain (even more so than Ronald Dowd had done in 1964) that epilepsy just as much as Iago was responsible for Otello's emotional state. The end of Act Three, where Iago kicked the prostrate hero down the sloping ramp of Ralph Koltai's hexagonal setting, had always been an impressive moment in Anthony Besch's production. On this occasion it was made still more malevolent by the fact that the body was a twitching one. Joan Carlyle, who had succeeded Luisa Bosabalian as Desdemona, gave a portrayal remarkable for the way she exploited her chest notes and for the splendid coherence she brought to the last act. Hers was not the most tender Desdemona imaginable, but it was a clear and admirable portrayal. Peter Glossop was again the Iago, and Alexander Gibson the conductor.

10. The Edinburgh Festival —Stravinsky

SOONER OR LATER, Scottish Opera was bound to get its chance to appear at the Edinburgh Festival. The question was when, and with what production or productions. Lord Harewood, during the last three years of his Festival directorship, felt it was still too soon for the Company to be thrown into the international spotlight. About Scottish Opera's standards he had no complaint: in an interview in *The Scotsman* in 1964 he had said that the Company was already something that could be treated completely seriously – "One can compare it with any other company, with the Scala if you like, and say where it is as good and where it isn't as good."

His main concern was that the available repertoire was not yet big enough to sustain a full three weeks at the King's; and if the Scottish Company was to share the theatre with a visiting one, thus enabling more operas to be offered, the rehearsal problems would be too severe for the wretchedly cramped stage facilities. Consequently, Lord Harewood thought he would wait until Scottish Opera could go it alone, with a season consisting of, say, one brand-new production, one from the previous year, one from further back, and perhaps a couple of one-act pieces, one a new production, the other older. It was his belief that by 1969 the Company would have a firm enough nucleus of works to choose from.

In retrospect, Lord Harewood's decision seems to have been perhaps excessively cautious. After all, he did not invariably insist that one company should sustain the full three weeks on its own, and indeed by 1965, his last year of office, Scottish Opera already had in its repertoire productions superior to the Munich *Così fan tutte* (sung in German, if you please), the Holland Festival *Don Giovanni*, and the English Opera Group *Albert Herring*, all of which he brought to Edinburgh that year. Nevertheless, he was surely right to recognise that it might be mistaken kindness to let Scottish Opera appear at the Festival too soon.

Nor did the Company get its chance the following year: 1966 was a year of transition, when Lord Harewood handed over the reins to his successor, Peter Diamand, who naturally – until he knew the lie of the land – preferred to play safe and invited a long-established German company, the Stuttgart Opera, to Edinburgh for the whole of the Festival that year. He was not to know that playing safe would prove, on this occasion, a mixed blessing, with a new production of *Wozzeck* cancelled after a single performance (through the sudden illness of the conductor, Carlos Kleiber, and the company's curious carelessness in failing to have a deputy on the spot) and a dull, dim *Magic Flute*, fortunately counterbalanced by a fascinating Wieland Wagner production of *Lulu* and a welcome, if less finely executed, *Lohengrin* from the same source.

Then, in 1967, Scottish Opera's opportunity came. Having by that time seen the Company at work, Mr Diamand decided to bring it into the Festival immediately and devised an imaginative way of doing so. Continuing the Harewood policy of "featuring" certain composers each year, Mr Diamand planned to make 1967 a year of Bach and Stravinsky; and since no large-scale Stravinsky survey could be called complete without his one full-length opera, *The Rake's Progress* (whose British premiere had been given in Edinburgh by the Glyndebourne company fourteen years earlier), Mr Diamand was faced with the choice of importing an established production or mounting a new one. Had I been the Festival director, I would have been tempted to bring over the famous Ingmar Bergman production from Stockholm. Instead, and perhaps more valuably, Mr Diamand commissioned Scottish Opera to prepare a *Rake's Progress* with Alexander Gibson as conductor, Peter Ebert as producer, and Alexander Young, the world's most distinguished Stravinsky-approved Tom Rakewell, in the title-role.

At first there was some indecision over who should be the designer. The Company favoured Peter Rice, who had recently designed its *Faust* and *Falstaff*, and whose *Ariadne auf Naxos* for Sadler's Wells suggested that he would have sound ideas on the neo-classicism of the *Rake*. Mr Hemmings however nominated Ralph Koltai, who had also worked with the Company (on *Otello*, *Don Giovanni* and *Boris*) and whose services, after some deliberation, were duly sought. It proved an exciting choice, for Mr Koltai's designs turned out to be among the most striking features of the production, even though some cost-cutting in building them resulted in their working less efficiently than they might have done if more expensive machinery had been available for the ingenious scene-changes.

No one, however, should therefore assume that it was a shoe-string production. People who believe it is "cheaper" for Mr Diamand to make use of Scottish Opera than to invite a foreign company to Edinburgh should remember that foreign companies are usually heavily subsidised by the cities and countries from which they come, whereas Scottish Opera's costs have to be paid largely by the Festival. The bill for *The Rake's Progress* that year ate a considerable distance into the Festival's annual budget. It amounted to £23,712 10s for the four performances – a sum which, by the standards of Covent Garden (where a new production can easily cost three or four times as much), was moderate, but which nevertheless made it seem all the more miraculous that only five years previously Scottish Opera launched its first season on the strength of the thousand pounds it had received from Scottish Television.

For those who wonder how the money for *The Rake's Progress* was spent, I

"Heut' oder Morgen . . ." Helga Dernesch as the Marschallin philosophises during her great scene at the end of Act One of Der Rosenkavalier.

Above: *a study in gold and silver. Janet Baker (Octavian) presents the rose to Elizabeth Harwood (Sophie) in Act Two of Der Rosenkavalier. Below: the assignation at the inn. Janet Baker, in her Mariandel disguise, plays up to Baron Ochs (Noel Mangin) in Act Three.*

(Left) Scottish Opera's first Edinburgh Festival production was of Stravinsky's The Rake's Progress. *Ralph Koltai's settings were both admired and criticised for their ingenuity—the opening scene, depicted here, was certainly striking but was deemed to be too claustrophobic and lacking its due verdant freshness. The cast included, left to right, David Kelly as Trulove, Alexander Young as Tom Rakewell, Elizabeth Robson as Ann Trulove, and Peter van der Bilt as Nick Shadow.*

(Right) Ralph Koltai's rich setting for the brothel scene was one of the memorable features of the 1967 production of The Rake's Progress.

include below a breakdown of the costs. It provides, I think, a useful indication of what it took to mount a major but by no means lavish production in the second half of the 1960s – those pendulum years among whose few saving graces, according to Bernard Levin, were the remarkable operatic experiences they managed to offer.

Singers and understudies	£3679	11	8
Chorus	1937	0	0
Music staff (repetiteurs, etc.)	724	15	6
Scottish National Orchestra	3517	3	6
Royalties/music	991	6	0
Producer/designer	1029	11	3
Sets and props	3267	11	6
Costumes	4324	6	0
Stage staff	2031	0	0
Stage incidentals	1210	4	7
Administration	1000	0	0
Total	£23,712	10	0

The Rake's Progress shared the King's Theatre that year with two visiting productions: Haydn's *Orfeo*, a Joan Sutherland/Richard Bonynge concoction which sprang (though limped might be a better word) from Vienna, and

(Above, left) An idyllic moment before "the progress of the rake begins". Elizabeth Robson and Alexander Young in Act One of The Rake's Progress. (Above, right) Sona Cervena, the Hungarian mezzo-soprano, was an incisive Baba the Turk. Beside her, Alexander Young—Stravinsky's personal favourite among latter-day exponents of the role of Tom Rakewell.

(Below) Perhaps the most haunting passage in Peter Ebert's production of The Rake's Progress was his handling of the final scene in Bedlam. John Warrack in the Sunday Telegraph made special mention of the "whey-faced man in woman's dress picking hopelessly at beads" (centre) and drew attention to the "walls deeply scored with scratches from the silent groups facing them."

Bellini's *I Capuleti ed i Montecchi*, which was imported, with Claudio Abbado as conductor, from the previous year's Holland Festival. Both these visiting productions were "serviced" by Scottish Opera – that is, Scottish Opera supplied the chorus and such local organisation as was necessary, and in the case of *Orfeo* the orchestra was the SNO.

How well did *The Rake's Progress* stand up to the competition? By common consent more than favourably, in spite of an initial doubt on the part of some members of the Company whether Stravinsky's opera, for all its qualities, was after all the ideal work with which to make a Festival debut. In spite, too, of an opening performance which was burdened with crises for the performers and discomforts for the audience – crisis and discomfort at one point converging when the interval between Acts Two and Three was grossly over-extended because Peter Ebert wanted to give the epilogue an extra rehearsal, and the audience found themselves excluded from the circle bar (as they had been earlier in the evening) because the Lord Provost, at that time Sir Herbert Brechin, was holding a reception there.

Fortunately the critics did not allow these irritations to interfere with their judgment, and most of them agreed that the production, while containing some unhappy details, was in general full of good things. But not, perhaps, outstandingly good things. Several writers made the point that, although the opening performance was up to Festival standard, it was an evening of promise rather than fulfilment; the assurance of presentation, now expected of Scottish Opera, was not wholly present. Peter Heyworth of *The Observer*, after praising the "right, flabby, complacent quality" of Alexander Young's Tom Rakewell, the stylishness of Peter van der Bilt's sardonic, firm-voiced Nick Shadow, the tension of Colin Tilney's harpsichord accompaniment in the great graveyard scene, and the fact that "both Peter Ebert's production and Ralph Koltai's severely stylised sets share a common determination to avoid easy routine," went on to say that these merits did not add up to a fully convincing performance. The rest of the principal singers, he felt, left something to be desired, and though Alexander Gibson's conducting "revealed a lot of meaty detail," he would have liked the energetic playing of the SNO to have contained more sharpness and wit.

David Cairns, in the *Financial Times*, praised the "lizard-like stillness and watchfulness" of Peter van der Bilt's Shadow, but considered that the Dutch baritone missed the "dynamic, actively malignant side of the fiend." Other critics, too, thought the part somewhat underplayed, Desmond Shawe-Taylor in the *Sunday Times* deeming this to be an advantage, Malcolm Rayment in the *Glasgow Herald* regarding it as a catastrophe. Martin Cooper of the *Daily Telegraph*, on the other hand, thought the whole cast admirable, even Elizabeth Robson's Ann Trulove (whom some critics had a down on), and he reserved a special word of praise for Sona Cervena's Baba the Turk, a role which, in previous productions, he had come to regard as a bore. Gerald Larner of *The Guardian* also felt that there was "no great musical weakness anywhere," though he was much more severe about Mr Koltai's settings.

It was these, indeed, that proved the most controversial feature of the production. Admirable and imaginative though some critics found them, it was generally agreed that they were perhaps too clever in their use of sliding platforms ("trays of puppets," as Joan Chissell called them in *The Times*) for some of the scene changes. As the *Musical Times* pointed out, "Ingenuity can be its own defeat"; and the writer went on to say that the designs drew too much attention to themselves, that they limited the acting area, and that they failed to provide the "sense of gradual contraction from the vernal freshness of the opening to the claustrophobia of Bedlam" – the opening scene, with its vertical patch of green (what looked like an upright square of carpet making do for a hedgerow) and surrounding darkness, already contained too much menace. On the other hand, the same reviewer paid tribute to the fact that a real attempt had been made to stage the music, not merely to decorate it.

So although the evening found the critics in mild disarray, they had all plainly found plenty to stimulate them. Much had been expected of the production (that in itself being a tribute to the rise of Scottish Opera) and it was judged by the highest international standards – except that allowances were made by some writers for the shortcomings of the King's Theatre, which were under attack even more strongly than usual that year (the Festival's twenty-first birthday), because the new opera house seemed no nearer and the Lord Provost had been threatening to reduce the Festival's annual subsidy from £75,000 to £50,000.

One aspect of the production that won special praise was the choral singing. This, to quote the *Musical Times* again, "showed not merely vigour and the expected choral skills, but evidence of real thought: the range of tone Arthur Oldham has encouraged from them could make possible the frenzied patter of the Auction Scene, the harsh response of the whores to Tom's 'Love too frequently betrayed' as if love were something outside their knowledge, merely a tiresome itch they knew how to deal with, and the all-passion-spent hollow octaves with which the madmen blurt 'Mourn for Adonis'. " Peter Ebert's flair for choreographing a chorus or ensemble, which had been remarked upon in previous years, came in for new admiration on this occasion, not least from John Warrack, who, in the *Sunday Telegraph*, spoke of the sure sense of general character which was imposed on the singers while allowing room for some very sharp individual sketches – "a whey-faced man in woman's dress picking hopelessly at beads [this in the Bedlam scene], the walls deeply scored with scratches from the silent groups facing them."

For all the minor flaws in its presentation, there was no Scottish Opera production which, until then, one felt more eager to see again, once its teething troubles had worn off. But alas, the ingenuity of its settings proved its defeat: because of mechanical troubles, the production was jettisoned.

The Rake's Progress, however, was not the Company's only contribution to the Edinburgh Festival's Stravinsky survey. At fairly short notice, it was agreed to mount a production of *The Soldier's Tale* as a morning event on the open stage of the Assembly Hall of the Church of Scotland during the last week of the

(*Above, left*) *As well as* The Rake's Progress, *Scottish Opera staged* The Soldier's Tale *during the Edinburgh Festival's Stravinsky year. Wendy Toye's production at the Assembly Hall was conceived on "Brechtian" lines, with simple props carried on and off by masked attendants and much use of banners and streamers—the Soldier's ride in the Devil's chariot, for instance, was suggested by twirling parasols and long coloured reins. Patrick Wymark (top left) was the Devil, Gordon Jackson (below) the Narrator. (Above, right) Una Stubbs, familiar to devotees of the Alf Garnett family, was the bright, brittle, mini-skirted Princess. (Below) The Devil wins the day. The Princess (Una Stubbs) is prevented by the border guards from joining the Soldier (Nicky Henson) at the end of* The Soldier's Tale. *At the left, the Narrator (Gordon Jackson) looks on.*

Festival. It proved an inspired idea. The Assembly Hall, which had been, and still is, one of the main settings for the Festival's dramatic events, had seldom if ever before been used for music. But Scottish Opera was quick to realise the possibilities, and perhaps in future some special musical use will be made of it in much the same way as the Rotunda at the rear of the Stockholm Opera has come to serve as an important setting for Swedish experimental works.

The days when *The Soldier's Tale* could be deemed an experimental piece, uniting opera, ballet and speech, were of course long since passed, but the freshness and inventiveness of Scottish Opera's presentation of it were a pleasure to eye and ear. At first one wondered whether the choice of Wendy Toye as producer would be altogether wise: the relentless crudeness and jokiness of her Offenbach romps at Sadler's Wells made one fear that she might do the same for Stravinsky. But fortunately these suspicions proved groundless. With the help of a well-chosen designer, Carl Toms, Miss Toye conceived what we like nowadays to call a "Brechtian" production, with simple props carried on and off by masked attendants, and much use of banners and streamers. Often the effect was beautiful and striking in an oriental sort of way, as when the Soldier's ride in the Devil's chariot was suggested by twirling parasols and long coloured reins, or when, in order to reach the Princess, the Soldier had to proceed through a kind of Chinese puzzle of closed doors.

The use of an English translation – the familiar one by Michael Flanders and Kitty Black – encouraged Miss Toye to take a number of liberties with the original text. But honour was done to Stravinsky and his librettist, C. F. Ramuz: there were no lapses of taste, no changes for the sake of change. Nor was there the hint of datedness from which *The Soldier's Tale* can sometimes suffer. There was a skilled, incisive cast, with Nicky Henson a likeably youthful Cockney Soldier, Gordon Jackson a relaxed, agreeable Narrator, casually dressed with a cigarette between his lips, Una Stubbs a bright, brittle, mini-skirted Princess, Patrick Wymark a hoarse-voiced Devil in black Czarist uniform.

The conductor, Alexander Gibson, and most of the seven instrumentalists were, like Mr Jackson, dressed casually in sweaters and slacks, but this casualness had no bearing on the playing, which was generally pointed and precise, with Sam Bor's solo violin earning special mention from the *Glasgow Herald*. Inevitably the layout of the hall, with its apron stage and absence of orchestra pit and curtains, meant that the musicians were in full view of the audience all the time; but, given the type of production which Miss Toye had devised, this added effectively to the theatre-workshop atmosphere of the occasion. The performances, which took place at the same time as the Festival's chamber concerts elsewhere in town, did not perhaps win enormous audiences – the largest, on the last morning, filled 67 per cent of the hall. Nor did the production win the amount of newspaper coverage allotted to *The Rake's Progress*, because by that time in the Festival the leading London critics had departed southwards. But for those who saw it, this *Soldier's Tale* left much that stuck in the mind; and when, three years later, Miss Toye created a new production for London, she felt confident enough to use the Edinburgh one as her model.

11. The Most Active Year Yet

TOWARDS THE END of the 1960s, Peter Hemmings coined two sayings about Scottish Opera which he repeated so persistently in public that they became something in the nature of political slogans. One was his famous declaration about the Company having as its target a twenty-week season by 1970; the other was his hopeful aphorism about how, if its subsidy were only 50 per cent larger, the Company would be able to double the length of its season.

His calculations, as things turned out, were by no means rash. By 1970 the twenty-week target was all but reached. By 1971 it was surpassed, and by that same year the Scottish Arts Council's grant, which in 1968 stood at £90,000 per annum, had risen steeply to £200,000 – not a vast sum by Covent Garden or Sadler's Wells standards, yet fairly spectacular by Scottish ones, especially if you kept in mind the absence of a deep-rooted operatic tradition and the fact that in 1962 the most the Arts Council could be coaxed into contributing was a mere £1000.

With the premiere of a new opera at Perth, a production at the Edinburgh Festival, a foreign trip, a visit to Newcastle, and a Christmas season in Edinburgh, 1968 was the Company's most active year yet and contained more innovations than any previous one. The spring season was ambitious – though the decision to confine the new opera, Robin Orr's *Full Circle*, to Perth seemed at first an uncharacteristic act of prudence on the part of a Company which had previously shown itself far from timid about staging modern operas. Fortunately this attack of cold feet was short-lived, and by the end of 1968 *Full Circle* had achieved the distinction of being the only work until then to have had two separate, and very different, productions by the Company.

Full Circle was Scottish Opera's first Scottish opera, a landmark in the history of a country which had previously offered scant outlets to composers with an ambition to write for the stage. Robin Orr's ambition, which had remained unfulfilled until he was fifty-nine years old, was finally brought to fruition with the support not only of the opera Company but also of Scottish Television, whose management had been showing renewed interest in the activities of Scottish Opera and wanted a short potentially televisual work for inclusion in a new series of programmes intended to bring opera to a wider audience.

After considering various subjects, the composer found the libretto he wanted in a radio play by the Scottish poet and dramatist, Sydney Goodsir Smith. Its title was *The Stick-Up*, which to my mind was more inviting as well as more explicit than the one ultimately favoured by the composer. Its setting was the Glasgow Gorbals, its accent was strongly Scottish, and its story concerned a Clydeside docker on the dole during the depression of 1930. From this, Orr fashioned a sharp little piece of Scottish *verismo* whose action moved quickly from the opening scene of the downhearted Davie and his wife in their squalid tenement, to armed robbery in a Glasgow back street, a fight in a sleazy pub, and a melodramatic climax of the I-didn't-know-the-gun-was-loaded variety.

The music, employing the same sort of small instrumental ensemble as Stravinsky's *The Soldier's Tale* (with which Scottish Opera proposed to couple it at Perth), was direct and lyrical in an apt post-Puccini way – if any other opera was brought to mind in listening to it, it was Puccini's *Il Tabarro*. Telling use was made of a beautiful, undulating theme that served on television as a sort of "River Clyde" motive but also haunted the rest of the score, reflecting in its most eloquent form the desolation of the wife, as she toiled in her wretched kitchen and worried about her husband. Into little more than half an hour, Orr crammed many striking touches: an ironic reference to the tune of "Scots wha hae" when the hero lamented his poverty, a gust of ragtime when the wife spoke longingly of a visit to the cinema, the poignancy with which the scene of the stick-up was counterpointed by the wife's offstage voice of conscience, the sudden eruption of the quarrel in the pub, the softly plaintive coda with the wife alone in her kitchen reiterating her husband's name after he has been arrested for killing the policeman.

All these features showed a strong, sure operatic sense, admirably conveyed by the young cast assembled for the occasion. William Elvin, a twenty-two-year-old Aberdonian who within a year or so was to be dividing his career between Scotland and Glyndebourne, portrayed Davie as a stocky Marlon Brando, and Sheila McGrow was equally convincing as Jean, his sad little waif of a wife. There were keen character sketches from Duncan Robertson as a pestering neighbour and William McCue as a brusque bartender, and Alexander Gibson drew vital accompaniments from an octet of players from the SNO.

Though Orr's decision to use a libretto in broad Scots aroused some initial controversy – the critics of the *Glasgow Herald* and one or two other newspapers claimed bafflement (a statement curiously at odds with the fact that those same critics had never seemed the least disconcerted by operas in any other language you cared to name) – the main battles at the time were waged over Michael Geliot's production. In *Boris Godunov* in Scotland in 1965, and in *The Rise and Fall of the City of Mahagonny* at Sadler's Wells, Mr Geliot had shown himself to have a persuasive way with what could be described as sociological opera; and it was no doubt with this in mind that he was invited to stage *Full Circle*.

The result, however, was by necessity a compromise production, which had to be geared both for the STV studios in Glasgow and for the Perth Theatre. The basic idea was exciting: in order to open out the action, Mr Geliot imaginatively set the opera in front of three giant screens on which photographs of

Some of the most eloquent music in Full Circle, *Robin Orr's opera about Glasgow slumland, depicted Jean (a delicate study by Sheila McGrow) toiling in her wretched kitchen and worrying about her out-of-work husband.* Full Circle *was the first Scottish opera to be presented by Scottish Opera.*

In Scottish Opera's second production of Full Circle *the slide projections were dispensed with and new revolving settings by Bernard Culshaw worked to telling effect. Here, as the opera approaches its violent climax, Davie (William Elvin) has a row with a bartender (John Graham) while the pestering neighbour Andra (John Robertson) eavesdrops in the background.*

seedy Glasgow streets and tenements were projected in quick succession, mingled and shuffled with shots of James Cagney and Edward G. Robinson (though the day of these film stars, as astute cinema buffs were quick to point out, was later than 1930) and with blow-ups of some of the props used in the story. A number of the pictures, such as the bullets from Davie's gun and his wife's kettle, were somewhat irritating statements of the obvious, but others had important comments to make on the action, as when the wife's face suddenly appeared on all three screens while Davie was counting the money he had stolen.

Unfortunately this fascinating but restless photographic tour of Glasgow slumland tended to compete too strenuously with the music. Its effect, instead of enhancing the opera, was sometimes merely distracting, especially as the projectionists appeared to have trouble getting the timing right – on the first night at Perth, screens were allowed to go blank or else presented the wrong picture. Nor, on television, did the idea work quite as well as intended, for there the use of the screens – admittedly quite striking in the theatre – came over more conventionally as a simple screen-within-a-screen technique.

The stage premiere on 10 April 1968 attracted a few of the English critics for the first time to Perth, and won from them moderately enthusiastic reviews. Stanley Sadie in *The Times* thought the music was stronger in terms of atmosphere than of personal character, but placed some of the blame on Sydney

Goodsir Smith's libretto, which made Davie seem too sympathetic and kindly a man to resort so readily to violence. Ronald Crichton made the same point more bluntly in the *Financial Times* when he described Davie's behaviour as "frankly daft," adding that "we are given no convincing indication why such an apparently nice and gentle man should suddenly and ineptly take to petty crime." Part of the trouble, as Stanley Sadie suggested, was the opera's shortness: thirty-five minutes was "barely time to establish character, let alone develop it."

Still, brevity in opera can be a fault on the right side; and when a new, more "traditional" production of *Full Circle* was prepared by Ian Watt-Smith, Scottish Opera's newly-appointed staff producer, for the Company's first Christmas season in Edinburgh, it became clear that brevity in this work was not necessarily a fault at all. This time, atmospheric revolving settings by Bernard Culshaw – representing kitchen, foggy street, and pub – enabled the music to make its own strong effect; and Mr Watt-Smith's production (whose expressiveness could be described as Bergian, as opposed to the Brechtian features of Michael Geliot's production) emphasised more strongly than the previous one the scheme of the opera – a series of short, intense scenes alternating with powerful instrumental interludes. There were moments – though Orr's music was less violent than Berg's – when you could imagine yourself to be watching a kind of Glasgow *Wozzeck*.

Obviously, one should beware of stating the case for *Full Circle* too highly. It had its faults. Yet when that most widely-travelled of opera critics, Andrew Porter, came to review the December performances for the *Financial Times*, he wrote that "in its terseness, in its sure small musical strokes, its unsentimental yet poetic text and music, its taut though not unlyrical texture, *Full Circle* strikes me as a masterly piece."

In the months between its two productions of *Full Circle* in 1968, Scottish Opera could scarcely have been accused of inactivity. *Götterdämmerung*, in the spring, brought the completion of the Company's *Ring* cycle a stage nearer; *The Marriage of Figaro* was added to the Mozart repertoire; and *Boris Godunov* and *Madama Butterfly* were revived for the first time since 1965. In August, the Edinburgh Festival's decision to feature the music of Britten and Schubert resulted in a new production of *Peter Grimes* and a concert performance of *Alfonso and Estrella* (there was also, less pertinently, a version of Monteverdi's *Il Ballo delle ingrate* staged as a late-night entertainment with the backing of the Scottish Gas Board). Finally, in an attempt to woo another sort of audience, a raid was made on the Gilbert and Sullivan market with a Christmas production of *The Gondoliers*.

By then, six years after it was founded, Scottish Opera had fully established itself as the best thing that had happened to Scotland since the launching of the Edinburgh Festival in 1947; and, in timely recognition of all that had been achieved, Glasgow Corporation enabled the Company that spring to acquire a stately new headquarters, far roomier than the one in Holland Street and even closer to the Glasgow theatre. For the previous sixty years the building had been the property of the Institution of Engineers and Shipbuilders in Scotland; but because in 1968 opera was very much an expanding world and shipbuilding an apparently retracting one, the three-storey block was put up for sale and bought by the Corporation for a sum in the region of £65,000. With the help of a grant of £25,000 from the ever-ready Scottish Arts Council, Scottish Opera was thereupon able to lease the premises, and this "Victorian palace," as Andrew Porter was to call it in the *Financial Times*, quickly gave the Company the kind of accommodation it had been dreaming of, solidly housed in surroundings of marble, stained glass, and rich wooden panelling. Here, in what was henceforward to be known as the Scottish Opera Centre, space was found for offices, rehearsal rooms, club rooms, a board room, workshops and wardrobe facilities, and a press office which was soon to become a gathering place for critics from all over Britain, congenially presided over by the energetic and refreshingly outspoken Thomson Smillie.

While Susanna (Catherine Gayer) strums a guitar, the Countess (Catherine Wilson) listens to Cherubino (out of the picture) singing "Voi che sapete" in Act Two of The Marriage of Figaro.

In this general atmosphere of expansion the spring season began on 9 April with *Figaro*, which was run in at Perth and then taken in repertory round the larger centres. With Alexander Gibson as conductor, Anthony Besch as producer, and John Stoddart as designer, things were thought to augur well for this attempt to cap the success of the previous year's *Così fan tutte*; too well, as it happened, for in the event *Figaro* failed to match the delights of that other production. Maybe, as Andrew Porter suggested, it was the expectation of miracles from this *Figaro* that was the basic cause of our disappointment. At any rate the interplay of the characters this time did not seem to have fired Mr Besch's imagination quite so powerfully – or else, perhaps, he did not succeed in drawing from a less than perfect cast the kind of characterisation he would have liked. Nor was the English translation, again by Ruth and Thomas Martin, quite so deft and illuminating as that for *Così*. As Stanley Sadie remarked in *The Times*, its failings included "lack of both style and social awareness, and a dispiriting reliance on transatlantic commonplaces." Apart from that, it was simply less witty than the familiar Dent translation favoured by Sadler's Wells,

Yet although the evening "did not provide that keen, intense pleasure. from minute to rapt minute, which *Figaro* usually can" (Andrew Porter again), it nevertheless had good things to offer. In Glasgow it gained a spontaneity it had lacked at Perth; and by then, too, Alexander Gibson had been able to increase the size of the orchestra, thereby adding greater bloom to the tone. His conducting, as in *Così*, was generally light and tender, with a nice ear for woodwind detail and for the curve of an appoggiatura. But there were times – and this was true also of Mr Besch's production – when prettiness and fluency of movement were allowed to make do for the deeper, stronger feelings of the opera.

Sometimes, not always: for in Catherine Gayer, an American soprano imported from the Deutsche Oper, Berlin, and thereafter to become a frequent visitor to Scotland, the Company found an unusually sympathetic Susanna

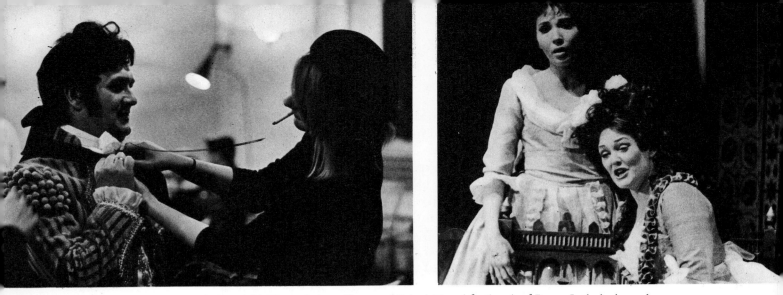

(Above, left) The wardrobe staff prepare Michael Maurel for the role of Figaro. In the background (right) Anthony Besch stands watching. Mr Besch's production of The Marriage of Figaro *in 1968 was a successor to his highly successful* Così fan tutte *the previous year.*

(Above, right) Moment of despair during the comings and goings of Act Two of The Marriage of Figaro. *The Countess (right) was Catherine Wilson. As Susanna, Catherine Gayer avoided the tiresome pertness so many singers bring to this role and suggested an instinctive awareness that all life's joys are transitory.*

(Opposite) Altercation between the Count and Countess (Peter van der Bilt and Catherine Wilson) in Act Two of The Marriage of Figaro *while Susanna (Catherine Gayer) stands out of sight.*

who delicately mingled impulsiveness with poise, was charming to look at and avoided the tiresome pertness so many singers bring to this role. When in Act Three she twice asked the question, "Who is as happy as I am?" she affectingly caught the tenderness of the moment and at the same time suggested an instinctive awareness that all life's joys are transitory. There was sadness as well as sweetness in Miss Gayer's Susanna, and when she was replaced later that year by two brasher exponents of the role (one of whom, if you please, actually pretended to catch a fly during a crucial ensemble in Act Three) her presence was sorely missed.

As for the rest of the cast, Catherine Wilson brought a passion and vibrancy to the Countess that made amends for a voice which on this occasion did not flow purely enough. Peter van der Bilt was a masculine, rangy Count, with a strong line in sulkiness and pigheadedness. Michael Maurel made a likeable Figaro, maybe a little too lightly characterised, yet effective in the last act. Cherubino was played alternately by two young Scottish singers, Patricia Hay and Josephine McQueen, the latter drawing a little paean of praise from Peter Heyworth of *The Observer*, who described her as "engagingly diminutive . . . a naughty, precocious twelve-year-old who apes his elders without really feeling the pressures that underlie their strange behaviour." For Mr Heyworth, Miss McQueen was the only character who seemed made of flesh and blood, though he also had a good word for John Stoddart's striking Andalusian settings. Certainly these and the costumes – Goya in Casa Pupo surroundings – added

personality to a production which was sometimes short of that commodity.

But if *Figaro* offered less than was expected, *Götterdämmerung* offered more, much more. Indeed, having felt its way somewhat cautiously into Wagner with *Die Walküre* in 1966 and *Das Rheingold* in 1967, the Company now went on to mount a *Götterdämmerung* of real international status – sung, conducted, presented with a flair that made one impatient for the completion of the only British *Ring* outside London (the Company bravely toured it in five pantechnicons from Glasgow to Aberdeen to Edinburgh, which was more than Sadler's Wells was by that time willing to do with even its simplest productions).

Rarely if ever before in the pit had Alexander Gibson drawn quite such consistently thrilling, scorching, exultant sounds from the SNO. In two years he had matured from a capable Wagner conductor into one who could get inside the music and bring off such passages as the Waltraute scene and Hagen's Dream with a keen sense of atmosphere, who could revel in the lusty outdoor music and capture the splendour and poignancy of the final cataclysm. Of course, there were also moments which seemed as yet less meaningful to him than others, and sometimes he was a little inclined to rush his fences, but as a first performance of a work of such a scale it was remarkably assured and alive.

Visually it was an impressive show. New and better permutations of Michael Knight's segmented ring were brought into play, the production worked with a naturalness that had formerly evaded the Company, and some effort was made to give the lighting and costumes a welcome new consistency and subtlety

In Götterdämmerung in 1968, Victor Godfrey made a vivid character out of Gunther— a touching, tragic dreamer, making a show of force that was not in keeping with his personality.

of style, a more communicative sense of colour. Scene changes, as in *Rheingold*, took place behind a gauze that managed simultaneously to evoke water, air and fire – basic elements of *The Ring* which modern productions are sometimes inclined to ignore.

More than in *Rheingold* and *Walküre*, Peter Ebert's approach proved to be a convincing compromise between the traditional and the abstractionist treatment of Wagner, without seeming "merely" a compromise. It elucidated the main events of the story without over-emphasising them, and created an admirable balance between stillness and movement. The assembling of Hagen's troops – to the sound of genuine steerhorns, resourcefully borrowed from Decca – and the subsequent wedding scene with the procession effectively entering above the trio of conspirators, showed the production working at its strong and intelligent best. The closing scene, in which the ring-shaped rostrum split across the middle and Hagen's body dropped into the crevice while the stage was flooded with light, was visually as well as musically moving. Though technically it did not work perfectly every time, it was nevertheless a minor miracle on stages as small and badly equipped as Scotland's.

The cast, a generally excellent one, mingled established Wagnerians with strong new talent. There was nothing routine about the singing, no feeling that international jet-set performers had dropped in *en passant* to enhance a local production: even the established singers were new to their parts, and it was exciting to hear Anita Välkki perform the *Götterdämmerung* Brünnhilde for the first time in her career, a full-toned, committed, very affecting portrayal. Charles Craig as Siegfried made up with warmth of tone what he lacked in acting ability. Victor Godfrey created a vivid character out of Gunther – a touching, tragic dreamer, oddly suggestive of an Anthony Eden making a show of force that was not in keeping with his personality. Helga Dernesch, making her British debut, was such a radiantly blooming Gutrune that it was plain that here Scottish Opera had made another of its international discoveries, from which audiences in Glasgow, Edinburgh and Aberdeen were in later seasons to benefit hugely. Elfego Esparza was a jumpy ox of a Hagen, whose fidgets were sometimes unintentionally comic. When Alberich asked him "Are you sleeping my son?" Mr Esparza replied (as Peter Heyworth caustically noted in *The Observer*) by scratching his nose. Not until the squat, black-voiced Texan returned in 1971 to sing Dr Bartolo in *The Barber of Seville* did Scottish audiences discover the true forte of this Hagen: an outstandingly comic Rossini singer. Mr Esparza was the sole example of miscasting in *Götterdämmerung*. Anna Reynolds was a magnificent, eloquent Waltraute, who made her scene with Brünnhilde one of the highlights of the evening. The Rhinemaidens – Patricia Hay, Josephine McQueen, Marjory McMichael – were well cast from local forces.

Most of the critics were quick to recognise the growing maturity of the Scottish *Ring*. In a review headed "Magnificent," Gerald Larner of *The Guardian* proclaimed, "At last Scottish Opera has made it with Wagner." William Mann of *The Times* admired the freshness of the performance, Colin Mason in the *Daily Telegraph* called it a "notable achievement," and Ronald Crichton in the

(Above, left) Helga Dernesch, making her British début, was such a radiant Gutrune in Götter-dämmerung in 1968 that it was plain that here Scottish Opera had made another of its international discoveries from which audiences in later seasons would benefit hugely. Here, in the Hall of the Gibichung, she is seated beside Gunther (Victor Godfrey).

(Above right) Anna Reynolds (right) was a magnificent, eloquent Waltraute in Götterdäm-merung in 1968, and made her scene with Brünnhilde (Anita Välkki) one of the highlights of the evening.

(Below) As Götterdämmerung proceeds towards its close, Gutrune and Hagen stand on either side of Siegfried's body. In this scene from the 1968 production, the Gutrune is Helga Dernesch and the Hagen is Elfego Esparza, the Texan bass who returned three years later to sing the very different role of Dr Bartolo in Scottish Opera's production of The Barber of Seville.

In the 1968 revival of Boris Godunov, *Joseph Rouleau succeeded David Ward in the title role. Here he is seen with Dennis Brandt as Shuisky.*

Financial Times thought it "nicer to look at than the schematic and cumbrous ring-complex at Covent Garden" – though he, like the critics of the Sunday papers, felt that the musical execution, for all its punch, was not yet as accurate as Solti's.

Of the season's two revivals, the *Boris Godunov* was a dim and unsatisfactory shadow of the 1965 performance, but *Madama Butterfly* emerged even better than before. In each case the reason, to be frank, lay at least partly in the conducting: Alexander Gibson, who had conducted the 1965 performances of *Boris* so admirably, now passed the opera on to David Lloyd-Jones, who certainly knew the music (he was responsible for the new English translation of the opera that was used for this revival) but seemed unable to galvanise the SNO and the Scottish Opera Chorus into anything resembling incisive action. The sounds were tame, stodgy, scraggy – so much so that for once one actually found oneself missing the brighter, brassier hues of the Rimsky version instead of the Mussorgsky original rightly preferred by Scottish Opera.

Had David Ward still been on hand to sing Boris, perhaps the performance would have made a stronger impression. But Mr Ward, though initially announced for the role, was in fact already booked to sing Wotan at La Scala, Milan. His replacement, Norman Treigle of the New York City Opera, likewise dropped out, before even arriving in Scotland, and the part was sung in the end

End of Das Rheingold. *Wotan (David Ward) gathers his gods and goddesses around him to lead them across the rainbow bridge into Valhalla. In this scene from the revival in the spring of 1971, Donner is played by John Graham, Loge by Joseph Ward, Fricka by Maureen Guy and Freia by Catherine Wilson.*

Two more scenes from Das Rheingold. *Above:* the argument between the gods and the giants (William McCue and Simon Estes) over the payment for Valhalla. *Below:* four of the gods: *Derek Blackwell as Froh, Maureen Guy as Fricka, John Graham as Donner, Joseph Ward as Loge.*

by Joseph Rouleau, the French-Canadian bass who had sung Méphistophélès so well in Gounod's *Faust* in 1964, but who missed the brooding melancholy and inwardness of Mr Ward's Boris. It was a strong, confident, resonant portrayal rather than a subtle one – an "effective" but not a moving Boris, better at conveying the Tsar's madness than suggesting its causes. Mr Rouleau's ornate, richly glittering robe, made specially for him by the Bolshoi in Moscow, looked magnificent. But it failed to disguise the fact that what Mr Rouleau gave was a performance rather than a true characterisation: emotionally he remained coolly on the outside of the role. Among the many other cast changes Josephine McQueen's Feodor was perhaps the most telling – sharply in focus, affecting in her silent contribution to Boris's death scene, charming in the earlier fun and games with the nurse, and giving us the rarely-heard parrot song as a welcome bonus.

If Alexander Gibson's presence was missed in *Boris*, it was strongly felt in *Butterfly*, which he was conducting for the first time since 1962. The way he savoured every strand of the music, drawing meltingly lyrical tones from singers and orchestra, was an object-lesson in how this opera must be put over if its finesse, its sweetness and sentiment are to ravish us as they should. As in the 1965 performances, the title-role was played by the coloured American soprano, Felicia Weathers, whose voice on this occasion seemed to have lost a little of its purity in the upper register but had gained a new richness down below. Her performance was enchanting – youthful, delicate, fastidious in its attention to Japanese graces, visually and vocally beautiful. Her entrance in Act One was exquisitely floated, and in the succeeding acts her joy as she prepared for Pinkerton's return, the pain of her disillusionment, were deeply felt and keenly projected. "One fine day" grew gently, naturally from the music, instead of being treated as a set piece. The little cry of pleasure she gave when Sharpless arrived was very touching – one of a number of true, vivid moments that added to the richness of the evening.

In Glasgow there was a new Pinkerton, Franco Bonisolli, previously known to British audiences only through his appearance with Anna Moffo in the Karajan film of *La Traviata*. It was a convincing portrayal, which presented the character as a handsome, attractively caddish G.I., refreshingly young and lithe, lightly fluent and glowing in voice. In Edinburgh and Aberdeen, Mr Bonisolli was replaced by Charles Craig, Scottish Opera's standard Pinkerton, harder and less romantic in character, more of a raddled and calculating businessman, but effective and vocally very reliable. Laura Sarti was again the sensitive Suzuki, and Ronald Morrison the humane, firm-toned Sharpless.

In 1968, as in 1967, Scottish Opera made its Edinburgh Festival appearance side by side with other opera companies – this time the Hamburg State Opera and the English Opera Group. Hamburg had originally been invited to give the British premiere of Alexander Goehr's *Arden Must Die* and Humphrey Searle's *Hamlet*, two new British works which that company, with characteristic enterprise, had added to its repertoire. But in the end these were deemed too elaborate for the stage facilities of the King's Theatre; and so instead, after what must have been considerable scraping of the barrel for productions which would fit, an elderly *Ariadne auf Naxos* (said to date back to the Hitler era) was dredged up and brought to Edinburgh along with a better, more recent, less vulgar *Elektra* and a fascinating Wieland Wagner version of *The Flying Dutchman*.

At Festival time, few years are good years for the reputation of the King's Theatre as a setting for opera, and 1968 was no exception. Rolf Liebermann, the Intendant of the Hamburg Opera, went out of his way to pronounce it the worst theatre his company had ever played in; and as if that were not enough, word leaked out that Howard & Wyndham – in what was to prove their last year of ownership of the theatre – were charging the Festival a fee of more than £1000 a performance for the privilege of putting on productions there.

Yet somehow, on top of this expense, the Festival managed to commission Scottish Opera to mount a new *Peter Grimes* – though for months beforehand rising costs threatened to put the production in jeopardy, and it was only with some extra help from the Scottish Arts Council and the chance to put on some performances in Newcastle directly after those in Edinburgh that this *Grimes* reached the stage at all. Had it failed to do so, Festival opera in 1968 would have looked very thin indeed and we would have lost the chance to see a production which, lovingly cast and prepared, revealed afresh the beauty of Britten's masterpiece.

Apart from the three church parables, presented by the English Opera Group, *Grimes* was the only Britten opera presented during the Festival's Britten year. But as Gerald Larner declared in *The Guardian*, "If it has to be only one, then it should be *Peter Grimes*, the first British opera for centuries to enter the international repertoire and stay in it for as long, so far, as twenty-three years." For the occasion, Scottish Opera invited Colin Graham, the most distinguished and experienced of Britten producers, to stage the piece. Surprisingly, he had never before worked on *Grimes*; nor had he hitherto worked with Scottish Opera. At first there was talk of asking Peter Pears, the earliest and most famous exponent of the role of Britten's anti-hero, to play the lead; but in the end it was thought that a new *Grimes* called for a new Grimes, and the American tenor Richard Cassilly – who had not previously appeared in Britain (a promised appearance in *Aida* at Covent Garden having been scotched by Equity, who had

(Opposite, top) Prologue to Peter Grimes: *Mayor Swallow (Harold Blackburn) advises Grimes during the court scene not to get another apprentice after a verdict of "accidental death" has been returned over the drowning of Grimes's latest boy. The American tenor Richard Cassilly (right) was originally to have played all performances of the title-role at the 1968 Edinburgh Festival, but because he was suffering from a throat complaint he shared the part with the English tenor, Nigel Douglas.*

(Opposite, bottom) An altercation between Ellen Orford (Phyllis Curtin) and Peter Grimes (Richard Cassilly) in Act Two of Britten's opera at the 1968 Edinburgh Festival. Eavesdropping in the background are Elizabeth Bainbridge as Auntie, Michael Maurel as Ned Keene, and William McAlpine as Bob Boles.

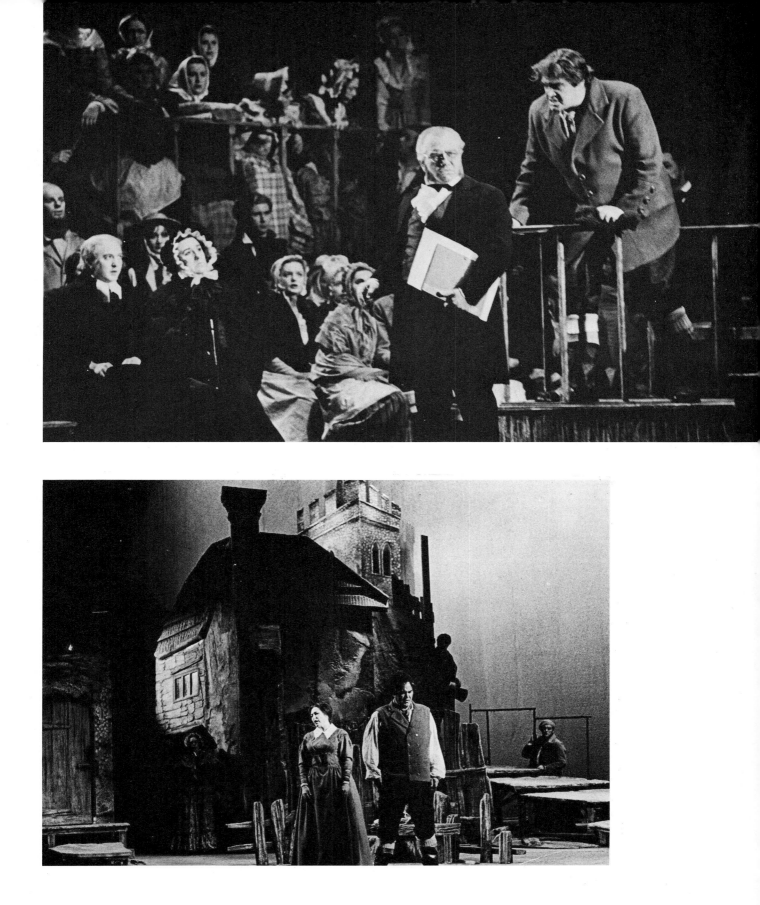

(Above) In the 1968 Edinburgh Festival production of Peter Grimes, Carter Hobson (John Graham) beats his drum as the mob make ready for the march to Grimes's hut. Among the crowd are (extreme left) Phyllis Curtin as Ellen Orford and John Shaw as Balstrode. On the right are John Robertson as the Vicar and Harold Blackburn as Mayor Swallow.

(Below, left) Nigel Douglas, the English tenor who was brought from the Zurich Opera to replace Richard Cassilly in some performances of Peter Grimes at the 1968 Edinburgh Festival.

(Below, right) Grimes (Richard Cassilly) and his latest apprentice (Dennis Sheridan) in Grimes's hut a few seconds before the boy falls to his death.

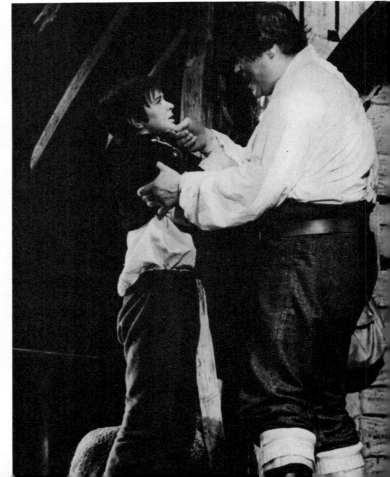

objected at the time to an American singing a role which could just as easily have been sung by Charles Craig) – was chosen for the part. The role of Ellen Orford also went to an American, Phyllis Curtin, who had sung Marguérite in Scottish Opera's *Faust* in 1966, and the large number of other parts were cast from London and local Scottish forces.

As things turned out, the opening night of the production seemed threatened with disaster. During final rehearsals, Mr Cassilly went down with a virus infection and in the first two of the four performances he had to be replaced by Nigel Douglas, a young British tenor who had been working with the Zürich Opera, where he had already sung Grimes in German. Happily there was nothing second-best about his performance – a taut, anguished, compelling portrayal, somewhat hard-toned yet keenly conveying the neurosis of the character. Britten himself attended one rehearsal as well as the first night of the opera, and his presence added to the sense of occasion. Overall this was a more successful and elating event than the previous year's *Rake's Progress*; and in 1971, when Britten was looking for someone for the role of Lechmere in *Owen Wingrave*, he remembered Mr Douglas's portrayal of Grimes in Edinburgh and chose him for the part.

Grimes, of course, is a great chorus opera, and Colin Graham and the conductor, Alexander Gibson, saw to it that both visually and vocally we were made intensely aware of this. In action and repose the Scottish Opera Chorus had a naturalness that drew one into the life of the East Anglian village, providing a convincing human backcloth against which the character parts could stand out. Phyllis Curtin was perhaps a little too cool and soignée for the role of Ellen Orford, but there were telling performances from John Shaw as a powerful Balstrode, Harold Blackburn as a lucid and resonant Swallow, and Michael Maurel as Ned Keene, with deft little character sketches from two Scottish singers, John Robertson and Johanna Peters, as the Rector and Mrs Sedley. Mr Gibson conducted the SNO with a vitality and sympathy that not only reinforced one's love for Britten's first successful opera, but also caught what might be called its deeply Verdian qualities – its lyrical fervour, its welling choruses, its sureness of pace. Mr Graham's production, without attempting to shed fresh light on the piece as Anthony Besch's *Albert Herring* had done in 1966, was fastidiously prepared and vividly executed. Alix Stone's likeably Dickensian settings, again conventional rather than experimental, showed how much can be achieved on the cramped stage of the Edinburgh theatre – provided one starts from scratch and does not attempt to shoehorn a larger production into it.

The performances won more consistently enthusiastic reviews than the Stravinsky in 1967. Joan Chissell in *The Times*, Ronald Crichton in the *Financial Times*, and Gerald Larner in *The Guardian* all exclaimed that much of the keen impact of the evening came from Mr Gibson's alert and vigorous conducting of the SNO; and though Gerald Abraham in the *Daily Telegraph* said he would not "pretend that the SNO is in the front rank of the world's orchestras," he nevertheless praised it for its thorough competence. Certainly it produced richer, more spine-tingling sounds than the Sadler's Wells orchestra during previous performances of *Grimes* in Scotland. On the social side, Lord Provost Brechin, who on the opening night of *The Rake's Progress* in 1967 had caused the circle bar to remain closed because he was holding a reception there, went to the opposite extreme on the opening night of *Grimes*. Having booked a block of seats for civic dignitaries from all over Europe, he changed his mind at the last moment, sent back the tickets, and took his burgomasters on a sail down the Clyde – where the weather replied by raining on them.

Mr Gibson and his Scottish forces, with an international team of soloists, were responsible also for the Edinburgh Festival's one real novelty in 1968 – a concert performance, on the closing night, of Schubert's *Alfonso and Estrella*. Previously heard in Britain only in a truncated Italian broadcast, the opera's appearance was heralded by an essay in *Opera News* in which the Schubert authority, Denis Vaughan, promised that we would encounter in Act Two one of the most atmospheric love scenes of the nineteenth century, and that the finales of the three acts would yield music ranking on the same plane as Mozart's. Although, in the event, one could not help feeling that Mr Vaughan had overstated his case, the performance nevertheless revealed *Alfonso* to be filled with lovely music, undermined only by Schubert's faulty sense of pace (the instinct he brought to Lieder evidently deserted him when he tackled the larger canvas of opera) and by a poor libretto that set the courtship of hero and heroine in a framework of warring armies, rival kings and bands of rebels. Mr Gibson conducted a trim, flowing performance, and although some of the soloists – who included Richard Lewis, Phyllis Curtin and Josef Greindl in leading parts – sounded less completely inside the music than the SNO and the lucid-voiced Scottish Opera Chorus, one had a clear enough impression of the opera to hope that one day it would be given a fully-fledged stage production in this country.

The Company's third Festival appearance in 1968 was its production of Monteverdi's *Il Ballo delle ingrate*, a fringe event sponsored by the Scottish Gas Board and staged as a late-night entertainment in the Adam Rooms of the George Hotel. Performances were preceded by international supper parties which displayed the merits of cooking by gas more effectively than the performances of Monteverdi displayed the merits of Scottish Opera. Peter Ebert's production and Jack Notman's designs had to be tailored to the hotel's very limited stage facilities, and as a result the occasion had the makeshift air of an Opera for All production. Of the principal singers – Heather Begg, Ann Baird, William McCue – only one seemed to have much of an idea of Monteverdian style. The few pleasures of the performance came from Roderick Brydon's sensitive direction of a group of string players from the SNO. The production was not revived in subsequent seasons, and its absence caused little regret – except that it served to stress the need for a full-scale Monteverdi production, of *The Coronation of Poppaea* or *Orfeo*, to be added to the Company's repertoire. What *was* regrettable was the fact that one of the rare examples of private sponsorship in the Company's history should have such an unmemorable outcome.

12. Florence

THOUGH THE Scottish National Orchestra took seventeen years to bring off its first foreign tour (to Austria, Germany and Holland in 1967), Scottish Opera succeeded in 1968 in exporting *Albert Herring* to the Florence Maggio Musicale with what must have seemed to all concerned a gratifying lack of problems. It was not, in fact, the Company's first chance to appear abroad – there had been previous invitations – but it was the first time that financial and artistic negotiations were together fruitfully resolved. The cost of the visit was estimated at £6000, of which the bulk was to be provided by Florence, with a contribution also from the ever-helpful Scottish Television; and for the first time, but not the last, Peter Hemmings publicly stated that it was cheaper for Scottish Opera to perform abroad than at home – a statement confirmed the following year when the German town of Augsburg paid more for a single performance of *Herring* than Aberdeen for a full week of Scottish Opera.

A date at the Florence Maggio Musicale, one of Europe's oldest-established festivals, was an undoubted coup for the Company. It was there, in the 1930s, that Vittorio Gui had launched his valuable Rossini revival, and, in the 1950s, that Maria Callas had sung some of her most famous roles. By 1968, however, both Gui and Callas had more or less retired from active musical life, and that year many of the performers at Florence were from Britain. Edward Downes conducted Verdi's *Otello*, with Jon Vickers in the title role; Joan Sutherland and Monica Sinclair appeared in Rossini's *Semiramide*; but, as the *Sunday Times* declared in a preview of the Festival: "It's to the Scottish Opera that the real honours go. That company, started seven years ago with two works and one week in Glasgow, will give two performances in Florence of its much-praised *Albert Herring*. And you can't establish yourself in this field much faster than that."

If the Company had any fears about appearing in Italy with a very English chamber opera in the same year as *Otello* and *Semiramide*, not to mention the Munich Opera's production of Stravinsky's *The Rake's Progress*, and an East Berlin version of the Dessau-Brecht *Puntila*, it need not have worried. A number of these events, it seems, flopped early in the Festival, and when *Albert Herring* arrived at the end it was thought to add a high and timely standard of performance to what had been the most fiercely criticised Maggio Musicale in memory.

Certainly the Italian newspapers gave the visitors a welcome, even though there was some confusion as to where Scottish Opera actually sprang from – one of the advance programme-leaflets had announced that the production was "della Scottish Opera di Aldeburgh," a statement contradicted by posters all over the city proclaiming the presence of "la Scottish Opera di Glasgow." But there was nothing ambiguous about the headline in *La Nazione* which described the production as a "Spettacolo bello e divertente," nor about Leonardo Pinzauti's accompanying review, which spoke of "musicality of the first order, united with settings full of fancy and comedy." The *Corriere della Sera* praised the "admirable" conducting of Roderick Brydon and the "adroit" singers, and another newspaper, *Il Messagero*, called the production "a great success," adding that the performance was "absolutely perfect."

As music critic of *The Scotsman*, I flew with the Company on its charter flight to Italy in order to write a "colour" piece about the visit and to review the performances. Florence, at the time, was still recovering from the destructive floods of the previous year (and when the Company arrived, at the height of a torrential thunderstorm, it seemed that further floods were imminent); but fortunately the beautiful old Teatro della Pergola had been fully renovated, and on June 17, within an hour or so of arriving, the singers began their final rehearsals in the theatre where, nearly 200 years earlier, Mozart's *Figaro* had had its Italian premiere and where, in 1847, Verdi's *Macbeth* had been baptised. For the performers it must have been tantalising to be in so great a city yet have so little spare time (a drawback also for visiting music critics, faced with the labour of wiring messages from an Italian post office where breakdowns in communications seemed a normal part of life). But the chance to appear in, to experience music in, one of the world's first-established opera houses was handsome enough compensation. "This is the theatre we'd like to take home," said some of the cast about this elegant Florentine antique, with its 1300-seat auditorium intimate enough to involve the audience closely in Britten's gallery of East Anglian portraits, yet big enough to let the lyrical vocal phrases, the sharply-drawn instrumental timbres, flower freely. Though the stage and backstage area proved by no means lavishly equipped by modern standards, they were nevertheless generously roomy; as Peter Hemmings commented, there was enough space to store Scottish Opera's complete stockpile of productions, whereas in the Scottish theatres there is scarcely space for one – when *Die Walküre* was staged in Glasgow in 1966, Hunding's tree had to be stored outside the stage-door of the King's Theatre.

A major task for Roderick Brydon during those final preparations was the need to beat the orchestra into shape. The usual SNO players had not been available for the visit, and the use of Italian players had been deemed impracticable. So for the occasion an *ad hoc* ensemble (said to be members of the English Chamber Orchestra) was recruited in London but sounded far from at ease in Britten's often awkwardly exposed scoring. Even on the opening night, the playing still had too many rough edges. That, however, was a fact that seemed happily to have escaped the Italian critics, whose knowledge of the piece was presumably scanty – it had never before been staged in Italy.

But if the orchestra was a comparative disappointment, so was the production's failure to attract the full houses that had been predicted at the box-office. The trouble, it turned out, was that although almost all the seats were reserved, they were reserved by serial ticket holders who tended to stay away from events they deemed to be too "difficult." Those who attended, however, obviously found *Herring* a very approachable piece, which on this occasion was made still more approachable because Anthony Besch, in order to ease the language barrier, had made his production visually more explicit than was necessary in Scotland.

Adam Pollock's settings looked well – travel had not yet begun to fray and splinter them. Gregory Dempsey and the rest of the cast were in good form. The applause sounded appreciative. And when, some weeks later, an enthusiastic review was written in the *Musical Times* by Jeremy Noble (not the easiest of critics to please), a final seal of approval seemed to have been placed on Scottish Opera's first foreign venture. Touring abroad now appeared likely to become a regular part of the Company's activities. As I wrote at the time in *The Scotsman*: "It seems plain that in *Herring* they have a 'useful' production, easily transportable, with a cast that has remained amazingly faithful to it from the time it was launched two years ago. One imagines that, if the Florence performances win international acclaim, then Scottish Opera will be invited to take *Herring* elsewhere next year."

The words proved prophetic. In 1969 *Herring* was successfully toured to Hanover, Dortmund and Augsburg in Germany, and in 1970 (along with *The Turn of the Screw*, by then another "useful" production) to Iceland. The transportability of *Herring* even gave rise to a question-and-answer quip that went the rounds at the time of America's first astronaut landing on the moon. The question: What will be the first lunar opera production? The answer: Scottish Opera's *Albert Herring*, of course.

The banner (corrected version) with which Florence celebrated Scottish Opera's visit to the 1968 Maggio Musicale. This was the Company's, and Albert Herring's, *first appearance in Italy. In subsequent years the production was taken to Germany and Iceland.*

"*The gloriously convincing Dido of Janet Baker, a performance that was noble, passionate, deeply responsive to every note and inflection of the music.*"

13. *The Trojans*

The Wooden Horse—"a very functional, barbaric-looking weapon standing eighteen and a half feet high, all wheels and pulleys, and so heavy that when it arrived in Glasgow it promptly broke through the floorboards of the King's Theatre."

THAT SCOTTISH OPERA would stage *The Trojans* in tribute to the Berlioz centenary was practically a foregone conclusion. It was in Glasgow in 1935 that the vast masterpiece had first been seen in Britain in that famous pioneering production by Erik Chisholm's dedicated amateurs; and though *Beatrice and Benedick*, *Benvenuto Cellini*, and *The Damnation of Faust* were doubtless on Alexander Gibson's and Peter Hemmings's list of possibles in 1969, it was plain that – as with their ventures into Verdi and Wagner – the final choice would be the musically most challenging one. The main question was not that the choice would be *The Trojans*, but how the Company would tackle it. Cut or uncut? With or without the ballet music? On a single night or spread across two? In French or English?

The problems were quickly resolved, and in the right way; and while France in 1969 was trying with typical perversity to forge an opera out of Berlioz's Requiem – the Lyons Festival that year actually staged a "version scénique" with 500 performers, including dancers – Scottish Opera succeeded in providing, at a single blow, the first major international event of the Berlioz year, the first performance of the Berlioz Centenary Committee's new edition of *The Trojans* score, and the first production in the world ever to offer the opera complete, in English, on a single evening.

Meanwhile, over in the composer's homeland, anyone wanting to experience *The Trojans* was faced with three choices: to make do with the brutally abbreviated "oratorio" version at the same Lyons Festival as took such pains to distort the Requiem; to wait for the Paris Opéra's revival, also viciously cut, at the end of the year (the cuts, it is said, provoked jeers from the gallery, which

Ann Howard, as Cassandra, may have been made to look a bit too like a Trojan Ava Gardner, but nevertheless this was a striking portrayal, with the edge and brilliance of tone needed to dominate the big crowd scenes. Here she is seen in duet with Choroebus (John Shaw).

suggested that at last someone in France had begun to care); or to come to Britain, either for the Scottish production in the spring or the Covent Garden one in the autumn.

To suggest that British musicians almost invariably respect Berlioz more highly and perform him better than French ones may seem a sweeping piece of patriotism, yet the evidence in its favour has long been substantial. For while the French habitually distrust the ability of Berlioz's music to stand on its own feet – a centenary article in *Figaro* complained that he "savait mal son métier" – the British simply get on with the job of performing it properly, of correcting the misprints in French editions of the scores, of writing about it with the love and understanding it deserves, and of preventing masterpieces like *The Trojans* from suffering what has become known as the "death by a thousand cuts" they traditionally receive in France.

A study in classical seriousness: Joseph Rouleau and Bernadette Greevy as Narbal and Anna, with Robert Thomas (right) as Iopas in The Trojans.

Janet Baker and Bernadette Greevy, as Dido and Anna, sing their long duet in The Trojans.

A heartfelt moment between father and son: Aeneas and Ascanius, as portrayed by Ronald Dowd and Patricia Hay.

No moment in The Trojans *was more touching than the entrance of the widowed Andromache and her son Astyanax, portrayed by Elaine McDonald of Scottish Theatre Ballet and five-year-old Alisdair McLean. Behind them, Ann Howard as Cassandra. The rapt clarinet obbligato which accompanied this scene was played by Keith Pearson of the Scottish National Orchestra.*

It was surely characteristic that it needed a British visitor to detect the presence of forgeries in the big centenary exhibition mounted at the Paris Bibliothèque Nationale; and characteristic, just over a hundred years earlier, that Berlioz was never enabled to hear the first part of his opera – the two acts comprising "The Capture of Troy." Not that what he heard of the second part was anything more than a travesty, for, to quote Ernest Newman, "the director, the singers, the machinists, all clamoured for cuts and still more cuts" (and their successors today are still doing so). Among the sections that were speedily sacrificed were some which now seem to us so indisputably inspired – the "Royal Hunt and Storm" and Hylas's haunting song – that the mind can only boggle at the crassness of the people who tampered with them. As Berlioz wrote after the final performance: "I am in my 61st year. I have neither hopes, nor illusions, nor great thoughts left. . . . My contempt for the folly and meanness of men, my hatred of their detestable ferocity, are at their height, and I say hourly to Death: 'When you will!' " He died six years later, broken by the defeat of *The Trojans* in Paris, and having produced during that time little music of consequence.

It was against that background that Scottish Opera set out afresh to champion a work whose greatness had been brought at least partly into view by a

German production at Karlsruhe in 1890 and by the first Covent Garden production in 1957, as well as by the valiant Chisholm performances. By interrupting the gradual creation of its *Ring* cycle to make way for *The Trojans*, Scottish Opera gave the composer the poetic justice he had deserved ever since the Paris Opéra in his lifetime rejected his masterly Virgilian epic in favour of *Tannhäuser*. And not only poetic justice, but textual justice. In preparing his performance, Alexander Gibson said he became more and more convinced that to cut the opera at all was to commit vandalism (eventually he did omit a few unimportant repeated bars); and to the old complaint that the opera is unperformable as Berlioz wrote it, both he and the producer Peter Ebert had ready answers. Mr Gibson, after approaching it – he said – with trepidation, found it far easier to rehearse than expected. Orchestrally, he discovered that it contained nothing like the sustained difficulty, the complications for string players, that are found in the Wagner operas; and because rehearsals went so smoothly, he had more time to go into detail, and concentrate on orchestral finesse, than he had the previous year with *Götterdämmerung*. His major problems tended to be mechanical ones, like where to place the chorus during the "Royal Hunt and Storm" so that they could be clearly heard.

Berlioz's unsurpassed ability to think orchestrally impressed him again and again. "The piano arrangements one uses in rehearsals [and which have long played their part in getting the opera a bad name] bear no resemblance to what it's all about," he remarked at the time. "Sometimes they don't even give a suggestion of important themes. And there are passages which sound marvellous on the orchestra, but which may, in the piano edition, look like nothing more than, say, a series of boringly reiterated chords."

For Mr Ebert, too, the opera held fewer problems than expected. Much of it, he felt, was characterised with an almost Mozartian subtlety and beauty. His main difficulties were the organising of the big choruses on the small Glasgow stage, and in toning down some of the wilder nineteenth-century stage directions. The fall of Troy, he thought, would lend itself to Brechtian treatment, with a grim setting of grey stone walls, in contrast with the warmer, more lyrical second part, where he planned to enclose the story of Dido and Aeneas in a gold framework with richer props.

The designs were to be by Hans-Ulrich Schmückle of the Augsburg Opera, where Mr Ebert had by then been appointed Generalintendant, while retaining his links with Scottish Opera. Mr Schmückle, a large, solemn-eyed, hatchet-jawed man who looked rather like a German Fernandel, was a new name in Scottish Opera circles, and much preliminary interest was naturally aroused by his design for the Wooden Horse. This turned out to be a very functional, barbaric-looking weapon standing 18½ feet high, all wheels and pulleys, and so heavy that when it arrived in Glasgow it promptly broke through the floorboards of the King's Theatre. Another evil-looking war-machine was promised by the firm of Ebert and Schmückle for the final scene of the opera.

Though the bill for the decor ran to £10,000 – high by Scottish Opera standards but nothing to what Covent Garden was to spend on its new production in the autumn – a contribution of 20 per cent came from the Augsburg company, which wanted to use the same settings the following year for its own production of *The Trojans*. Augsburg also promised to store the settings for Scottish Opera, because (such are the financial intricacies of the opera world) it would be cheaper to keep them in Germany and ship them back when needed than to store them in Glasgow.

After arousing more anticipation than perhaps any other Scottish Opera production, *The Trojans* was finally unveiled in Glasgow on 3 May 1969 – a historic date in the Company's evolution. The performance (the first of five that spring) proved so profoundly affecting, so absorbing, so elating that at the time it was hard to know where to begin to describe its riches. One was left – like that German music-lover who attended the first Covent Garden production twelve years earlier – with just a single thought in mind: "When can I hear this music again?"

There were two features, however, that cried out for pride of place: the gloriously convincing Dido of Janet Baker, a performance (though she was suffering that night from a serious virus infection which made it uncertain, until the moment she actually stepped on to the stage, whether she would be able to appear) that was noble, passionate, deeply responsive to every note and inflection of the music, as great a living, vibrant, tragic portrayal as her Dorabella in *Così* had been a sublimely, touchingly comic one; and the warmth and vitality of the SNO under Alexander Gibson, who became overnight a Berlioz conductor to reckon with, and who with his players revelled in the music's force and drive, its sudden surging outbursts, its grandeur and purity and melancholy. As David Cairns, most renowned of British writers on Berlioz, was to declare later in the *New Statesman*, Mr Gibson had mastered the style and scale of the score "to an extent that leaves criticism silent." No other Berlioz performance Mr Gibson had until then conducted in Scotland had prepared us for quite such an intense involvement in the music, such a tireless flow of sensitive, beautiful tone from the SNO, such keenly pulsing rhythms and expressive phrasing. It was all there, and one could only listen and listen and be carried along by the tide of the music as it moved from Troy to Carthage and on towards Italy.

The casting, both in major and minor roles, proved rewardingly good, with few weak links. Ronald Dowd, an experienced Aeneas in concert-hall performances, brought a thrilling vehemence to his portrayal, though hampered by a vulgar wig and tunic that recalled Claude Rains in *Caesar and Cleopatra*. Cassandra was sung by Ann Howard, the tall and elegant Fricka of the Company's *Die Walküre* in 1966, with the edge and brilliance of tone needed to dominate the big crowd scenes. Bernadette Greevy was a tender, gentle-voiced Anna (how apt it seemed to find an Irish girl in an opera by Berlioz!), John Shaw and Joseph Rouleau were the sturdy Choroebus and Narbal, and Duncan Robertson brought the right nostalgic sweetness to Hylas's song. Patricia Hay, one of the Company's rising local singers, made a likeable young Ascanius.

Though one saw why, and how easily, the ballet music was cut from previous

Father and daughter. A striking portrait study of David Ward as Wotan and Helga Dernesch as Brünnhilde during Wotan's long monologue in Act Two of Die Walküre. *The picture is from the 1971 revival of Peter Ebert's production at the Edinburgh Festival.*

Two more scenes from the Edinburgh Festival performance of Die Walküre. Above: *Siegmund (Charles Craig) recounts his adventures to Sieglinde (Leonore Kirschstein) and Hunding (William McCue) in Act One.* Below: *Wotan (David Ward) caught between wife and daughter. Anna Reynolds (left) was Fricka in this revival of the opera, and Helga Dernesch (right) Brünnhilde.*

productions of *The Trojans*, it was good to have it restored, for it is full of delightful, inimitably Berliozian ideas – much better than most operatic ballet music. In Part One, with members of the Scottish Theatre Ballet (as the Western Theatre Ballet was now called after its decision to leave Sadler's Wells and, with support from the Scottish Arts Council, make its home in Glasgow) weaving their way through the crowd, the effect looked a little fussy; but the series of dances in Part Two were more tellingly done, and the "Royal Hunt and Storm," superbly played by the SNO, had ample atmosphere.

Atmosphere, or at any rate the right atmosphere, was not always so present in Mr Ebert's production and Mr Schmückle's settings. There were things to be said in their favour – especially for the decision to leave the stage largely uncluttered, so that people had space to move. But the visual impression was too Germanic, Straussian rather than Berliozian. The Wooden Horse, a massive Heath Robinson contraption, certainly looked well, but the fact that it disgorged its troops outside instead of inside the Trojan wall seemed strategically wrong. During Part Two, one missed the suggestion of sea and starry Carthaginian night, so magically evoked by the orchestra (Hylas in this production was a landlubber, though his music directly contradicted this). The death of Dido, vocally so eloquently realised by Janet Baker, deserved more effective treatment from Mr Ebert than it received, and the unveiling of the promised "war machine" in the closing bars, though an impressive *coup de théâtre*, could not be said to clarify the end of the opera (one critic thought it was a plough) any better than Berlioz's own and very different idea – a grandiose vision of Rome.

Nor did the costume designs by Sylte Büsse-Schmückle, wife of the stage designer, really rise to the occasion. The effect was dowdy, the colours drably mixed, and Mr Dowd was not the only singer to be inaptly dressed – Cassandra, in a cocktail dress, looked like a Trojan Ava Gardner, and Andromache (touchingly played by Elaine McDonald of Scottish Theatre Ballet in a scene which Mr Ebert captured more tellingly than any other) wore black instead of classical funereal white.

But such details, though they often irritated and seemed surprisingly muddle-headed, did not seriously hamper the musical glories of the evening. These grew even greater in subsequent performances, not least in the choral department, where Arthur Oldham's singers excelled themselves; and though in 1969 there was no special train to bring Berlioz connoisseurs north from London, as there had been in 1935, the production nevertheless received extensive and admiring coverage from visiting critics, almost all of whom had their priorities right: the evening was a triumph for Mr Gibson, for his singers and players, and above all it was a triumph for Berlioz.

Point of departure: Aeneas (Ronald Dowd) stands among his men before setting sail for Carthage.

14. *Così* Again

So GREAT WAS the expense and effort of mounting *The Trojans* in 1969 that no other new production was launched that spring, and the rest of the season was devoted to revivals of *Così fan tutte*, *Albert Herring*, *The Gondoliers*, and *Full Circle*. But since *The Trojans* offered what was tantamount to two masterpieces for the price of one, with the option of a skilfully-organised supper in between, only the anti-Berlioz lobby had grounds for complaint. Most of that lobby (never strong in Britain) remained silent – a spent force – and it was left to a correspondent from East Lothian to attempt to stoke the anti-Berlioz fire single-handed when, in a letter to *The Scotsman*, he fumed about Berlioz's gross inferiority to Wagner and attacked Scottish Opera for its weak-mindedness in interrupting its *Ring* cycle for the sake of so feeble a Frenchman.

Among professional writers, only Kenneth Elliott in the *Times Educational Supplement* had misgivings to air, though his reason for doing so – namely that Berlioz was a vandal, bordering at times on insanity, in his treatment of Virgil – seemed simply to be a denial of one of the basic tenets of opera: that it is the composer, not the librettist or author, who is the dramatist. Britten's *A Midsummer Night's Dream*, after all, is a masterpiece not because it happens to stick to the text of Shakespeare's play, but in spite of it. The point about *The Trojans* is that Berlioz (himself the most Shakespearian of composers) took from Virgil only what he needed to inspire him, and the result is Berlioz's *Trojans*, not Virgil's.

Of the other productions that spring, *Così fan tutte* was in some respects even better than in 1967, for Elizabeth Harwood's Fiordiligi had lost the slight coolness and reserve that had previously been present (she had meanwhile sung the role at the Aix-en-Provence Festival) and had gained an authority, a bloom and passion that made her portrayal as fully alive as Janet Baker's still entrancing Dorabella and Peter van der Bilt's dashing Guglielmo. The rest of the cast were newcomers to the production. John Shirley-Quirk, making his first appearance with Scottish Opera since his solitary performance of Arkel in *Pelléas et Mélisande* in 1962, brought a likeable, faintly professorial air to the part of Don Alfonso, sang mellowly and intimately, had the ability to make an aside really sound like an aside, and seemed quicker-witted and more genuinely Mozartian (though not necessarily more effective) than his endearingly avuncular predecessor, Inia Te Wiata.

The two other newcomers, both making their first operatic appearance in Britain, were more of a mixed blessing. The young Danish tenor, Kurt Westi, proved a pleasantly lyrical but small-voiced Ferrando who, because he consistently forced his tone, began to disintegrate vocally long before the end of each performance. His shape, short and tubby compared with the lanky Peter van der Bilt, was also against him, and some of the romance of the evening was thereby lost. The Canadian soprano, Carrol Anne Curry, was a neatly musical, wide-eyed young Despina, welcomely avoiding exaggerating her impersonations of the doctor and lawyer, but lacking the experience to bring real personality to the part – though in Edinburgh she was beginning to make more of it than she had done in Glasgow.

As before, the conductor was Alexander Gibson, who drew firm, smooth, well-moulded playing from the SNO. The string tone was light and fluent, woodwind and brass had plenty of character, and, though the gait of the performance remained unhurried, rhythms had more fibre and intensity than two years earlier. Anthony Besch's production retained its beauty and polish. To the question worriedly voiced by *The Scotsman* at the start of the season – "Can this *Così* come alive again?" – the performances provided a reassuringly affirmative answer.

Mr Besch's other production, *Albert Herring*, was also in good shape in its performances in Perth and Glasgow before it departed on its second foreign tour, this time to Hanover, Dortmund and Augsburg. With the original cast still preserved almost intact, its teamwork seemed more telling than ever. Roderick Brydon's conducting continued to unveil fresh subtleties, though his latest instrumental ensemble – a combination of two Edinburgh chamber groups in place of the SNO – lacked body and muscle.

The SNO, on the other hand, produced more delicate, graceful string tone for James Loughran in *The Gondoliers* than his own orchestra, the BBC Scottish Symphony, had done when Joan Cross's congenial production was launched the previous December; and in Edinburgh it was *The Gondoliers* – not, alas, *Così fan tutte* – which had the honour of being the first Scottish Opera production to win the presence of the Queen, the Duke of Edinburgh, and Princess Anne, who were in the city to attend the General Assembly of the Church of Scotland. What they saw was not, it must be owned, one of the Company's special pieces or sharpest productions, but at least it conveyed the charm and sweetness of Sullivan's music more tellingly than a traditional D'Oyly Carte performance. It also enabled a number of rising Scottish singers, dominated by William McCue's ripe portrayal of Don Alhambra, to show their paces and to meet the Royal party after the show.

Robin Orr's *Full Circle*, which now served as a somewhat uneasy prelude to two one-act pieces by the freshly-established Scottish Theatre Ballet, was weakened by some cast changes among the character parts; but William Elvin and Sheila McGrow, as the amateur gangster and his sparrow of a wife, remained keenly in focus in Ian Watt-Smith's sympathetic production.

In 1968, when the spring season was over, Scottish Opera had had the extra excitement of preparing *Peter Grimes* for the Edinburgh Festival. In 1969 there were no such thrills, for Peter Diamand had chosen to make Italy his special theme that year and decided to give the Florence Opera the run of the King's Theatre for the full three weeks. If there was inevitably some disappointment among members and supporters of Scottish Opera, Mr Gibson and Mr Hemmings were quick to make plain that they regarded a place in the Festival as an honour, not a right. The chance to hear the Florentine company in Edinburgh was an important one which did not come every year or even every ten years; its repertoire, and character, promised to be stimulatingly different from Scottish Opera's; and its visit was to be subsidised by Italy to the tune of more than £100,000, whereas (contrary to popular opinion) a production by Scottish Opera caused and still causes the Festival to dig much deeper into its coffers than any production imported from abroad.

But welcome though the opportunity was to experience the Florence Opera, and rich the subsidy it promised to bring, there was a period during the planning when it seemed unlikely that there would be any opera at all at the Edinburgh Festival that year. The trouble, which reached crisis proportions, lay in the rift which developed between Howard & Wyndham, the then owners of the King's Theatre, and Sir Herbert Brechin, the then Lord Provost of Edinburgh. To put it briefly, Howard & Wyndham wanted to sell the King's Theatre to Edinburgh Corporation (just as they wanted to sell their other remaining regional theatres to other corporations), but Sir Herbert deemed the price too high.

If there was an irony in the fact that the sum asked by Howard & Wyndham was only slightly in excess of the amount which Italy was prepared to spend on sending the Florence company to Edinburgh for three weeks, it seemed to escape Sir Herbert. Howard & Wyndham delivered an ultimatum: either buy the King's Theatre or it will be transformed into an office block.

For a while Sir Herbert prattled about the Festival no longer being able to afford opera (which, considering what foreign companies were willing to pour in by way of subsidy, was quite a statement) and opined that the Festival City could survive without the King's. Even after the Scottish Arts Council and an anonymous donor had between them offered to contribute £100,000 towards the cost, and after he had been reminded that Scottish Opera had its needs as well as the Festival, the Lord Provost continued to dig in his heels. But in the end, though not before a storm of criticism had erupted in the correspondence columns of *The Scotsman*, Sir Herbert bowed to the inevitable. Four days before the contract with Florence was due to be signed, Edinburgh Corporation agreed to buy the theatre. Thus ended an affair which *The Scotsman* on its leader page crisply summed up as an unwise piece of brinkmanship.

Meanwhile, ever resourceful, Scottish Opera was planning to take part in the 1969 Edinburgh Festival under its own steam. Though deprived of a place in the official programme, it immediately bobbed up on the fringe, where it had the assistance of its regular *deus ex machina* in the guise of Scottish Television. At short notice, and for the sum of £1000, STV commissioned a one-act opera from the young Scottish composer, John Purser, to be given a series of late-

(Opposite) The Gondoliers *with a* Così *cast: perhaps Scottish Opera did not succeed in making its first Gilbert and Sullivan production quite as musically distinguished as was hoped, though it was sensitively conducted by James Loughran and the singers included Janet Coster and Anne Pashley as Tessa and Gianetta (front left and right) and Ronald Morrison and John Wakefield as Guiseppe and Marco (rear).*

(Right) The Gondoliers *may not have been one of Scottish Opera's sharpest productions, but at least it conveyed the charm of the music and enabled a number of rising Scottish singers, dominated by William McCue's Don Alhambra, to show their paces. Here Mr McCue (left) is seen with Ian Wallace, Johanna Peters, and Jill Gomez as the Plaza-Toro family and (behind) John Robertson as Luiz.*

(Left) John Purser's The Undertaker—*a sort of* Heure espagnole *with coffins instead of clocks—was first seen in 1969 as part of the Edinburgh Festival fringe. Nan Christie and Frederick Bateman (in the foreground) were the young lovers; Ronald Morrison and Patricia Hay (behind) were the Abbot and the Prostitute.*

(Below) The Undertaker *drew its humour, mildly black, from the fact that the coffin shop was also a wine cellar. Here Frederick Bateman and Patricia Hay, as Pierre and Marie, sample the house wine.*

night performances along with Robin Orr's *Full Circle* at the Gateway Theatre, which the television company had newly acquired for use as a colour studio. In that way the renovated auditorium would be handsomely handselled, a new Scottish opera would be baptised before a discriminating festival public, and one of the performances would be tele-recorded for future transmission.

The resultant double-bill perhaps did not boast the excitement or glamour of a new production at the King's Theatre, but at least it was something. Or was it? Certainly Reginald Barrett-Ayres of Aberdeen University, writing in the Aberdeen *Press and Journal*, clearly thought not. "At this year's Festival," he asserted, "the [Florence] Teatro Comunale made Scottish Opera look ridiculous." Perhaps, in declaring *Full Circle* to have been "very badly done" and Purser's *The Undertaker* to be "the kind of thing written by inexperienced students of composition, without even skill or craftsmanship," he overstated his case. After all, the Florence Opera brought one thoroughly bad production along with others ranging from mediocre to outstanding; and though Ian Watt-Smith's once-sharp production of *Full Circle* had been gradually degenerating, it was hardly yet as feeble as Barrett-Ayres made out.

There was, however, more than a grain of truth in what he said, for surely it was not Scottish Opera's job to stage a prentice piece as thin as Purser's at an international festival, nor was it the job of the Company's musical director, Alexander Gibson, to conduct it. Yet that was what happened, and no one's reputation – not the composer's, not Scottish Opera's, not Scottish Television's – could be said to have benefited much from the experience.

To be fair to Purser, he no doubt did what he could in the time he had. He had never before composed an opera, and for this first attempt he compounded his problems by electing to write his own words (a decision which prompted *Opera* magazine to say he had crucified himself on his libretto). The plot in itself was not a bad one. A sort of *Heure espagnole* with coffins instead of clocks, it concerned an undertaker's shop in the south of France which served also as a wine cellar. Its action – comic, amorous, tipsy, and finally supernatural – moved fast, but dramatically it was weakly motivated and the denouement was confusing.

The music, with its brittle, obsessive rhythms and lyrical effusions, never rose above a superficial level and too often fell between several stools, with Orff and Stravinsky on the one hand vying with early Britten on the other. Yet there was something there. Whatever its flaws, it had enough exuberance and sense of theatre to carry it along; and though Arthur Jacobs in *Opera* caustically remarked that if STV had known as much about opera as it presumably did about plays, it would not have given *The Undertaker* programme space, the opera was thought by Winton Dean in the *Musical Times* and Ronald Crichton in the *Financial Times* to be at the very least a promising start, and by myself to be "notable chiefly for the hints it provided of the very much better opera Purser may one day write."

Ian Watt-Smith's energetic production did *The Undertaker* proud, Mr Gibson and his octet of instrumentalists made much of the lithe, bright music, and the spirited cast included Nan Christie and Frederick Bateman as a convincing pair of young lovers, William McCue and Patricia Hay as undertaker and local prostitute, and Ronald Morrison as an Abbot who turned out to be a relative of Britten's Mr Gedge. Maybe the evening rated only a minor place in the annals of Scottish Opera, yet all the same it set a precedent: it established that the Gateway, if STV would release it for opera from time to time, could be an important acquisition – the sort of studio theatre, complete with pit, that Purser and other young composers need in order to develop their theatrical talents.

15. *Fidelio*

THE LACK OF a new Scottish Opera production at the 1969 Edinburgh Festival made it seem all the more vital that the Company should repeat the idea, successfully tried out the previous year, of a Christmas season in Edinburgh. Only in this way could proper continuity be achieved – and continuity was now the heartcry of the Company – but the problem as usual was one of money. Before he could go ahead with his plans, Peter Hemmings had to obtain the financial blessing of the Scottish Arts Council. Not for the first time, this meant exclaiming that the Company would be in jeopardy if a December season proved impossible. Not for the first time, the Scottish Arts Council was politely blackmailed into acquiescence. And so, on 5 December 1969, a new production of Rossini's *La Cenerentola* was presented at the King's Theatre, with Patricia Kern in the title-role, Colin Graham as producer, Emanuele Luzzati as designer, and Bryden Thomson as conductor.

Mr Graham had already worked with the Company on *Peter Grimes* the previous year, but the other protagonists (including the composer) were new-comers. With the Christmas market in mind, the title of the opera was trans-lated as *Cinderella*. Along with a revival of *Albert Herring* and Scottish Theatre Ballet's new version of *Beauty and the Beast*, for which Colin Graham wrote the script and Thea Musgrave the music, it ran in repertoire for ten days and proved a fair box-office success – by the last of the four performances, attendance had risen to 81 per cent.

Artistically, *Cinderella* rose to about the same level of achievement so long as Miss Kern was in the cast, but dropped appreciably the following spring when it was revived with two other singers sharing the title-role. Indeed, without Miss Kern to enhance it, this was latterly to seem one of Scottish Opera's few routine productions, though at least it was seldom less than good routine. At Christmas, however, its shortcomings were largely unobtrusive, thanks to the way Miss Kern appeared to find new subtleties, new graces and delights in a role she had sung many times – but surely never more truly or eloquently – at Sadler's Wells and elsewhere.

Thanks also to the refreshingly serious regard which Mr Graham had for the opera, *Cinderella* emerged as something more than a tale of rags to riches. That aspect of the story had its part, of course, but was not allowed to hide the moral of the piece – which tells how goodness and virtue, not the glamour of wealth and rank, bring loving hearts together. To have reverted, as many producers do, to the familiar fairy-tale, and to have introduced Cinderella to her prince by magic, would have been to miss the point of the opera. It was one of the pleasures of Mr Graham's production that he made the lovers discover each other, and test their love, by entirely human means.

That is not to say, however, that the evening lacked spectacle. Mr Graham, with Mr Luzzati's assistance, drew a fine distinction between what he described as "man magic" (which was another way of saying that the scene-changing would be skilful and striking) and fairy-tale magic. The aim was to create an adult *Cenerentola* which would nevertheless, under the title of *Cinderella*, have sufficient fun and glitter to appeal to children. By implication, the production was perhaps therefore something of a compromise. But with Miss Kern casting her own particular magic over the performance, it worked.

The supporting cast was, well, very much a supporting cast. Seriousness in *Cenerentola* is a good thing, but Mr Graham permitted the Ramiro and Dandini, Frederick Bateman and Ronald Morrison, to be excessively serious. On the other hand, Ian Wallace as Don Magnifico and Ann Baird and Patricia Clark as the ugly sisters gave fairly standard comic portrayals, admirable of their kind and very neatly timed, yet somehow working in opposition to the rest of the opera. In this, if in little else, one sensed what was in fact true: that this *Cenerentola* was Mr Graham's first venture into Rossini. More troublesome than this apparent contradiction, however, was the fact that so many roles were rather under-sung. Even the rare and welcome chance to hear Alidoro's aria restored to the crucial scene before Cinderella departs for the ball was to some extent squandered by the strain with which John Graham (who otherwise handled the part very engagingly) shaped its charming if not strongly Rossinian phrases.

The performances were given in English, in Arthur Jacobs' lively translation. Lively, too, was Bryden Thomson's conducting, though he missed the tenderness and sentiment of the music and was variably served by the BBC Scottish Symphony Orchestra, much of whose playing sounded thin and scrappy. Nor did Mr Luzzati's bright, mobile settings move as smoothly as they should have done; and the visiting London critics, who had seen similar Luzzati settings in productions of other operas and had become tired of what Alan Blyth in the *Financial Times* aptly described as their "familiar, too familiar, tuppence-coloured, doll's-house vein," were disturbed (as was *The Scotsman*, though not the *Glasgow Herald*) by the fussiness of the decor, which seemed out of keeping with the rest of the treatment of the opera.

These faults were magnified in the spring of 1970 when – first with the young French-Canadian singer Josephte Clément as Cinderella and then with the American Rosalind Elias – the performances failed to muster the kind of glow Miss Kern had been able to give them. Fortunately the rest of the spring season, which included new productions of *Fidelio* and *The Turn of the Screw* and a revival of *Don Giovanni*, was strong enough to carry the comparative failure of *Cinderella* (which was still identified by its English title, though this time audience figures fluctuated between a capacity house at Perth and 44 per cent during the

In staking an early claim on the services of Helga Dernesch, Scottish Opera was "reaping the harvest of foresight" said Peter Heyworth of The Observer *in his review of* Fidelio. *As a result, he added, the production was "crowned by a Leonore as finely sung as any I have heard."*

An unusually fatherly portrayal of Rocco the jailer by William McCue was deemed one of the assets of the production of Fidelio. *Rightly he was allowed to sing his Act One aria, which some productions omit. Here it is seen in progress, with Josephine McQueen (Marzelline) and Helga Dernesch (Leonore) as audience.*

Company's second visit to Newcastle); and with the addition of a lively if controversial *Magic Flute* during the Edinburgh Commonwealth Games and a superlative production of Henze's *Elegy for Young Lovers* at the Edinburgh Festival, 1970 proved as diverse and successful a year as any in the Company's history to date.

Like dozens of other opera companies all over the world, Scottish Opera had planned its *Fidelio* in honour of the Beethoven bicentenary, which fell that year. But it had one special advantage which no other company had at that time but which Herbert von Karajan was to pounce on for his Salzburg Easter Festival performances of the opera in 1971: namely the presence of Helga Dernesch as Leonore. Scottish Opera, of course, had staked a claim on Miss Dernesch two years previously when she made her British debut in Glasgow as Gutrune in *Götterdämmerung*. Like Janet Baker, Miss Dernesch had quickly found that she liked the atmosphere of Scottish Opera; and before 1970 was over she had signed an agreement to appear the following year as Brünnhilde in the *Ring* cycle the Company was planning to complete, and also to re-learn the role of the Marschallin in English for Scottish Opera's new production of *Der Rosenkavalier*. So frequently was she in Scotland during this period that she could be thought just as much Scottish Opera's property as Karajan's or anyone else's; and considering that she was already being widely hailed as the new Nilsson and even the new Flagstad, Scottish Opera's achievement in capturing her

The Act One quartet in Fidelio, *with (left to right) Josephine McQueen as Marzelline, Werner Krenn as Jacquino, William McCue as Rocco, and Helga Dernesch as Leonore. Rocco's home—a kind of outhouse to the prison—was effectively raised at the end of this scene to reveal the prison behind.*

services seemed all the greater. Not for the first time, as Peter Heyworth remarked in *The Observer*, the Company was "reaping the harvest of foresight, and as a result its new production of *Fidelio* at the King's Theatre in Glasgow is crowned by a Leonore as finely sung as any I have heard."

Mr Heyworth chose his words carefully – for in common with several others among the battalion of critics who descended on the King's Theatre he felt that Miss Dernesch's singing abilities had for the moment outstripped her acting technique. As Andrew Porter pointed out in the *Financial Times*, "she kept her gaze downcast, which inhibited communication," and as Ronald Crichton suggested in the same paper, her portrayal "so far remains a little statuesque, emotionally objective." But concerning Miss Dernesch's vocal equipment there was nothing but praise. To quote Peter Heyworth again, "In one of the most notoriously testing of all soprano roles only an isolated B flat in 'Komm, O Hoffnung' revealed the least evidence of strain, and in the closing scene her singing had a radiance and ease that few present-day sopranos can equal."

Though the rest of the performance had less vocal distinction, it nevertheless had a number of strong features. On the opening night in Glasgow, the Florestan, Ronald Dowd, was said to be unwell, yet he brought a characteristic nervous energy to his portrayal and performed convincingly in spite of a beard and tattered gown that made him look more like the old man of the woods than a political prisoner. William McCue was a genial, fatherly Rocco, "very much the master of his family circle," as Ronald Crichton pointed out, "but shrinking into insignificance as soon as Pizarro appears."

The decision to cast a visiting Canadian, Morley Meredith, in the latter role

Pizarro (Morley Meredith) objects to Rocco's permissiveness in allowing the prisoners to come out of their dungeons into the sunlight. The lighting at this point in the production was imaginatively conceived by Charles Bristow so that it seemed to be coming through an overhead grille.

was a shot in the dark – and not, as things turned out, a wholly successful shot. "Dramatically," declared Peter Heyworth, "he hardly gets closer to villainy than a headmaster in a rage," and Ronald Crichton detected a "superficial streak" in his performance which was "confirmed at curtain call when Mr Meredith blew kisses to the audience, as if he had been singing not Beethoven but Lehar." Nevertheless, he did succeed in making one critic's flesh creep. "Never," wrote Malcolm Rayment in the *Glasgow Herald*, "have I seen this role portrayed in a more sinister way. This Pizarro reminded me forcibly of the Third Reich." Mr Rayment's statement was amusingly counterpointed the same morning in *The Scotsman*, where Mr Meredith's Pizarro was described as a "vain, handsome film star, with an aura of romance about him more dangerous perhaps than the more familiar treatment of the part as a snarling Nazi." That sort of portrayal, however, did turn up later in the run when Mr Meredith was replaced by Donald McIntyre, whose performance proved on the whole more idiomatic and effective.

But if Helga Dernesch was the heroine of the evening, Alexander Gibson was the hero. He gave, said Peter Heyworth, "a big-boned yet finely detailed reading, and his growing artistic stature was apparent in the manner in which dramatic excitement was never imposed on the music but grew out of its inner movement." Mr Gibson tended to favour fast speeds, which made this *Fidelio* surely one of the shortest on record – especially as there was no performance of the overture "Leonore No. 3" to eke out Act Two. As one who had served his prentice years at Sadler's Wells, Mr Gibson knew the value of moving straight from the dungeon scene into the radiance of the finale, whatever

Finale of Fidelio: *Leonore (Helga Dernesch) is reunited with Florestan (Ronald Dowd). Behind are Rocco and his family, and on the left Don Fernando (Ronald Morrison).*

problems it might give Peter Ebert on the production side. For the man who, some months earlier, had anonymously offered Mr Gibson a handsome bribe if he would omit the intrusive "Leonore No. 3" there was no problem at all. He got what he wanted because that was what Mr Gibson intended in any case; whether Scottish Opera accepted the bribe the story does not say!

Peter Ebert's production proved generally sound, very good at conveying the domestic atmosphere of Rocco and his family, excellent at placing the choruses: the affecting simplicity of the prisoners, as they groped timidly towards a small central pool of light, was rightly one of the most memorable moments of the evening. Lightness and darkness were the basis of Mr Ebert's treatment of the opera. Praise for Charles Bristow's lighting came from almost all the critics, especially from William Mann in *The Times* who thought it as imaginatively lit an opera production as he had ever seen.

For his settings, Mr Ebert went once again to Hans-Ulrich Schmückle of the Augsburg Opera, who, since his *Trojans* designs the previous year had seemed almost *Fidelio*-like in their claustrophobic atmosphere, was widely deemed a suitable choice. What he supplied was an impressively sturdy, menacing structure, with a huge prison gate as its focal point. A specially telling visual moment was when this gate was raised at the start of the finale, and sunlight of blinding intensity streamed in through the huge aperture. Such moments helped to make this *Fidelio* the special experience a bicentenary production should have been; they also helped to make it a repertory production of high and distinctive quality, though once again the costume designs by Sylte Büsse-Schmückle lacked the taste and cohesion one had come to expect of Scottish Opera.

16. Eight New Productions

BETWEEN THE SPRING of 1970 and early summer of 1971, Scottish Opera succeeded in mounting no fewer than eight new productions – a princely total which many leading European opera houses, not least Covent Garden, would regard as far beyond their personal realms of possibility. And when one considers the list of pieces chosen, which reads like a rich and varied roll-call of operatic greatness, the achievement seems all the more remarkable: *Fidelio, The Turn of the Screw, The Magic Flute, Elegy for Young Lovers, La Traviata, Der Rosenkavalier, Siegfried, The Barber of Seville*, not to mention a revival of *Don Giovanni* so substantially rethought that it was tantamount to a new production – could any opera company offer a prouder repertoire?

So many important new productions, of course, must have placed an enormous strain – financial, physical and intellectual – on the Company's resources. As early as January 1970, Peter Hemmings had publicly stated that the gross expenditure for the following twelve months would be "the largest ever"; and the *Daily Telegraph*, in a report headed "Rosy future for Scottish Opera," had announced that £300,000 was to be spent on new productions, an increase of £50,000 on the previous year. But if the rosy future was not to be rapidly curtailed by red bank statements, guarantees of a good deal more money were going to be required over the next few seasons. The Scottish Arts Council, recognising this, increased its grant from £125,000 to £210,000 between 1970 and 1971. Glasgow Corporation followed suit with a contribution of £15,000 – £8750 more than before; and not long afterwards Edinburgh Corporation passed "without comment" a motion to increase its subsidy from £8000 to £9000, in spite of protests in the correspondence columns of the Edinburgh *Evening News*, where angry citizens complained of the waste of public money and pointed puritanical fingers at the Corporation, remarking "Will they never learn?"

Yet grants were still far below what Mr Hemmings considered to be a reasonable level for the Company at that stage in its development. An Endowment Trust Fund had been launched by now to help pay for a variety of special projects, but private enterprise in Scotland had long been notoriously unsympathetic to the Company's needs, nor was it yet showing much sign of a change of heart. In Ireland the Wexford Festival receives generous backing from the

Part of the strength of Anthony Besch's production of The Turn of the Screw *derived from the remarkable portrayals of the children which he drew from eleven-year-old Timothy Oldham as Miles and Nan Christie as Flora, here seen in the "Tom, Tom, the piper's son" sequence of Act One.*

Guinness breweries, and in Denmark the artistic ventures supported by Carlsberg are legion; but Ireland and Denmark are not Scotland, and Scottish Opera had failed so far to find a brewery or distillery similarly eager to subsidise opera. Among many relevant stories quoted about Scottish meanness was one concerning a prosperous London firm which agreed to give the Company a donation. In the interests of etiquette, the firm decided to refer the matter to its Scottish office. The Scottish office, regarding the whole idea as tiresomely frivolous, thereupon refused to cough up the money.

By this time, with 110 performances planned for 1971, and with an itinerary likely to stretch as far south as Liverpool, Mr Hemmings felt that the Company should be receiving grants proportionately comparable with those of Covent Garden and Sadler's Wells. A heading in *The Guardian* in 1970 – "Funds low, but opera expands" – seemed oddly reminiscent of some of the headings which newspapers had been bestowing on the Company's activities as far back as 1963. Referring to the Scottish Arts Council's subsidy, Peter Hemmings declared challengingly at a press conference that it compared "very unfavourably" with the £850,000 then received by Sadler's Wells and the £1½ million by Covent Garden.

"I would think," he said, "that Scottish Opera and the Welsh National Opera, in view of the fact that between them they now bear the brunt of opera provision outside London, should be getting between £300,000 and £500,000 each." He added that Scottish Opera's "slice of the Government cheque" was unfair in view of the decreasing number of regional performances undertaken by Sadler's Wells; and he predicted that the £300,000 required for Scottish Opera productions in 1970 would jump to £450,000 in 1971. Of this, with audiences now averaging about 85 per cent, about one-third would be recouped from the box-office and the rest would have to be met by grants.

As it happened, Mr Hemmings's prediction of £450,000 proved in the end to be fairly conservative. When the 1971 season came to be costed, the estimated gross expenditure amounted to £467,000; and since the figures for 1971 make a fascinating comparison with those for the abortive 1961 season (see page 11), I quote them in full:

Estimated Gross Expenditure

Permanent salaries and fees	£55,000
Accommodation, office, etc.	37,000
Scenery and costumes	25,000
Spring season	177,000
Autumn season	106,000
Winter season	37,000
Opera for All	24,000
Opera for Schools	6000
	£467,000

Estimated Income

Box-office (including guarantees)		
Spring season	£70,000	
Autumn season	85,000	
Winter season	15,000	
	£170,000	(36½%)

Scottish Arts Council Grants

Basic grant	£200,000	
Opera for All	24,000	
	£224,000	(48%)

Other Sources

Rents, hires, administration charges	£16,500	
Grants and donations	5000	
Local authorities	40,500	
	£62,000	(13½%)
	£456,000	(98%)
Estimated Deficit	£11,000	(2%)
	£467,000	(100%)

Above: *the forging scene from Act One of* Siegfried, *with Ticho Parly, the Danish tenor, in the title role. Below: Mime (Francis Egerton) attempts to poison Siegfried in the forest scene. In the background, just visible, the corpse of the dragon, which Siegfried has just slain.*

Two scenes from Götterdämmerung photographed during Scottish Opera's first complete cycle of The Ring *in December 1971. Above: Berit Lindholm as Brünnhilde with John Shaw as Gunther in Act Two; behind them, Hagen's troops, with Hagen himself (Louis Hendrikx) in the centre. Left: Brünnhilde and Siegfried (Berit Lindholm and Ticho Parly) in Act One of the opera.*

(*Above*) *Wherever the good or evil was meant to lie in Anthony Besch's production of* The Turn of the Screw, *there was little ambiguity about the expression on Nan Christie's face, when, as Flora, she prepared to steal away from the dozing Mrs Grose (Judith Pierce).*

(*Below*) *Final scene between the Governess (Catherine Wilson) and Miles (Timothy Oldham) as* The Turn of the Screw *approaches its tragic close.*

The above figures were accompanied by a number of interesting footnotes, of which two in particular spoke powerfully for themselves. The first was that the average cost of a Scottish Opera performance was now about £4640 per night – more than twice the estimate had been for the whole 1961 season. The other was that a capacity house in Glasgow yielded a box-office return of £2200 at £3 top price. The Company might have added, as proof of the prudence with which it runs its affairs, that the £25,000 estimated for scenery and costumes in 1971 was less than half the sum Covent Garden has been known to spend on a single production.

But apart from the financial strain of mounting eight new productions in quick succession, there was also the physical and intellectual one; and the fact that the bulk of them were conducted by Alexander Gibson made one inclined to wonder to what extent it was brave, to what extent foolhardy, to tackle so much in little more than a year. Had enough time for preparation really been allowed? In one or two instances it seemed not; and indeed, even in the case of a major production such as *Der Rosenkavalier*, there was evidence (amid much that was outstanding) of insufficient orchestral rehearsal and of corners occasionally being cut – if such a phrase can be used of what was almost certainly the first complete performance of Strauss's opera ever to have been given in a British theatre.

Yet Scottish Opera has always appreciated a challenge; and of the series of challenges it met during this period, almost all were mastered and at least one – the Edinburgh Festival production of Hans Werner Henze's *Elegy for Young Lovers* – was hailed by Peter Heyworth in *The Observer* as "the finest thing Scottish Opera has as yet achieved." But first there was *The Turn of the Screw*, with which the Company opened its 1970 spring season in Aberdeen. For some time Scottish Opera had been planning to add another Britten chamber opera to its repertoire, and to allot it to the same team – Messrs Besch and Brydon – who had been responsible for the highly successful *Albert Herring*. And obviously, if another Britten chamber opera was to be done, then *The Turn of the Screw* had top priority. Not only was it arguably the greatest of all Britten's works, it was also one which would fit neatly into the Scottish theatres, which could be cast from some of the same singers as *Herring*, which would unquestionably stimulate Mr Besch's imagination as a producer, and which would enable Mr Brydon to build on the experience of the work he had gained when he conducted it a few years previously for John Calder's country-house festival at Ledlanet in Kinross-shire. The latter production, which actually took place in the hall and on the staircases and balconies of a house uncommonly like Bly (there are even a tower and a lake at Ledlanet, but these, alas, could not have been used without moving the performers and audience in and out of the building – something beyond the ingenuity of even John Calder), was a very special, not to say unique, treatment of the opera; and it left an impression which could not be completely erased by the new production, for all its qualities.

Yet the new production was extremely good, well up to the standard of *Herring*, masterfully thought out by Mr Besch, and realised musically by Mr Brydon and his admirable cast. In its approach, it cut skilfully across the two basic ways of performing *The Turn of the Screw*. Mr Besch could have followed, if he had wished, the English Opera Group's traditional precedent, whereby the piece is presented as the simple story of a brave governess attempting to save two children from the evil spirits that haunt them. Or, as had been done in a Morley College production in London in 1966, he could have shown the evil to lie at least partly in the governess's own overwrought imagination, conjuring up (as the Morley programme-note put it) "two ghostly adversaries, endowing them with seductive, sensuous qualities absent in herself. . . . So many revealing phrases of pride, sexuality and frustration fall from her lips that, in the end, sides cannot be taken in deciding where the evil lay."

The Scottish production scrupulously avoided taking sides, and thereby achieved the full ambivalence which is so fascinating a feature not only of Henry James's *conte* but also of all Britten's operas. As Roderick Brydon remarked about the production in an interview in *The Scotsman*, "It is not a straightforward ghost story any more than it is a straightforward study in neurosis. What we're trying to do is to explore, as it were, every cul-de-sac and so achieve maximum ambiguity. . . . To say that the opera presents a collision between good and evil is too naïve a distinction – the two overlap constantly and that is where the problem lies."

The resultant labyrinth of good and evil was laboriously explored by Mr Besch's production, in which various clues were planted, some pointing one way, some another. On the one hand, he made the ghosts seem very tangible menaces by casting two powerful, incisive singers – Gregory Dempsey ("a red-haired version," as one critic observed, "of the practical joker with sheet and floured face") and Milla Andrew – in these awkward roles. On the other hand, during the important colloquy between the ghosts at the start of Act Two, the governess was visibly present – thus implying, or so it seemed, that the ghosts were figments of her imagination.

Earlier, even the prologue had been brought ingeniously into the action; for instead of the traditional tenor narration, sung in front of a closed curtain, Mr Besch chose to illustrate the words with a mimed tableau in which we saw the governess being hired by the children's guardian and – effective touch – the guardian was recognisably Gregory Dempsey in a different wig from the one he wore later as the ghost. In order to make this point, the production had to indulge in the luxury of two tenors – one to sing the anonymous prologue, the other to double as guardian and ghost – yet in the circumstances it seemed money well spent.

For some critics, notably Gerald Larner in *The Guardian*, the mimed tableau – gratuitous though it was – served as proof that Mr Besch considered that the ghosts did not exist, and that Quint was merely the product of the governess's secret love for the guardian. But others were not so sure, and Stephen Walsh in *The Observer* expressed a longing for something more tendentious in place of a production which, he claimed, was "all very balanced and equivocal, and all slightly unhelpful." In Aberdeen that spring, there seemed indeed to be something a little too cool and objective about Mr Besch's handling of the piece, something almost too carefully calculated, too intent on providing evidence for and against, so that the result was a little bloodless, almost like a lecture. It was all very beautiful, adorned as it was with filmy, floral, softly dappled settings by John Stoddart, and subtly and intricately lit by Charles Bristow; what was lacking was a strong feeling of active, creeping malignancy – the audience tended to be kept at arm's length instead of being immersed in the drama.

But by the time it reached Glasgow and Edinburgh (it was also taken to Newcastle, where it had a considerable success) the production had gathered force. Catherine Wilson's portrayal of the governess, originally a shade constrained, now carried remarkable authority and intensity, and her pleas, her outbursts, her perplexed musings were delivered in consistently assured, heartfelt tones, enunciated with high clarity. Her exclamation of the one word, "Dead!", on learning that the man she had just seen at the window had expired of a head injury the previous winter, was one of the most spine-chilling moments of the evening. As in Aberdeen, eleven-year-old Timothy Oldham – son of the Company's chorusmaster – seemed perhaps a little young for the part of Miles, and had not quite enough wind to cope with its arduousness. Yet as more than one critic commented, the Company in choosing him had made a sound investment – he would obviously grow into the role, he would have plenty of time to do so before his voice broke, and in any case he had a quality of vulnerable innocence which was very affecting.

One respect in which the production scored strongly over previous ones was in the casting of a young Ayrshire singer, Nan Christie, as Flora. Most performances of *The Turn of the Screw* make do with a mature soprano in this part, ineffectually disguised to look like a kid sister. As played by Miss Christie, however, Flora was a big sister, a slim, blonde teenager, fresh and delicate-voiced, very convincing indeed. The way she played the first of the lakeside scenes (not a lake in this production but a swamp overgrown with twisted plants) was extraordinarily telling, for she somehow succeeded in looking simultaneously oblivious and aware of the presence of the ghost of Miss Jessel standing behind her. Even as I write a year after watching Miss Christie in the part, the memory of her face, of the way she sat during those moments, remains vivid.

Judith Pierce's plump, doddery Mrs Grose showed her in very different light from her magisterial Lady Billows in *Albert Herring*; but the light in which Roderick Brydon, the conductor, was shown was again that of an outstandingly perceptive Britten exponent, drawing sharp, colourful, sensitive tone from his orchestra – this time a new one, Leonard Friedman's Scottish Baroque Ensemble, a bold, alert young body of players who were to become increasingly useful to Scottish Opera in the months ahead when there were more performances than could be undertaken by the SNO or the BBC Scottish Symphony Orchestra.

So although to begin with this *Turn of the Screw* threatened to lack complete spontaneity, it soon developed into one of the Company's most satisfying productions. Modern opera, of course, has always been a *forte* of Scottish Opera; and in August 1970 we were to be reminded of this again when *Elegy for Young Lovers* was presented at the Edinburgh Festival. But before that there were other events worth chronicling. Not, perhaps, the lacklustre revival of *Cenerentola*; certainly, however, the return of *Don Giovanni*. Sung now in Italian instead of the Dent translation previously used, this came a step or two nearer the ideal presentation towards which the Company had been reaching ever since 1964. Apart from the presence of Peter van der Bilt in the title-role, the cast was new; so too the producer, Ian Watt-Smith, who replaced Peter Ebert and brought a number of fresh ideas to the manipulation of the singers and of Ralph Koltai's sliding abstract settings. After a gap of several years it was exciting to see again those powerful, menacing black and white panels, which this time, even more strongly than before, enabled the action to move relentlessly forward without the stop-go scene changes that so hamper the Zeffirelli production at Covent Garden. The fact that the panels served almost as characters in the drama inspired Mr Watt-Smith to invent a striking *coup de théâtre* for the close: as Giovanni's final encounter with the Commendatore reached its climax, the two main panels advanced on him from either side of the stage and crushed him between (as it were) the forces of Heaven and Hell. In the circumstances it seemed apt that Giovanni should meet his fate not at the hands of the Commendatore himself but by way of Mr Koltai's designs, which in 1970 as in 1964 and 1965 continued to dominate the evening.

Moreover, musically and dramatically, the presentation of the opera as a whole had undoubtedly deepened and tautened. There was both a passion and a grace in Alexander Gibson's conducting that kept the score coursing forward without skimping its expressive detail; and in the clear acoustics of the Aberdeen theatre the SNO's accompaniments sprang warmly to life, with full, eager bass tone, bright, lively woodwind and upper strings. Later in the run, in Glasgow and Edinburgh, there was some slackening of tension in the performances, and an element of routine entered the singing. But meantime one was able to admire many of the ideas brought to the production: the sight of Giovanni and Leporello circling like jackals round Donna Elvira during her opening aria; the reminder, when Elvira started weeping during "Madamina," that Leporello's familiar, jocular catalogue song is cruel as well as comic.

After five years, Mr Van der Bilt seemed a bolder, more rapacious Giovanni; and of the newcomers, Stafford Dean proved a spry, active Leporello, bringing plenty of incisiveness and a whiff of *commedia del'arte* to his portrayal; Milla Andrew was a refreshingly sultry Anna, and Luisa Bosabalian an Elvira who, in big and expressive if not ideally beautiful tones, caught the pathos of her role – in "In quali eccessi" she sang her music touchingly to Giovanni's cloak, left behind on the stage. Patricia Hay and John Graham, two resident singers who had profited from a recent period of tuition in Italy, were a nicely amorous

Zerlina and Masetto. The only really controversial portrayal was Werner Krenn's Ottavio. Mr Krenn, a young Viennese tenor and former member of the Wiener Sangerknaben, had already been acclaimed for some excellent recordings and his appearances under Karajan and other conductors; but in Aberdeen his voice – the result, it was said, of a throat infection – was muted to the point of inaudibility. The infection, if such it was, persisted throughout the season: in Glasgow, Newcastle and Edinburgh the voice remained damped, nor was much compensation provided by Mr Krenn's acting abilities which, even in a role that placed few demands on them, seemed slight. Yet the voice, though tiny, was unquestionably a beautiful instrument – so musical, so exquisite, so precise in the shaping of the decorated twists and turns of the two arias that he justified his journey from Vienna to Scotland.

After the close of the spring season and the start of the Edinburgh Festival, the Company succeeded in plugging another of the gaps in its activities by arranging to give a week of performances of *The Magic Flute* in Edinburgh's civic playhouse, the Royal Lyceum Theatre. The reason, or excuse, for the new production was the Commonwealth Games, which had arrived in Edinburgh much sooner than the long-awaited opera house – which was still an untidy, embarrassing hole in the ground next door to the Lyceum but which apparently failed to inspire feelings of guilt in those civic dignitaries who had managed to achieve at lightning speed the expensive construction of the swimming pool, stadium, and all the other facilities required by the Games.

(Opposite) The shifting of the action of The Magic Flute *from Egypt to a multi-racial never-never-land far to the East of Suez was a pleasant fancy at the time of the Commonwealth Games. Here Pamina, sung by Jill Gomez, is seen with the Three Spirits (left to right, Moyra Paterson, Ann Baird, Sheila McGrow) costumed by Alex Reid in Siamese style. The costume for Tamino (David Hillman, far left) also had a distinctly Far Eastern look.*

(Right) *As the Queen of the Night in* The Magic Flute, *Rhonda Bruce looked effectively like a bird of prey but could not quite muster the vocal ferocity her costume seemed to demand.*

If Scotland was to display its sports facilities to so many thousands of visitors, it was argued, then it should also display something of its cultural assets at a time – the end of July – when not much is usually happening. Since there was no new opera house to show off, the next best thing seemed a new opera production by the Company which (along with the Edinburgh Festival) had done so much to put Scotland on the international map. And so it came about that Clive Perry, the lively young director of Edinburgh's civic theatre company, fulfilled one of his many enterprising ambitions, which was to put on Scottish Opera at a period when his own company was on holiday. Edinburgh was apparently willing to make some extra funds available for the occasion; a shallow orchestra pit was designed to replace the narrow gulley where palm-court trios had once been accustomed to play; the only question was what opera would be likely to fill the theatre (which looks a good deal smaller than the King's but is in fact almost as big) for a week. The magic name was *The Magic Flute*, and by the third of the six performances attendances had risen above 90 per cent, where they remained for the rest of the week.

The production, it must be owned, was less magical and revealed something of the rush with which it had been planned, cast and rehearsed. Attempts to capture *The Magic Flute*, of course, bite the dust more easily than any other Mozart production, and the Company was well aware that its chances of an artistic success were slighter than with either *Così* or *Giovanni*. Certainly, of the marvellous matching of sight and sound, the ability to make us think afresh about the opera, the desire to probe beneath the surface, the keen feeling for time and place which were such memorable features of *Così*, there was little hint. The chance to present, in a friendly, intimate theatre, the kind of light, fleet *Flute* one often dreams of, was largely missed – partly because the opera was saddled with settings by Geoffrey Scott (one of the Lyceum's resident designers) which proved generally clumsy and unhelpful, partly because the cast, while it reflected the internationality of the Commonwealth Games, was in the main moderate, and partly because Alex Reid's costumes, while bright and cheerful (gaudy even), served only to emphasise the lack of considered thought that seemed to have been given to the evening.

The producer was Peter Ebert who, we were told beforehand, had "ideas" about the *Flute*. And so he had – some of them good, some of them attractive, but not in sum quite convincing enough to make the resultant changes seem worthwhile. The rearranging of Act Two so that the solemnity of the trial by fire and water came after instead of before the Papageno-Papagena love duet carried a certain logic without actually seeming an improvement. The shifting of the action from Egypt to a multi-racial never-never land far to the East of Suez was a pleasant fancy at the time of the Games but did not make the opera any more coherent.

Still, there was a potentially fine Pamina in Jill Gomez – tall, slim, beautiful, pure and sensitive-voiced, if not yet quite full enough toned for the role. David Hillman, Tamino, sang boldly, musically, but his voice was a little lacking in charm. Michael Maurel, better at singing than playing his pipes, was an engaging Papageno with some good Edinburgh jokes to add to the Ruth and Thomas Martin translation which the Company chose to use. Simon Estes, a coloured Sarastro imported from New York, lacked weight and variety of tone, and had trouble reaching down to his bottom notes, but was welcomely more human, less pompous, than the general run of high priests. Alexander Gibson drew well-paced if somewhat dry playing from the BBC Scottish Symphony Orchestra, which continued to lack the SNO's finesse in the pit.

Musically, then, the production had possibilities, some of which were more fully realised when it was brought into the general repertoire later in the year; but the sight of a gauze instead of temples and doors in the finale to Act One, the steps that trundled automatically (and noisily) out of Sarastro's dais, the idea of producing the Queen of the Night from a kind of revolving oyster-shell on top of a pinnacle and of placing one of the Three Ladies behind a kind of masonic television screen at the start of Act Two were all aspects of the evening that grew increasingly tiresome to live with.

The Edinburgh Festival production of *Elegy for Young Lovers*, however, was another matter, for here was the kind of event – imaginatively conceived, scrupulously prepared, lovingly presented – on which Scottish Opera had built its reputation. That the Company would one day stage an opera by Hans Werner Henze, and would do so ahead of Covent Garden and Sadler's Wells, was a foregone conclusion. Alexander Gibson had been established for some time as Britain's leading Henze conductor, with a salutary list of British orches-

Hans Werner Henze, composer and musical jack-of-all-trades, was himself the producer of Elegy for Young Lovers *at the 1970 Edinburgh Festival. Here he explains a gesture to Jill Gomez, who played the role of Elisabeth Zimmer. On the right John Shirley-Quirk who took the leading role of the poet Mittenhofer—a part originally written for Dietrich Fischer-Dieskau.*

tral premieres to his credit. What he had not yet conducted was one of Henze's operas, and it was his desire to do so which prompted Peter Diamand to make an important feature of Henze in the 1970 Festival.

At a time when *King Stag, The Young Lord,* and *The Bassarids* were still awaiting British productions, *Elegy for Young Lovers* at first seemed a self-indulgent choice – after all, it had been performed in Britain before, by Glyndebourne in 1961; but Henze's stature as a composer and man of the theatre was not then fully established, and the Glyndebourne production was not a success. The idea, therefore, was to give *Elegy* an opportunity to re-establish itself in the light of our latter-day appreciation of Henze, and in a production which would give us the music complete instead of truncated as at Glyndebourne and in the various Continental productions it had received in the interim.

Since Henze was to be coming to Edinburgh for the Festival, the opportunity was taken to invite him to produce his opera himself – a musical jack-of-all-trades, he had already been responsible for at least two previous productions of the work, at Schwetzingen and Berlin, and for the latter production had even designed the settings and costumes. This time, however, the settings were to be by Ralph Koltai, and the resultant triumvirate of Koltai, Henze and Gibson was an uncommonly successful one. The treatment of the piece was an inventive mixture of the realistic and abstract, of the romantic and satirical. It made

a rich, substantial and rewarding evening, a valuable contribution to Edinburgh's Henze year and to the Company's repertoire.

Elegy is a portrait of the artist as a vain old man. The action revolves round a famous poet, Gregor Mittenhofer, who exploits every person, every situation that may be of use to him in his work and his private life. The most distinguished exponent of this evil genius has always been Dietrich Fischer-Dieskau, but Henze, with the backing of Alexander Gibson and presumably Peter Diamand, felt it was time to shed different light on the role. As a result, the part went to John Shirley-Quirk, an intelligent and sensitive baritone who had already (on television) successfully portrayed another vain anti-hero, Eugene Onegin, and had appeared with Scottish Opera in 1969 as Don Alfonso.

For those who had never seen Fischer-Dieskau as the poet, Mr Shirley-Quirk's performance was doubtless easy to accept. But for anyone acquainted with the German singer's overwhelming, cannibalistic portrayal, Mr Shirley-Quirk's dessicated, crotchety creature, looking faintly like Robert Helpmann as Dr Coppelius in the Beecham film of *The Tales of Hoffmann*, must at first have been disconcerting. The voice, and the personality, seemed several sizes smaller.

Yet once you had grown accustomed to it – and there were later, post-Festival performances in Glasgow and in Aberdeen that enabled this to be done – his portrayal carried its own conviction. Here was not a lofty, awe-inspiring Mittenhofer but a petulant *petit maître* whose tantrums were more comic than frightening, but not because of that any less dangerous; indeed, he performed his atrocities with a whimsical, knowing, spidery glee which made them seem all the nastier. Vocally, by necessity, Mr Shirley-Quirk was better at capturing the half-tones of his part than the big outbursts. His rage at the end of Act Two was small-scale, waspish (interesting how insects kept coming to mind in watching him) rather than leonine; but then, he was singing the original English version of the Auden-Kallman libretto, not the German translation used by Fischer-Dieskau – and of course German is a more impressive language to be angry in than English.

Of the five main characters in the poet's *entourage*, almost all were superbly

(Opposite, top left) Jill Gomez and David Hillman as the young lovers whose death on the mountainside was indirectly caused by the poet Mittenhofer and later celebrated by him with an elegy. A scene from Henze's Elegy for Young Lovers *at the 1970 Edinburgh Festival.*

(Opposite, top right) John Shirley-Quirk (right) made the poet Mittenhofer a dessicated, crotchety creature, who performed his atrocities with a whimsical, spidery glee. Scarcely less striking in this production was Sona Cervena's portrayal of the poet's secretary-cum-patroness.

(Opposite, below) Ralph Koltai's characteristically abstract designs for Elegy for Young Lovers *were inevitably a controversial feature of the production. With tubular scaffolding to represent the slopes of the Hammerhorn, the result for one critic was "the only stage mountain I have ever wanted to climb." Others longed for something more clearly representational. In this picture the characters (left to right) are Jill Gomez and David Hillman as the young lovers, Sona Cervena and John Shirley-Quirk as patroness and poet.*

Catherine Gayer's portrayal of the widow, Hilda Mack, whose mysterious visions are the basis of Mittenhofer's poems, had already been made world-famous by the West Berlin production of Henze's Elegy for Young Lovers; *but in Edinburgh she seemed to gain fresh nuances.*

taken. Catherine Gayer's study of the widow, Hilda Mack, whose mysterious visions are the basis of Mittenhofer's poems, was already famous from the Berlin production; but in Edinburgh it seemed to gain fresh nuances, and the zigzagging bravura phrases of the vocal line were, if anything, even more brilliantly executed. Sona Cervena, like Miss Gayer a sterling (if rougher-voiced) exponent of twentieth-century opera, was admirable in a part which Peter Heyworth in *The Observer* described as a "dedicated yet resentful blue-stocking who serves as patroness and secretary as well as doormat"; and Jill Gomez and David Hillman, in music very different from Pamina's and Tamino's, were convincing young lovers, though they did not have at their disposal the more inspired passages of Henze's score.

Unlike the Glyndebourne production, which faithfully recreated the period atmosphere of the opera's Alpine setting, Mr Koltai's decor evoked time and place in strikingly modern terms. Spare and skeletal, it consisted of a flight of stairs, a grandfather clock, and a few basic pieces of furniture to represent the mountain inn where the action takes place, and a magnificent construction of tubular scaffolding and Perspex to represent the looming Hammerhorn on which the lovers perish. For one or two critics this proved irksome – Malcolm Rayment in the *Glasgow Herald* longed for something more natural, and Stanley Sadie in *The Times* complained about the stylisation being unnecessarily discordant with Fausto Moroni's period costumes. But Noël Goodwin in the *Daily Express* crisply stated the case for the defence by declaring Mr Koltai's Hammerhorn to be the only stage mountain he had ever felt keen to climb, and even Mr Sadie felt disposed to praise the storm scene in the last act – "marvellously effective projections on to a scrim, with the various jagged lines brilliantly suggestive of the mountain in upheaval."

Minor grumbles apart, no other production in the history of the Company received such unanimously enthusiastic reviews as this. Mr Sadie, it is true, was a little uncertain about the portrayal of Mittenhofer "not merely as unscrupulous but also as downright absurd, a small man, a trivial, pretentious socialite hypocrite who surely must be a charlatan," and he asked in his very thoughtful notice if it was "not unreasonable to wonder whether Henze's recently acquired political philosophies have obscured for him the real validity of his own opera"; but he described the actual mechanics of the production as a superb, and a superbly theatrical, piece of work. "Its detail is meticulous, its observation precise to the text and the interaction of the characters constantly revealing: a technical triumph for Henze and Scottish Opera."

Peter Heyworth's high regard for the production has already been quoted. For Andrew Porter in the *Financial Times* it was likewise "one of the high achievements of Scottish Opera"; for Gerald Larner in *The Guardian* it was "one of the finest [productions] ever seen at the Edinburgh Festival"; and though Desmond Shawe-Taylor in the *Sunday Times* suggested that Henze's score contained "too much cuisine and a shortage of meat," he called the production "distinguished," and like everyone else singled out Alexander Gibson for the insight he brought to the music. Indeed, as Peter Heyworth observed, Mr Gibson conducted what was "in every way an outstanding musical performance," which was realised by the SNO "with a delicacy and definition unequalled in my experience."

As soon as the Festival was over, the Company embarked on its most extensive autumn tour so far, culminating in performances of *Albert Herring* and *The Turn of the Screw* at Reykjavik in Iceland – the first time a British opera company had performed there. Then in December came the unveiling of the last new production of 1970. For some time it had been felt that the repertoire needed another Verdi opera. Verdi connoisseurs would unanimously have named *Don Carlos* as first choice, a masterpiece long overdue in Scotland; but with *Otello* and *Falstaff* already available (though the latter had not been seen since 1966) it was considered that Verdi connoisseurs had already fared pretty well – and so one of the earlier, more manifestly "popular" operas, *La Traviata*, was chosen as the mainstay of the latest Christmas season in Edinburgh. At first it was hoped to include revivals of *Fidelio* and *The Magic Flute* during the same short visit; but because the King's Theatre had been reserved by Stanley Baxter for a new pantomime, this idea had to be modified. Fortunately the Royal Lyceum once again proved available, which at least enabled the season to take place even though it meant changing the repertoire. To accommodate the Verdi, Clive Perry agreed to extend the orchestra pit he had kindly provided earlier in the year; but it was obvious that *Fidelio* would have to be dropped, and the programme finally consisted of *Traviata*, *The Magic Flute*, and some guest performances of a vivacious new production of Purcell's *King Arthur* by the English Opera Group.

Coming so soon after *Elegy*, the unexpectedly old-fashioned treatment of *La Traviata* made an odd impression. Of course, operagoers with cherished memories of the Carl Rosa fell on it thankfully, and so far as the box-office was concerned the production was a popular success (the three performances of *Elegy* in Edinburgh had drawn, at best, a 65 per cent house – not bad, all the same, for an uncompromising modern piece, and certainly far better than *Volo di notte* in 1963). Yet no one could call the *Traviata* production typical of Scottish Opera. It was, as Gerald Larner pointed out in *The Guardian*, "not the customary integrated ensemble performance but a quite uncharacteristic star display."

The stars in question were Clarice Carson and Franco Bonisolli – not yet big names in Britain (where Miss Carson, in fact, was appearing for the first time and where Mr Bonisolli was known chiefly for his portrayal of Pinkerton in Scottish Opera's 1968 revival of *Madama Butterfly* and of Alfredo in the Karajan film of *Traviata*) but singers with a stage demeanour and limited range of gesture suggestive of the world's most backward-looking, canary-fancying opera houses such as the New York Metropolitan – in which Miss Carson, indeed, is a prized soprano. To quote Gerald Larner again, Miss Carson dominated the stage in "the grand old-fashioned manner with a timing which is all her own and with singing which is not exactly refined or utterly accurate but which is physically exciting and compulsive listening." Mr Larner added that when she was not

With incense rising all round him, John Shirley-Quirk as Mittenhofer delivers his elegy. The final, memorable scene of the 1970 Edinburgh Festival production of Elegy for Young Lovers.

Bernard Culshaw's stark yet glittering settings, with their suspended mirrors, added a touch of implied fin-de-siècle immorality to the production of La Traviata. *Even in Violetta's death scene (pictured here with Clarice Carson as Violetta and Moyra Paterson as her maid) these omnipresent mirrors, one of them directly over her bed, reminded us of what her profession had been.*

singing sometimes she was coughing, in anticipation of her doom, and anyone with notes to produce had to put up with it.

The result, then, was pure operatic escapism. For anyone who, like Malcolm Rayment of the *Glasgow Herald*, has no special affection for *Traviata* this perhaps did not matter; and Mr Rayment was able to report that, so far as he was concerned, the performance was well presented and well sung. But for anyone who, like Joseph Kerman in *Opera as Drama*, regards *Traviata* as one of Verdi's most homogeneous and meaningful dramatic masterpieces, the production was disappointing. It was certainly hard to recognise it as the handiwork of Ian Watt-Smith, who earlier in the year had presented so interesting a *Giovanni*. One could only assume that he found Miss Carson's Violetta and Mr Bonisolli's pleasantly sung but wooden Alfredo too intractable to do much about; nor did he draw anything more than a very straightforward, mellow-voiced account of Germont from Ronald Morrison – though from Moyra Paterson, in the part of Violetta's maid, he obtained a deft little character sketch which suggested that, given material he can work with, he may yet have things to tell us about *Traviata*.

The handling of the crowd scenes on the small stage looked adept if somewhat provincial; but Bernard Culshaw's stark yet glittering settings, with their use of mirror effects above and behind the singers, added a lively touch of implied *fin-de-siècle* immorality to the occasion. Even in Violetta's death scene these omnipresent mirrors, one of them directly over her bed, reminded us of what her profession had been. Perhaps, however, it was poetic justice that what some of us saw in them was the reflection of the conductor, James Loughran, who with the BBC Scottish Symphony Orchestra had been the evening's main source of eloquence.

17. *Rosenkavalier*, the *Ring*, and the Future

FOR ITS TENTH year of activity – or eleventh really, if one counts the ill-fated 1961 season which was stillborn for want of a £1700 subsidy from the Arts Council – Scottish Opera planned a repertoire which was rightly intended as a celebration but which never degenerated into one of those acts of self-indulgence (an all-star *Aida*, say, or a *Daughter of the Regiment* with the reigning coloratura, in which a better-endowed or more frivolous-minded company might have been tempted to wallow.

In one way, of course, the new *Rosenkavalier*, with Helga Dernesch, Janet Baker, and Elizabeth Harwood in three of the main parts, may have looked suspiciously like wallowing. But the addition of a Strauss opera to the repertoire had become an obvious need; and though the presence of Miss Dernesch, Miss Baker, and Miss Harwood in one single production may have seemed like star casting, these three singers were in fact regular members – even, to some extent, discoveries – of the Company.

Scottish Opera, after all, had won Miss Dernesch's services before she became a Karajan star, and continued to provide her with the kind of working conditions she liked even after Karajan had elected her his new Brünnhilde and Leonore. For the sake of appearing in *Rosenkavalier*, she was willing to learn the Marschallin's role in English translation. Janet Baker had made no secret of her affection for Scottish Opera – an affection generated, like Miss Dernesch's, by working conditions which she found to be more inspiring than those of many a longer-established company, and in particular by the chance to make music with a conductor, Alexander Gibson, who appeared to have a deep, instinctive understanding of how a singer breathes and thinks. In enabling Miss Baker to explore and extend the range of her operatic talents, first as Dorabella, then as Dido, now as Octavian, Scottish Opera further earned her gratitude. As for Miss Harwood, she, too, though she was already destined to be Karajan's next Countess at Salzburg, was attracted by the idea of returning to Scotland, not least because she would once more be singing opposite Janet Baker.

In choosing *Rosenkavalier*, Scottish Opera again revealed its eagerness to tackle big, challenging works – next time, said Alexander Gibson, it would be *Die Frau ohne Schatten*. But, in addition, the spring season was to include a new *Siegfried* and revivals of *Traviata*, *The Magic Flute*, *Albert Herring*, and *The Turn of the Screw*; the

Rosenkavalier, *Act One: While Baron Ochs (Noel Mangin) sings of his wedding plans, Mariandel/Octavian peers from her hiding-place behind the Marschallin's bed.*

Rosenkavalier, Act Two: *Sophie (Elizabeth Harwood), fresh from her convent education, listens in rapture to Octavian as the Knight of the Rose.*

summer was to see a new *Barber of Seville;* the Edinburgh Festival a revised *Walküre;* and the autumn a second and new production of *The Rake's Progress.* Riches indeed!

Neither *Traviata* nor *The Magic Flute,* with their original casts preserved fairly intact, seemed much better than before – indeed Geoffrey Scott's tiresome settings for the Mozart were subsequently donated to the Glasgow Grand Opera Company, thus putting paid, so far as Scottish Opera was concerned, to a production that had been neither more nor less successful than most other present-day *Flutes. The Barber,* on the other hand, went uncommonly well. Like the Mozart and Verdi productions, it was geared in the first place for the Royal Lyceum Theatre in Edinburgh, where it was to have a week of performances in July while the resident drama company was on holiday.

As a box-office attraction it did not quite measure up to the Mozart of the previous year, though all the same it drew good houses. Artistically, it had plenty to offer: a zestful, creatively comic production by Ian Watt-Smith, who here had more flexible singers than in *Traviata;* a conductor (the Israeli, Gary Bertini, working for the first time with the Company) who was keen to take a fresh look at the music, cleaning up the orchestration and restoring a number of passages that are usually cut; uncluttered decor by Bernard Culshaw, whose practical structure of a stage-within-a-stage, with curtained cubicles at the rear and overhead lighting gantries exposed to the eye, made this seem something of a Brechtian *Barber;* and a cast which, though it may have been stronger on teamwork than on vocal quality, certainly made a better case for the former commodity than *Traviata* did for the latter.

The most distinguished singing came from Anne Howells, a Glyndebourne protégé on whom Scottish Opera had had its eye for some time. A true mezzo, she was able to bring an exciting dark cutting edge to her lower notes, though her portrayal of Rosina seemed sometimes unexpectedly brash – more a Carmen than a future Countess Almaviva. In some ways Patricia Hay, who alternated with Miss Howells, seemed more naturally mischievous and charming, even if her voice was lighter and lacked Miss Howells's smokier tones.

There was no doubt, however, about the success of Elfego Esparza's Dr Bartolo. His unerring sense of timing, his relish of words (a modification of the Dent translation was used), his facial expressions and gestures (owing more to Oliver Hardy and early Hollywood comedies, perhaps, than to Beaumarchais, but very funny) all served to make this a brilliantly detailed comic study. The only danger was that so vivid and resourceful a Bartolo might tend to dominate the production; and with a lightweight but likeable Figaro (Michael Maurel) and a particularly genial Don Basilio (William McCue) this very nearly happened. Yet these, along with David Hillman's deft Almaviva (excellent in his two disguises) and Judith Pierce's busty Berta, were all most engaging portrayals.

Compared with *Rosenkavalier,* of course, the *Barber* was a low-budget production, albeit an enjoyable one. *Rosenkavalier,* however, was one of those very special pieces with which, from time to time, Scottish Opera has caught the public's imagination long before the performance actually reaches the stage. Strauss's opera had not been seen in Scotland since the Hamburg production at the 1952 Edinburgh Festival. All five of the Edinburgh and Glasgow performances were quickly sold out. The news that not only would the cast include two of the *Così* singers in plum roles, but that the opera would be in the hands of Alexander Gibson, Anthony Besch, and John Stoddart (the same conductor, producer, and designer who had worked together so creatively on *Così*) suggested that another major success was on the way. Even the knowledge that Mr Gibson, after exhaustive study of the score, had decided to do away with traditional cuts and treat us to every note the composer wrote, gave the promised production an added fillip.

This, one felt, was what Scottish Opera had come to mean: a desire to face and overcome difficulties, to question and re-examine traditions, to treat the composer's intentions where possible as sacrosanct, to stage each opera with the care and sensitivity which one expects under festival conditions but which are not always so easy to achieve in the course of a busy season. At Covent Garden, for instance, an unabridged *Rosenkavalier* would scarcely have been feasible, simply because big international opera houses inevitably rely on jet-set singers flying in and out, expecting standard cuts to be observed and discomfited if they are not. In 1971, Scottish Opera's spring season continued to have that festive air which the Company had succeeded in maintaining each year.

Yet the very fact that each year Scottish Opera had managed to mount at least one outstanding production which stuck indelibly in the memory meant that a great deal, perhaps even too much, was expected of *Rosenkavalier*. And certainly, when the production was finally unveiled on May 20 at the King's Theatre, Glasgow, there were moments of disappointment among the many pleasures which the evening yielded. In the orchestral hubbub which introduces Act One, the SNO sounded unexpectedly uncouth; and in the act as a whole there were passages when momentum seemed to sag, when ragged edges drew attention to themselves, and when Noel Mangin, who had been recruited from Hamburg to play Baron Ochs, seemed ill at ease in his role – vocally he was content to make do with splintery speech-song declamation, depriving his music of proper line and flow.

Rosenkavalier, Act Two: Octavian presents the ceremonial silver rose to Sophie, Baron Ochs's intended bride.

The second and third acts, fortunately, were a different story. By then, many of the earlier tensions appeared to have resolved themselves and the performance steadily gathered force. Mr Mangin acted well, even if he still failed to live up to one's ideas of how an Ochs should sound; but it was above all the triumvirate of Dernesch, Baker, and Harwood, with Miss Baker as its apex, which was the special glory of the evening and which inspired William Mann to write in *The Times* that "a more intelligent or emotionally moving, let alone convincing *Rosenkavalier* would be hard to find." Part of this conviction derived from the fact that this was a truly youthful *Rosenkavalier*. The librettist, Hofmannsthal, had envisaged the Marschallin as being "32 years at the most" and Ochs not more than 35. Opera-goers accustomed to more middle-aged, even elderly, portrayals, must have found Scottish Opera's unusually authentic

Rosenkavalier, *Act Two: Baron Ochs* (Noel Mangin), *wounded in the arm by Octavian* (Janet Baker), *bellows in imaginary pain.*

treatment of the work (with a Marschallin even younger than 32) quite startling in its effect.

As a producer, Anthony Besch has always revelled in clarifying operatic situations such as those which exist between the Marschallin, Octavian, and Sophie; and on this occasion he explored their relationships in what Andrew Porter in the *Financial Times* considered to be a refreshingly unsentimental way. Not that the resultant performance was at all cold: indeed Miss Baker's Octavian was quite remarkably ardent (though she was also adept at capturing the priggish, less likeable side of the young man) and the opera's multiplicity of character sketches were lovingly attended to, from Thomas Hemsley's masterly, distraught Faninal, Nigel Douglas's gleeful Valzacchi, and Joan Davies's stunningly beautiful Annina right down to the perfectly observed Leopold of Peter Lyon. In grace and humour, in overall balance, in fluency of movement, handsomely framed by John Stoddart's settings, this was a *Rosenkavalier* which in most ways fulfilled expectations. By the time it reached Edinburgh, it had gained under Alexander Gibson a musical sheen that had sometimes been lacking in Glasgow; and in Aberdeen, where Michael Langdon appeared as Ochs, it received what some members of the Company thought to be the best performance of all.

Siegfried in the spring season, and the greatly revised and improved *Walküre* at the Edinburgh Festival, showed what strides the company's *Ring* had been making since 1966. Under Mr Gibson, the SNO was now learning to make a true Wagner sound, to bring each opera to strong, expressive life, to convey the symphonic grandeur and heart-rending beauty of the music. Among *Siegfried*'s vocal assets were David Ward's Wotan, a warm and characteristically human portrayal, unusually good at suggesting the god's sardonic humour. The start of Act Three emerged, as in all good performances it should, as perhaps the greatest, most crucial passage in the entire *Ring*. Here the performance was enhanced by Mr Gibson's surging yet not overweighted accompaniment, and by Patricia Purcell's very promising Erda. Earlier it had been a pleasure to encounter Francis Egerton's sharp little Mime, a sly, fidgety, comically moody portrayal, not perhaps sufficiently evil, yet good at suggesting the childishly wheedling side of the dwarf. Helga Dernesch was the sort of golden, lissom, full and even-toned Brünnhilde whom every Wagnerian must dream of meeting at the end of *Siegfried*; and if Ticho Parly's portrayal of the title-role, familiar in London and continental opera houses, seemed by then to be audibly tiring, he had earlier brought impressively powerful, forthright, if somewhat rough-hewn tone to his part.

As for *Walküre*, the drabness which had been a dispiriting feature of the production in 1966 had largely gone; and though there was still a good deal of darkness about the stage, there was also a more imaginative use of colour, with a front gauze and follow-spotlights effectively deployed. Here, as in *Siegfried*, Peter Ebert's conception of *The Ring* seemed increasingly assured and even Michael Knight's settings were more flexible than had originally seemed possible. David Ward as Wotan and Charles Craig as Siegmund repeated and enhanced the performances they had given five years previously; Anna Reynolds was an incisive Fricka; Leonore Kirschstein, a new Sieglinde from Munich, looked lovely, but her voice did not gain real beauty of line until she returned to sing the role in Glasgow in December.

Before that, however, the company had much else to do. Various sorties were made into England. Liverpool was visited for the first time, and the week of performances in that city was ecstatically greeted by Michael Kennedy of the *Daily Telegraph*. Two acts of *Siegfried* were performed in a concert version at the London Proms, and served to remind Londoners that it was high time the Company was invited to present a season at Covent Garden (not that Peter Hemmings yet placed a London appearance very high on his list of priorities). Newcastle, where Scottish Opera now had solid support, was visited again.

More important, for Scotland at least, was the opening of the Company's autumn season with *The Rake's Progress* at the newly-built MacRobert Centre of Stirling University. This was not the stimulating if arguably over-ingenious production which had been seen at the 1967 Edinburgh Festival but an entirely new one, specially prepared for Stirling by the latest of the Company's young staff producers, David Pountney. Entirely new – and, one might add, surely entirely different from any other *Rake* that had hitherto been seen on a professional stage. For instead of attempting to match Stravinsky's neo-classical music to a neo-classical production, Mr Pountney chose to jolt it out of its traditional framework and to present it in a mixture of styles and costumes.

The result was disconcerting, and for some people distasteful and infuriating. Ralph Koltai's latest settings, with their emphasis on ladders, pulleys, and lengths of wire, carried Koltai austerity into the realms of self-parody. Yet it was the sort of production of which opera companies too frequently fight shy – one which was prepared to take risks, and to jolt the audience as well as the opera itself. Whatever the flaws of the evening (and some of Mr Pountney's ideas seemed tiresomely overdone) its aims were admirable. Less admirable, at

Rosenkavalier, *Act Three:
In the closing scene, the tender
woman in love of Act One gives
way to the great lady that the
Marschallin (Helga Dernesch)
truly is.*

Stirling at least, was its execution. The new 500-seat theatre, though comfortable and exciting to sit in, turned out to have acoustical problems which prevented the performance from making any great impact. Voices, such as Jill Gomez's, which at Covent Garden can sound big, here sounded muffled. Orchestral tone was clear but dry, and Alexander Gibson seemed to have difficulty making the Scottish Baroque Ensemble play Stravinsky's score with the rhythmic élan it needed.

Away from Stirling, however, the performance began to flower; and at the King's Theatre, Edinburgh, later in the tour (where it shared a repertoire with *The Barber* conducted by Roderick Brydon and an uneven revival of *Don Giovanni* conducted by Bryden Thomson) one got a better impression of its qualities. Though one could not help feeling that the Company had been over-hasty in jettisoning Peter Ebert's 1967 production, the graveyard scene, blackly enacted in and around a vast coffin, was nevertheless a chilling *tour de force*, grimly sung by Alexander Young and Peter van der Bilt as Rakewell and Shadow. Jill Gomez made a charming young Ann, and Johanna Peters doubled the roles of Mother Goose and Baba the Turk, each to superbly fruity effect. By now, too, the Scottish Baroque Ensemble was playing as if it knew and loved every note of the score; and Roderick Brydon, who had replaced Alexander Gibson as conductor, was able to demonstrate how useful an alternative to the SNO this Edinburgh-based orchestra was in the process of becoming.

By now, however, everybody's thoughts were racing ahead to *The Ring*. This, the first complete performance of Wagner's tetralogy in Scotland for nearly half a century, was to form the climax of the company's first ten years. For various reasons – not really economic ones, as was rumoured, but mainly because the SNO would not be available for a prolonged period in the middle of its winter season – only one cycle was planned, though an extra performance of *Götterdämmerung* was to be thrown in as prelude.

When public booking opened in November, with seat prices as high as £7, all tickets were sold almost at once – which meant that, of the £35,000 the cycle was expected to cost, about £22,000 would be recouped from the box-office. Then, a week before the season opened, Friedelind Wagner arrived in Glasgow to take part in an imaginatively-planned teach-in at the King's Theatre. Rehearsals were now in full flood, and outside the theatre Scottish Opera's poster made a stunning sight: a vast red sheet of flame, with the words *Der Ring des Nibelungen* starkly etched into it. Here indeed was the culmination of a decade of growth, courage, flair, ambition.

The performances were all and more than one hoped for, beset though they were by last-minute illnesses. Helga Dernesch, confined to Vienna by bronchitis, was sadly missed, but the chance to hear Margaret Kingsley and Berit Lindholm as her substitutes gave the cycle a fresh and special interest. Miss Kingsley, a young English soprano, had appeared in *Walküre* in several major foreign opera houses but not until now in Britain; and her bright, brave little Brünnhilde, well sung and affectingly acted, was one of the triumphs of the week. As for Miss Lindholm, she came to Scotland from Stockholm with unimpeachable references. She had been Bayreuth's Brünnhilde earlier that year, and was booked to be Covent Garden's new Brünnhilde in 1973. That Scottish Opera should choose her – as a stand-in, if you please, for the indisposed Dernesch – gave some indication of the standard at which the Company now aimed.

At first Miss Lindholm's voice and manner threatened to be disappointingly monotonous; but as the cycle progressed, she blossomed as a Wagner singer and actress of real quality. In Act Two of the final *Götterdämmerung*, and in her Act Three monlogue, she was expressive, ardent, very moving. But like all good performances of *The Ring*, this was one which was greater than the sum of its parts. Along the way, one could savour John Dobson's subtle Loge and Louis Hendrikx's imposing Hagen, but it was the magnificent growth of Alexander Gibson's conception of the cycle, the virile yet sensitive playing of the SNO, the increased assurance of Peter Ebert's production, the mounting intensity of David Ward's Wotan which made the week the most enthralling event in the history of the Company and of music in Scotland.

In the *Financial Times*, Andrew Porter exclaimed how Mr Gibson had developed from an "admirable" conductor into a "superb" one, and deemed the performance to be of a quality usually associated with Furtwängler, Knappertsbusch, and Reginald Goodall. Even Stanley Sadie of *The Times*, seldom a critic who lets himself get carried away, wrote with euphoria that Scottish Opera's could yet "become supreme among present *Ring* productions."

As a full-scale operation, the cycle was a success on every level. A daily fleet of buses carried Edinburgh supporters back and forward; three opera restaurants and a special car park were brought into action; visitors came from Aberdeen, Elgin, London, even America; and Bernard Levin was there, adding one more *Ring* to his collection. Yet above the excitement, clouds were darkly gathering. Between *Siegfried* and *Götterdämmerung*, Robin Orr announced that in 1972 there would be a new, celebratory production of *Pelléas et Mélisande* but added grimly that the Scottish Arts Council's grant, which now rested at a potential £210,000, fell £60,000 short of the Company's needs, thus placing many activities in jeopardy; staff would have to be cut, and an Edinburgh Festival revival of *The Trojans*, with Janet Baker, and Helga Dernesch as Cassandra, abandoned.

Alexander Dunbar, latest of the Arts Council's directors in Scotland, stated bluntly that the company must learn to live within its means, but he would have gained a more sympathetic hearing if he had admitted, simply, that it was under-subsidised. However, the *Glasgow Herald* backed him up, scolding Scottish Opera for being too ambitious. For a moment it seemed as if history was repeating itself and we were back in 1962, when people did not realise what a miracle they had in their midst. Happily, a begging letter circulated to the audience at *Götterdämmerung* had quick results. Such was the goodwill the Company had inspired that the £60,000 was raised by December 31. Scottish Opera could now proceed into 1972, to new productions and new adventures, head high, fearless as ever.

Cast Lists

1962 King's Theatre Glasgow
June 5 to June 9

MADAMA BUTTERFLY
Puccini in Italian
3 performances

F. B. Pinkerton	Charles Craig
Goro	Andrew Gold
Suzuki	Laura Sarti
Sharpless	John Cameron
Cio-Cio-San	Elaine Malbin
Imperial Commissioner	John Shiels
The Bonze	William McCue
Prince Yamadori	John Shiels
Trouble	Lindsay Marshall
Kate Pinkerton	Norma Goldie

Conductors	Alexander Gibson (2)
	James Lockhart (1)
Producer	Denis Arundell
Designer	Mark King
Lighting	Charles Bristow

PELLÉAS ET MÉLISANDE
Debussy in French
3 performances

Golaud	Louis Maurin
Mélisande	Micheline Grancher
Geneviève	Laura Sarti
Arkel	Joseph Rouleau (2)
	John Shirley-Quirk (1)
Pelléas	Emile Belcourt
Yniold	Ingrid Gywther
A Physician	John Shiels

Conductor	Alexander Gibson
Producer	Denis Arundell
Designer	Mark King
Lighting	Charles Bristow

1963 King's Theatre Glasgow
May 27 to June 1
King's Theatre Edinburgh
June 3 to June 8

OTELLO
Verdi in Italian
4 performances

Montano	William McCue
Cassio	Emile Belcourt
Iago	Peter Glossop
Roderigo	Edward Byles
Otello	Charles Craig
Desdemona	Luisa Bosbalian
Emilia	Laura Sarti
Lodovico	Don Garrard
A Herald	John Graham

Conductor	Alexander Gibson
Producer	Anthony Besch
Designer	Ralph Koltai
Lighting	Charles Bristow

IL SERAGLIO
Mozart in English
4 performances

Belmonte	John Wakefield
Osmin	Inia Te Wiata
Pedrillo	Adrian de Peyer
Selim	Moultrie Kelsall
Constanze	Rae Woodland
Blonda	Marion Studholme

Conductor	Leon Lovett
Producer	Peter Ebert
Designer	Peter Rice
Lighting	Charles Bristow

VOLO DI NOTTE
Dallapiccola in English
4 performances
British premiere

Rivière	Don Garrard
Leroux	Russell Cooper
Pellerin	Jon Andrew
Inspector Robineau	William McCue
Four Officials	Thomas Thompson
	Michael Wakeham
	Russell Cooper
	John Worthley
Radio Operator	Raymond Nilsson
Mrs Fabien	Marie Collier
A Voice	Laura Sarti

Conductor	Alexander Gibson
Producer	Peter Ebert
Designer	Ralph Koltai
Lighting	Charles Bristow

in a double bill with
L'HEURE ESPAGNOLE
Ravel in English
4 performances

Concepcion	Marie Collier
Gonzalez	Emile Belcourt
Torquemada	Edward Byles
Ramiro	Peter Glossop
Don Inigo Gomez	Howell Glynne

Conductor	Brian Priestman
Producer	Anthony Besch
Designer	Peter Rice
Lighting	Charles Bristow

1964 King's Theatre Glasgow
May 14 to May 23
King's Theatre Edinburgh
May 26 to May 30

FAUST
Gounod in French
5 performances

Faust	André Turp
Méphistophélès	Joseph Rouleau
Wagner	John Shiels
Valentin	Julien Haas
Siebel	Laura Sarti
Marguérite	Andréa Guiot
Martha	Johanna Peters

Conductor	Alexander Gibson (3)
	Roderick Brydon (2)
Producer	Anthony Besch
Designer	Peter Rice
Lighting	Charles Bristow

DON GIOVANNI
Mozart in English
6 performances

Leporello	Harold Blackburn

Donna Anna	Elizabeth Fretwell (3)
	Jennifer Vyvyan (3)
Don Giovanni	Peter van der Bilt
Commendatore	David Ward (2)
	William McCue (4)
Don Ottavio	Alexander Young
Donna Elvira	Marilyn Tyler
Zerlina	Elizabeth Robson
Masetto	Michael Maurel
Conductor	Leon Lovett
Producer	Peter Ebert
Designer	Ralph Koltai
Choreographer	Shelah Wells
Lighting	Charles Bristow

OTELLO
Verdi in Italian
5 performances

Cast as 1963 except

Cassio	David Hughes
Roderigo	John Robertson
Otello	Ronald Dowd (2)
	Sergio Barlottini (1)
	Charles Craig (2)
Lodovico	Harold Blackburn

1965 King's Theatre Glasgow
May 14 to May 22
His Majesty's Theatre Aberdeen
May 25 to May 29
King's Theatre Edinburgh
June 1 to June 5

BORIS GODUNOV
Mussorgsky in English
6 performances

Nikitich	William McCue
A Woman	Dorothy Miller
Mitiukha	John Shiels
Shchelkalov	Raymond Hayter
Prince Shuisky	Emile Belcourt
Boris Godunov	David Ward
Pimen	Norman Lumsden
Grigory	William McAlpine
The Hostess	Elizabeth Bainbridge
Missail	Frances Egerton
Varlaam	Donald McIntyre
Xenia	Catriona Gordon
Feodor	Anne Pashley
Xenia's Nurse	Johanna Peters
Boyar	John Robertson
Simpleton	Duncan Robertson
Khrushchev	Ronald Morrison
Lavitzky	John Robertson
Chernikovsky	John Shiels

Conductor	Alexander Gibson
Producer	Michael Geliot
Designer	Ralph Koltai
Lighting	Charles Bristow

MADAMA BUTTERFLY
Puccini in Italian
8 performances

Cast as 1962 except

Goro	Francis Egerton
Sharpless	Robert Savoie
Cio-Cio-San	Felicia Weathers
Imperial Commissioner	Ronald Morrison
The Bonze	Victor Godfrey (1)
	William McCue (7)
Prince Yamadori	Ronald Morrison
Trouble	Conrad Brown
Conductors	Norman del Mar (5)
	Roderick Brydon (3)
Producer	Peter Ebert
Designer	David Wilby
Lighting	Charles Bristow

DON GIOVANNI
Mozart in English
5 performances

Cast as 1964 except

Leporello	Ian Wallace
Donna Anna	Janice Chapman
Commendatore	Donald McIntyre
Don Ottavio	Donald Pilley
Donna Elvira	Ava June
Zerlina	Margaret Price
Conductor	Alexander Gibson

1966 King's Theatre Glasgow
May 6 to May 21
King's Theatre Edinburgh
May 24 to June 4
His Majesty's Theatre Aberdeen
June 7 to June 11

FALSTAFF
Verdi in Italian
7 performances

Sir John Falstaff	Geraint Evans (6)
	Robert Savoie (1)
Dr Caius	Dennis Brandt
Bardolph	Francis Egerton
Pistol	Ian Wallace
Meg Page	Laura Sarti
Alice Ford	Luisa Bosabalian
Mistress Quickly	Elizabeth Bainbridge
Nanetta	Elizabeth Robson

Fenton	Ryland Davies (4)
	Duncan Robertson (3)
Ford	John Shaw
Conductor	Alexander Gibson
Producer	Peter Ebert
Designer	Peter Rice
Lighting	Charles Bristow

FAUST
Gounod in French
5 performances

Cast as 1964 except

Faust	William McAlpine
Méphistophélès	Donald McIntyre
Wagner	Ronald Morrison
Valentin	Robert Savoie
Siebel	Josephine McQueen
Marguérite	Phyllis Curtin (4)
	Luisa Bosabalian (1)
Conductor	Roderick Brydon

ALBERT HERRING
Britten in English
7 performances

Lady Billows	Rae Woodland
Florence Pike	Johanna Peters
Miss Wordsworth	Patricia Clark
Mr Gedge	Ronald Morrison
Mr Upfold	Francis Egerton
Superintendent Budd	William McCue
Emmie	Sheila McGrow
Cis	Jennifer Bermingham
Harry	Charles Begbie
Sid	Michael Maurel
Albert	Gregory Dempsey
Nancy	Catherine Wilson
Mrs Herring	Anna Reynolds
Conductor	Roderick Brydon
Producer	Anthony Besch
Designer	Adam Pollock
Lighting	Charles Bristow

DIE WALKÜRE
Wagner in German
8 performances

Siegmund	Charles Craig
Sieglinde	Elizabeth Fretwell
Hunding	Donald McIntyre
Brünnhilde	Anita Välkki
Wotan	David Ward (6)
	Hubert Hofmann (2)
Fricka	Ann Howard
The Walkyries	
Gerhilde	Josephine Allen
Ortlinde	Catherine Wilson

Waltraute	Ann Howard
Schwertleite	Marie Hayward
Siegrune	Laura Sarti
Grimgerde	Johanna Peters
Rossweisse	Patricia Brigenshaw

Conductor	Alexander Gibson
Producer	Peter Ebert
Designer	Michael Knight
Lighting	Charles Bristow

1967 Perth Theatre
April 12 to April 15
King's Theatre Glasgow
May 6 to May 20
His Majesty's Theatre Aberdeen
May 23 to May 27
King's Theatre Edinburgh
May 30 to June 10

COSÌ FAN TUTTE
Mozart in English
9 performances

Ferrando	Ryland Davies
Guglielmo	Peter van der Bilt (8)
	John Kitchiner (1)
Don Alfonso	Inia Te Wiata
Fiordiligi	Elizabeth Harwood
Dorabella	Janet Baker
Despina	Jenifer Eddy

Conductor	Alexander Gibson
Producer	Anthony Besch
Designer	John Stoddart
Lighting	Charles Bristow

DAS RHEINGOLD
Wagner in German
5 performances

Woglinde	Dorothy Robertson
Wellgunde	Josephine McQueen
Flosshilde	Josephte Clément
Alberich	Gwyn Griffiths
Wotan	Forbes Robinson (2)
	David Ward (3)
Fricka	Anna Reynolds
Freia	Elizabeth Fretwell
Fasolt	Victor Godfrey (4)
	William McCue (1)
Fafner	Richard Angas
Froh	Ramon Remedios
Donner	Ronald Morrison
Loge	Joseph Ward (2)
	Richard Holm (3)
Mime	Francis Egerton
Erda	Patricia Purcell

| Conductor | Alexander Gibson |

Producer	Peter Ebert
Designer	Michael Knight
Lighting	Charles Bristow

LA BOHÈME
Puccini in Italian
7 performances

Colline	Inia Te Wiata
Schaunard	Ronald Morrison
Marcello	Robert Savoie
Rodolfo	George Shirley
Benoit	Malcolm King
Mimi	Luisa Bosabalian (6)
	Joan Carlyle (1)
Parpignol	John Robertson (6)
	James McJannet (1)
Alcindoro	John Graham
Musetta	Barbara Rendell (6)
	Maria Pellegrini (1)
Official	Ramon Remedios
Sergeant	John Graham

Conductor	Roderick Brydon
Producer	Peter Ebert
Designer	Peter Rice
Lighting	Charles Bristow

ALBERT HERRING
Britten in English
4 performances

Cast as 1966 except
| Lady Billows | Judith Pierce |

OTELLO
Verdi in Italian
5 performances

Cast as 1964 except
Cassio	William McAlpine
Iago	John Shaw (3)
	Peter Glossop (2)
Otello	Charles Craig (3)
	Pier Miranda Ferraro (2)
Desdemona	Joan Carlyle
Lodovico	Richard Angas

1967 Edinburgh Festival

THE RAKE'S PROGRESS
Stravinsky in English
4 performances

Tom Rakewell	Alexander Young
Ann Trulove	Elizabeth Robson
Trulove	David Kelly
Nick Shadow	Peter van der Bilt
Mother Goose	Johanna Peters
Baba the Turk	Sona Cervena
Sellem	Francis Egerton

| Keeper | Ronald Morrison |

Conductor	Alexander Gibson
Producer	Peter Ebert
Designer	Ralph Koltai
Lighting	Charles Bristow

THE SOLDIER'S TALE
Stravinsky in English
6 performances

Narrator	Gordon Jackson
Soldier	Nicky Henson
Devil	Patrick Wymark
Princess	Una Stubbs

Conductor	Alexander Gibson
Producer	Wendy Toye
Designer	Carl Toms
Lighting	Charles Bristow

1968 Spring – Perth Theatre
April 9 to April 13
King's Theatre Glasgow
May 3 to May 18
His Majesty's Theatre Aberdeen
May 21 to May 25
King's Theatre Edinburgh
May 28 to June 8

GÖTTERDÄMMERUNG
Wagner in German
5 performances

First Norn	Johanna Peters
Second Norn	Laura Sarti
Third Norn	Patricia McCarry
Brünnhilde	Anita Välkki
Siegfried	Charles Craig
Gunther	Victor Godfrey
Hagen	Elfego Esparza
Gutrune	Helga Dernesch
Waltraute	Anna Reynolds (4)
	Patricia Purcell (1)
Alberich	Gwyn Griffiths
Woglinde	Patricia Hay
Wellgunde	Josephine McQueen
Flosshilde	Marjory McMichael

Conductor	Alexander Gibson
Producer	Peter Ebert
Designer	Michael Knight
Lighting	Charles Bristow

THE MARRIAGE OF FIGARO
Mozart in English
11 performances

Figaro	Michael Maurel
Susanna	Catherine Gayer
Doctor Bartolo	William McCue
Marcellina	Johanna Peters

Cherubino	Patricia Hay (3)
	Josephine McQueen
	(8)
Count Almaviva	Peter van der Bilt
Don Basilio	Kevin Miller
Countess	Catherine Wilson
Almaviva	
Antonio	John Graham
Don Curzio	John Robertson
Barbarina	Ann Baird
Peasant Girls	Margaret Leigh-
	Hamilton
	Karen Russell
Conductors	Alexander Gibson (7)
	Leonard Hancock (4)
Producer	Anthony Besch
Designer	John Stoddart
Lighting	Charles Bristow

MADAMA BUTTERFLY
Puccini in Italian
6 performances

Cast as 1965 except

F. B. Pinkerton	Franco Bonisolli (3)
	Charles Craig (3)
Goro	John Robertson
Sharpless	Ronald Morrison
Imperial	William Elvin
Commissioner	
The Bonze	John Graham
Prince Yamadori	William Elvin
Trouble	Alisdair McLean
Kate Pinkerton	Patricia Hay

BORIS GODUNOV
Mussorgsky in English
6 performances

Cast as 1965 except

Nikitich	Ronald Morrison
Shchelkalov	William Elvin
Prince Shuisky	Dennis Brandt
Boris Godunov	Joseph Rouleau (5)
	Don Garrard (1)
Pimen	Don Garrard (5)
	William McCue (1)
The Hostess	Gita Denise
Varlaam	Victor Godfrey
Xenia	Ann Baird
Feodor	Josephine McQueen
Simpleton	Duncan Robertson
	(5)
	Athole Still (1)
Khrushchev	Norman White
Lavitzky	John Graham
Conductor	David Lloyd-Jones

FULL CIRCLE
Orr in English
3 performances

Jean	Sheila McGrow
Davie	William Elvin
Andra	Duncan Robertson
Stranger	Ronald Morrison
Barman	William McCue
Bystander	John Shiels
Policeman	Ronald Morrison
Conductor	Alexander Gibson
Producer	Michael Geliot
Designer	Neil Parkinson
Lighting	Charles Bristow

THE SOLDIER'S TALE
Stravinsky in English
3 performances

Cast as 1967 except

The Narrator	Job Stewart
The Soldier	Ray Davis
The Princess	Clover Roope

1968 Maggio Musicale
Fiorentino

ALBERT HERRING
Britten in English
2 performances

Cast as 1967

1968 Edinburgh Festival

PETER GRIMES
Britten in English
4 performances

Hobson	John Graham
Swallow	Harold Blackburn
Peter Grimes	Richard Cassilly (2)
	Nigel Douglas (2)
Mrs Sedley	Johanna Peters
Ellen Orford	Phyllis Curtin
Auntie	Elizabeth Bainbridge
Captain Balstrode	John Shaw
Bob Boles	William McAlpine
Rev Horace	John Robertson
Adams	
First Niece	Ann Baird
Second Niece	Patricia Hay
Ned Keene	Michael Maurel
John	Dennis Sheridan
Dr Crabbe	Norman White
Conductor	Alexander Gibson
Producer	Colin Graham
Designer	Alix Stone

IL BALLO DELLE INGRATE
Monteverdi in English
5 performances

Cupid	Ann Baird
Venus	Heather Begg
Pluto	William McCue
Conductor	Roderick Brydon
Producer	Peter Ebert
Designer	Jack Notman
Choreographer	Alexander Bennett

1968 Autumn – Theatre Royal
Newcastle September 10 to
September 14

THE MARRIAGE OF FIGARO
Mozart in English
2 performances

Cast as spring 1968 except

Susanna	Lee Venora
Doctor Bartolo	Richard van Allan
Cherubino	Patricia Hay
Count Almaviva	Ronald Morrison
Conductor	Alexander Gibson

PETER GRIMES
Britten in English
2 performances

Cast as 1968 Edinburgh Festival except

Peter Grimes	Nigel Douglas
Captain Balstrode	John Shaw (1)
	Neil Easton (1)
Ned Keene	William Elvin
Dr Crabbe	Robert Harvey

1968 Winter – King's Theatre
Glasgow December 12 to
December 21

THE GONDOLIERS
Sullivan in English
5 performances

Fiametta	Ann Baird
Francesco	Martin Lane
Giulia	Pamela Molcher
Antonio	John Graham
Giorgio	John Leishman
Vittoria	Karen Russell
Marco Palmieri	John Wakefield
Giuseppe Palmieri	Ronald Morrison
Tessa	Janet Coster
Gianetta	Anne Pashley
The Duke of	Ian Wallace (4)
Plaza-Toro	Lawrence Richards
	(1)
The Duchess of	Johanna Peters (3)
Plaza-Toro	Gillian Knight (2)

Casilda	Jill Gomez
Luiz	John Robertson
Don Alhambra	William McCue
Annibale	Bruce Clark
Inez	Elsa Kendal
Conductor	James Loughran
Producer	Joan Cross
Designer	Jack Notman
Choreographer	Clover Roope

THE MARRIAGE OF FIGARO
Mozart in English
3 performances

Cast as autumn
1968 except

Susanna	Joan Summers
Doctor Bartolo	William McCue
Marcellina	Johanna Peters (2)
	Janice Chapman (1)
Count Almaviva	Peter van der Bilt (2)
	Ronald Morrison (1)
Conductors	Alexander Gibson (2)
	Leonard Hancock (1)

FULL CIRCLE
Orr in English
2 performances

Cast as spring 1968
except

Stranger	Bruce Clark
Policeman	John Leishman
Producer	Ian Watt-Smith
Designer	Bernard Culshaw

1969 Spring – Perth Theatre
April 5 to April 12
King's Theatre Glasgow
May 3 to May 17
King's Theatre Edinburgh
May 19 to May 24
His Majesty's Theatre Aberdeen
June 3 to June 7

COSÌ FAN TUTTE
Mozart in English
11 performances

Cast as 1967 except

Ferrando	Kurt Westi
Guglielmo	Peter van der Bilt
Don Alfonso	John Shirley-Quirk (10)
	Ronald Morrison (1)
Despina	Carrol Anne Curry
Conductors	Alexander Gibson (9)
	Leonard Hancock (2)

FULL CIRCLE
Orr in English
4 performances

Cast as winter 1968 except

Andra	John Robertson
Barman	John Graham
Conductor	Alexander Gibson (3)
	Leonard Hancock (1)

ALBERT HERRING
Britten in English
3 performances

Cast as 1968 except

Miss Wordsworth	Patricia Clark (2)
	Ann Baird (1)
Harry	Walter Wright
Mrs Herring	Anna Reynolds (1)
	Joan Clarkson (2)

THE TROJANS
Berlioz in English
5 performances

Part One – The Fall of Troy

Cassandra	Ann Howard
Choroebus	John Shaw
Andromache	Elaine Macdonald
Astyanax	Alisdair McLean
Priam	John Graham
Hecuba	Joan Clarkson
Aeneas	Ronald Dowd
Helenus	John Robertson
Ascanius	Patricia Hay
Pantheus	William McCue
Ghost of Hector	Joseph Rouleau

Part Two – The Trojans at Carthage

Dido	Janet Baker
Anna	Bernadette Greevy
Ascanius	Patricia Hay
Aeneas	Ronald Dowd
Iopas	Robert Thomas
Hylas	Duncan Robertson (4)
	John Robertson (1)
Narbal	Joseph Rouleau
Pantheus	William McCue
First Soldier	Ronald Morrison
Second Soldier	John Graham
Ghost of Cassandra	Ann Howard
Ghost of Choroebus	John Shaw
Ghost of Hector	Joseph Rouleau
Ghost of Priam	John Graham
Mercury	Brian Kemp
Conductor	Alexander Gibson
Producer	Peter Ebert
Set designer	Hans-Ulrich Schmückle

Costume designer	Sylte Büsse-Schmückle
Choreographer	Laverne Meyer
Lighting	Charles Bristow

THE GONDOLIERS
Sullivan in English
9 performances

Cast as winter 1968 except

Fiametta	Ann Baird (6)
	Nan Christie (3)
Francesco	Robert Ferguson
Giulia	Barbara Walker
Tessa	Janet Hughes
Gianetta	Patricia Hay
The Duke of Plaza-Toro	Ian Wallace
The Duchess of Plaza-Toro	Johanna Peters
Casilda	Jill Gomez (6)
	Ann Baird (3)

1969 Foreign Tour – Dortmund, Hanover, Augsburg

ALBERT HERRING
Britten in English
3 performances

Cast as spring 1969 except

Miss Wordsworth	Patricia Clark
Mrs Herring	Anna Reynolds

1969 Edinburgh Festival – The Gateway Theatre September 1 to September 11

THE UNDERTAKER
Purser in English
10 performances

Juliette	Nan Christie
Pierre	Frederick Bateman
The Undertaker	William McCue
Marie	Patricia Hay
The Abbott	Ronald Morrison
Conductor	Alexander Gibson
Producer	Ian Watt-Smith
Set designer	Ken Wheatley
Costume designer	Alex Reid

FULL CIRCLE
Orr in English
10 performances

Cast as winter 1968 except

Stranger	John Leishman
Conductor	Alexander Gibson

1969 Winter – King's Theatre
Edinburgh December 6 to
December 15

CINDERELLA
Rossini in English
4 performances

Tisbe	Ann Baird
Clorinda	Patricia Clark
Angelina	Patricia Kern
Alidoro	John Graham
Don Magnifico	Ian Wallace
Don Ramiro	Frederick Bateman
Dandini	Ronald Morrison
Conductor	Bryden Thomson
Producer	Colin Graham
Designer	Emanuele Luzzati
Lighting	Colin Graham

ALBERT HERRING
Britten in English
2 performances

Cast as foreign tour 1969 except
Mr Upfold	Francis Egerton (1)
	John Robertson (1)
Cis	Ann Baird
Harry	Timothy Oldham

1970 Spring – His Majesty's
Theatre Aberdeen March 26 to
April 4
Theatre Royal Newcastle
April 7 to April 10
Perth Theatre April 14 to April 18
King's Theatre Glasgow
May 1 to May 16
King's Theatre Edinburgh
May 19 to May 30

THE TURN OF THE SCREW
Britten in English
9 performances

Prologue	John Robertson
The Governess	Catherine Wilson
Flora	Nan Christie
Miles	Timothy Oldham
Mrs Grose	Judith Pierce
Quint	Gregory Dempsey
Miss Jessel	Milla Andrew
Conductor	Roderick Brydon
Producer	Anthony Besch
Designer	John Stoddart
Lighting	Charles Bristow

FIDELIO
Beethoven in German
8 performances

Jacquino	Werner Krenn
Marzelline	Josephine McQueen (7)
	Heather Howson (1)
Rocco	William McCue
Leonore	Helga Dernesch
Don Pizarro	Donald McIntyre (4)
	Morley Meredith (4)
1st Prisoner	Derek Blackwell
2nd Prisoner	John Leishman
Florestan	Ronald Dowd (7)
	Gregory Dempsey (1)
Don Fernando	Ronald Morrison (7)
	John Graham (1)
Conductor	Alexander Gibson
Producer	Peter Ebert
Set designer	Hans-Ulrich Schmückle
Costume designer	Sylte Büsse-Schmückle
Lighting	Charles Bristow

DON GIOVANNI
Mozart in Italian
10 performances

Leporello	Stafford Dean
Donna Anna	Milla Andrew (9)
	Josephte Clément (1)
Don Giovanni	Peter van der Bilt
Commendatore	Joseph Rouleau
Don Ottavio	Werner Krenn (9)
	John Robertson (1)
Donna Elvira	Luisa Bosabalian
Zerlina	Patricia Hay
Masetto	John Graham
Conductor	Alexander Gibson
Producer	Peter Ebert
Set designer	Ralph Koltai
Costume designer	Nadine Baylis
Staff producer	Ian Watt-Smith
Choreographer	Marjorie Middleton
Lighting	Charles Bristow

CINDERELLA
Rossini in English
13 performances

Cast as winter 1969 except
Tisbe	Sheila McGrow (6)
	Ann Baird (7)
Clorinda	Patricia Clark (12)
	Heather Howson (1)
Angelina	Josephte Clément (6)
	Rosalind Elias (7)

1970 Commonwealth Games –
Royal Lyceum Theatre
June 20 to July 25

THE MAGIC FLUTE
Mozart in English
6 performances

Tamino	David Hillman
Three Ladies	Patricia Hay
	Josephte Clément
	Claire Livingstone
Papageno	Michael Maurel
The Queen of the Night	Rhonda Bruce
Monostatos	John Robertson
Pamina	Jill Gomez
Three Spirits	Sheila McGrow
	Ann Baird
	Moyra Paterson
The Speaker	Bruce Martin
Sarastro	Simon Estes
First Priest	Alexander Morrison
Second Priest	John Graham
Papagena	Nan Christie
First Armed Man	Derek Blackwell
Second Armed Man	Norman White
Conductors	Alexander Gibson (4)
	Christopher Seaman (2)
Producer	Peter Ebert
Set designer	Geoffrey Scott
Costume designer	Alex Reid
Lighting	Charles Bristow

1970 Edinburgh Festival
King's Theatre Edinburgh
August 25, 27, 29

ELEGY FOR YOUNG LOVERS
Henze in English
3 performances

Hilda Mack	Catherine Gayer
Carolina Grafin von Kirchstetten	Sona Cervena
Dr Wilhelm Reischmann	Lawrence Richard
Toni Reischmann	David Hillman
Gregor Mittenhofer	John Shirley-Quirk
Elisabeth Zimmer	Jill Gomez
Josef Mauer	John Graham
Conductor	Alexander Gibson
Producer	Hans Werner Henze
Set designer	Ralph Koltai
Costume designer	Fausto Moroni
Lighting	Ralph Koltai

1970 Autumn – King's Theatre
Glasgow September 15 to
September 19
His Majesty's Theatre Aberdeen
September 22 to September 26
Theatre Royal Newcastle
October 12 to October 17

FIDELIO
Beethoven in German
4 performances

Cast as spring 1970 except
Jacquino   Alexander Oliver
Marzelline   Heather Howson
Don Pizarro   Werner Mann
Florestan   Ronald Dowd
Don Fernando   Ronald Morrison

ELEGY FOR YOUNG LOVERS
Henze in English
2 performances

Cast as 1970 Edinburgh Festival

THE MAGIC FLUTE
Mozart in English
7 performances

Cast as 1970 Commonwealth Games
except
Pamina   Jill Gomez (4)
                  Elizabeth Robson (3)
Three Spirits   Sheila McGrow
                  Ann Baird
                  Moyra Paterson (4)
                  Shirley Powley (3)
Sarastro   Simon Estes (4)
                  Stafford Dean (3)
First Priest   Alexander Morrison
                  (4)
                  Athole Still (3)
First Armed Man   Derek Blackwell (4)
                  Athole Still (3)
Second Armed   Norman White (4)
  Man   Bruce Martin (3)

Conductor   Alexander Gibson (2)
                  Christopher Seaman
                  (4)
                  Leonard Hancock (1)

1970 Foreign Tour – Iceland

THE TURN OF THE SCREW
Britten in English
2 performances

Cast as spring 1970 except
Flora   Sheila McGrow

ALBERT HERRING
Britten in English
2 performances

Cast as winter 1969 except
Florence Pike   Patricia Purcell
Mr Upfold   Francis Egerton
Miss Wordsworth   Patricia Clark
Mrs Herring   Claire Livingstone

1970 Winter – Royal Lyceum
Theatre Edinburgh December 11
to December 19

THE MAGIC FLUTE
Mozart in English
3 performances

Cast as autumn 1970 except
The Queen of   Jessica Cash
  the Night
Pamina   Elizabeth Robson
Three Spirits   Sheila McGrow
                  Ann Baird
                  Moyra Paterson
Sarastro   Stafford Dean
First Priest   Alexander Morrison
Papagena   Laureen Livingstone
First Armed Man   Derek Blackwell
Second Armed   Norman White
  Man

Conductor   Alexander Gibson (2)
                  Christopher Seaman
                  (1)

LA TRAVIATA
Verdi in Italian
3 performances

Violetta Valéry   Clarice Carson
Marquis d'Obigny Peter Lyon
Baron Douphol   John Graham
Doctor Grenvil   Bruce Martin
Flora Bervoix   Patricia Hay
Gastone   Alexander Morrison
Alfredo Germont   Franco Bonisolli
Annina   Moyra Paterson
Guiseppe   Alan Windsor
Giorgio Germont   Ronald Morrison
A Messenger   Norman White
Gypsies   Nancy Gottschalk
                  Alexandra Gordon

Conductor   James Loughran
Producer   Ian Watt-Smith
Set designer   Bernard Culshaw
Costume designer Alex Reid
Lighting   Charles Bristow

1971 Spring – Perth Theatre
March 11 to March 20
His Majesty's Theatre Aberdeen
March 25 to April 3
Theatre Royal Newcastle
April 6 to April 10
Royal Court Theatre Liverpool
April 12 to April 17
King's Theatre Glasgow
May 7 to May 22
King's Theatre Edinburgh
May 25 to June 5
His Majesty's Theatre Aberdeen
June 8 to June 12

ALBERT HERRING
Britten in English
4 performances

Cast as Iceland 1970 except
Lady Billows   Judith Pierce (3)
                  Rae Woodland (1)
Miss Wordsworth   Patricia Clark (3)
                  Ann Baird (1)
Cis   Ann Baird (3)
                  Heather Howson (1)
Albert Herring   Gregory Dempsey (3)
                  John Robertson (1)
Mrs Herring   Patricia Purcell

Conductors   Roderick Brydon (3)
                  Leonard Hancock (1)

THE TURN OF THE SCREW
Britten in English
4 performances

Cast as Iceland 1970 except
Mrs Grose   Judith Pierce (3)
                  Janet Edmund (1)
Quint   Gregory Dempsey (3)
                  John Robertson (1)

LA TRAVIATA
Verdi in Italian
15 performances

Cast as winter 1970 except
Violetta Valéry   Clarice Carson (14)
                  Catherine Wilson (1)
Doctor Grenvil   Norman White
Giorgio Germont   Ronald Morrison
                  (14)
                  Brian Kemp (1)
A Messenger   John Leishman
Gypsies   Nancy Gottschalk
                  Madeleine Morrison

Conductors   James Loughran (14)
                  Leonard Hancock (1)

THE MAGIC FLUTE
Mozart in English
8 performances

Cast as winter 1970 except

The Queen of the Night	Alexandra Gordon
Pamina	Jill Gomez (5)
	Heather Howson (3)
Three Spirits	Sheila McGrow
	Ann Baird (3)
	Grace Joss (5)
	Moyra Paterson
The Speaker	John Graham
Sarastro	Simon Estes
Papagena	Nan Christie (3)
	Ann Baird (5)
Conductor	Christopher Seaman

DAS RHEINGOLD
Wagner in German
9 performances

Woglinde	Patricia Hay
Wellgunde	Nancy Gottschalk
Flosshilde	Josephte Clément
Alberich	Raymond Myers
Wotan	David Ward (8)
	Victor Godfrey (1)
Fricka	Maureen Guy (5)
	Anna Reynolds (4)
Freia	Catherine Wilson
Fasolt	William McCue
Fafner	Simon Estes
Froh	Derek Blackwell
Donner	John Graham
Loge	Joseph Ward
Mime	Francis Egerton
Erda	Patricia Purcell
Conductor	Alexander Gibson
Producer	Peter Ebert
Designer	Michael Knight
Lighting	Charles Bristow

SIEGFRIED
Wagner in German
5 performances

Mime	Francis Egerton
Siegfried	Ticho Parly
Wotan	David Ward (4)
	Victor Godfrey (1)
Alberich	Raymond Myers
Fafner	Simon Estes (3)
	Norman White (2)
The Woodbird	Sally Le Sage
Erda	Patricia Purcell
Brünnhilde	Helga Dernesch
Conductor	Alexander Gibson
Producer	Peter Ebert
Designer	Charles Bristow

DER ROSENKAVALIER
Strauss in English
7 performances

The Feldmarschallin	Helga Dernesch
Count Octavian	Janet Baker
Page to the Princess	Nicholas Korankye
The Princess's Footmen	Ian Adam
	Anton Elder
	Ken Thomson
	John Leishman
Baron Ochs auf Lerchenau	Noel Mangin (5)
	Michael Langdon (2)
A Noble Widow	Nancy Gottschalk
Three Noble Orphans	Patricia Hay
	Moyra Paterson
	Claire Livingstone
Major-Domo to the Princess	John Robertson
A Milliner	Ann Baird
An Animal Seller	Alexander Morrison
A Scholar	Tom Scratchley
A Hairdresser	Gaetano Rea
A Notary	John Graham
Cook	John Austin
Boots	Anthony Feltham
Valzacchi	Nigel Douglas
Annina	Joan Davies
Kitchen Boy	Andrew McRobb
Messenger	David Ellis
A Tenor	Derek Blackwell
A Flute Player	David Little
Leopold	Peter Lyon (6)
	David Pountney (1)
Herr von Faninal	Thomas Hemsley (6)
	Peter Lyon (1)
Sophie	Elizabeth Harwood
Marianne	Judith Pierce
Major-Domo to Faninal	Clifford Hughes
Notary's Clerk	Andrew McRobb
Baron Ochs' Retinue	Ian Westrip
	Iwan Guy
	Anthony Feltham
	Kenneth Thomson
	John Leishman
A Doctor	Norman White
A Landlord	Alexander Morrison
Waiters	David Ellis
	John Austin
	Iwan Guy
	Michael Lanchberry
A Commissioner of Police	William McCue
Conductor	Alexander Gibson
Producer	Anthony Besch
Designer	John Stoddart
Lighting	Charles Bristow

1971 Royal Lyceum Theatre
Edinburgh July 26 to July 31

THE BARBER OF SEVILLE
Rossini in English
6 performances

Fiorello	John Graham
Count Almaviva	David Hillman
Figaro	Michael Maurel
Rosina	Anne Howells (3)
	Patricia Hay (3)
Doctor Bartolo	Elfego Esparza
Ambrogio	Peter Lyon
Berta	Judith Pierce
Don Basilio	William McCue
Sergeant	John Graham
Notary	Ian Westrip
Conductor	Gary Bertini
Producer	Ian Watt-Smith
Set designer	Bernard Culshaw
Costume designer	Alex Reid
Lighting	Roger Jackson

1971 Edinburgh Festival
King's Theatre Edinburgh
August 26, 28, 31

DIE WALKÜRE
Wagner in German
4 performances

Siegmund	Charles Craig
Sieglinde	Leonore Kirschstein
Hunding	William McCue
Wotan	David Ward
Brünnhilde	Helga Dernesch
Fricka	Anna Reynolds
The Valkyries	
Gerhilde	Heather Howson
Ortlinde	Nancy Gottschalk
Waltraute	Patricia Purcell
Schwetleite	Johanna Peters
Helmwige	Patricia Hay
Siegrune	Phyllis Cannan
Grungerde	Joan Clarkson
Rossweisse	Claire Livingstone
Conductor	Alexander Gibson
Producer	Peter Ebert
Designer	Michael Knight
Lighting	Charles Bristow

1971 Autumn – MacRobert Centre
Stirling September 27 to
October 9
Theatre Royal Newcastle
October 12 to October 16
King's Theatre Edinburgh
October 19 to October 23
King's Theatre Glasgow
October 26 to October 30

THE BARBER OF SEVILLE
Rossini in English
9 performances

Cast as summer 1971 except
Rosina	Anne Howells (5)
	Patricia Hay (4)
Conductor	Roderick Brydon

THE RAKE'S PROGRESS
Stravinsky in English
6 performances

Cast as Edinburgh Festival 1967 except
Ann Trulove	Jill Gomez
Baba the Turk	Johanna Peters
Sellem	John Robertson
Keeper	Uncast
Conductor	Alexander Gibson (2)
	Roderick Brydon (4)
Producer	David Pountney

DON GIOVANNI
Mozart in Italian
9 performances

Cast as spring 1971 except
Donna Anna	Luisa Bosabalian
Don Ottavio	Derek Blackwell (7)
	John Robertson (2)
Donna Elvira	Yvonne Fuller
Conductor	Bryden Thomson
Producer	Ian Watt-Smith

1971 Winter – King's Theatre
Glasgow December 11 to
December 18

DAS RHEINGOLD
Wagner in German
1 performance

Cast as spring 1971 except
Wellgunde	Heather Howson
Flosshilde	Claire Livingstone
Wotan	David Ward
Fricka	Anna Reynolds
Fafner	Louis Hendrikx
Donner	John Shaw
Loge	John Dobson

DIE WALKÜRE
Wagner in German
1 performance

Cast as Edinburgh Festival 1971 except
Brünnhilde	Margaret Kingsley

SIEGFRIED
Wagner in German
1 performance

Cast as spring 1971 except
Wotan	David Ward
Fafner	Louis Hendrikx
Brünnhilde	Berit Lindholm
The Woodbird	Alexandra Gordon

GÖTTERDÄMMERUNG
Wagner in German
2 performances

First Norn	Johanna Peters
Second Norn	Anna Reynolds
Third Norn	Heather Howson
Brünnhilde	Berit Lindholm
Siegfried	Ticho Parly
Gunther	John Shaw
Hagen	Louis Hendrikx
Gutrune	Catherine Wilson
Waltraute	Anna Reynolds
Alberich	Raymond Myers
Woglinde	Patricia Hay
Wellgunde	Heather Howson
Flosshilde	Claire Livingstone
Conductor	Alexander Gibson
Producer	Peter Ebert
Designer	Michael Knight
Lighting	Charles Bristow

In the compilation of these cast lists some performances were inadvertently omitted. These are two performances of *Albert Herring* in Perth in 1966; a performance of *The Gondoliers* in Glasgow in 1968 (six performances not five); two performances of *Albert Herring* and one performance of *The Turn of the Screw* in Newcastle in the Autumn of 1970. *Die Walküre* received three performances, not four, at the Edinburgh Festival of 1971.

Index